W9-BVQ-276

Why struggle through the Postal exam all alone?

Make the score...

Get the job!!!

with

PATHFINDER

Free Live Support

Just listen to what others have to say about Mr. Parnell's study guides ...

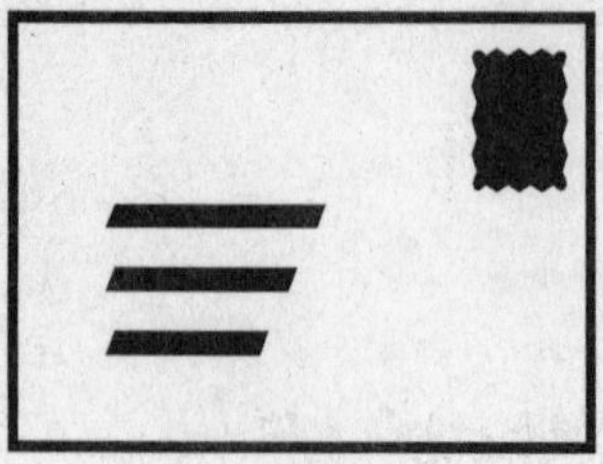

I used your book and got a job. I am living proof that at age 47 you can do it with good instruction and proper strategies. - J. G., Virginia

Buying your book was the best money I ever spent. Your book is easy to understand and has awesome strategies. The Postmaster offered me a job the very day I got my score in the mail. - J. D., Arkansas

I still can't believe that I got a score of 100! When people ask how I did it, I tell them to go buy your book. Your practice tests are ***EXACTLY*** *like the real thing, and your test taking tips are an absolute lifesaver. - J. B., New Hampshire*

After purchasing your course and another book, I realized that your course was much easier to use. I received a score of 100! Your book made all the difference in the world. - K. I., Missouri

I didn't even get the book until the day before the exam, and I still scored a 95.4. This book is a must for anyone who wants to score high enough to really get a job. - S. S., Michigan

Postal Exam 473 & 473-C

Copyright © 2005 by T. W. Parnell • Illustrated by Susie Varner • All rights reserved.
Pathfinder Distributing Company, the publisher, is a private firm not affiliated with the U.S. Postal Service.

The material in this book is believed to be current and accurate as of the publish date to the best of the author's knowledge. The information presented herein is based upon the author's experience, observations of Postal procedures, comments from Postal employees, and comments from experienced Postal exam applicants.

Code 473473C-00641

Mr. Parnell welcomes feedback from his customers.

Send us your score. Let us know how well this study guide worked for you.

Pathfinder Distributing Co., P.O. Box 1368, Pinehurst, TX 77362-1368.

info@pathfinderdc.com

To my children - Sarah, Sam, and Savannah

Copyright © 2005 by T. W. Parnell
All rights reserved including the right of reproduction in whole or in part by any means.

Published by Pathfinder Distributing Company, P.O. Box 1368, Pinehurst, TX 77362-1368
ISBN 0-94-018226-2 (The Original Postal Exam 473 & 473-C Study Guide)
ISBN 0-94-018227-0 (Complete Postal Exam 473 & 473-C Training Program)
ISBN 0-94-018228-9 (New Postal Exam 473 & 473-C Computer-Based Course)
Manufactured in the United States of America

A message from the author ...

The Postal Service strikes again!

It's not like the old exam wasn't hard enough. Taking any Postal exam ranks right up there with other fun filled activities like going to the dentist for a root canal.

So, what do they do? While our backs are turned, they sneak a new test in on us - the 473 - to replace the old 470 exam.

Thank goodness for friends. My Postal buddies gave me a heads up on the 473 exam six months before it was released. The new exam was first given in December 2004 at several locations scattered across the U.S. So, I spent that week bouncing around the country taking the exam.

Like everyone else who takes a Postal exam unprepared, my first couple of experiences with the 473 were miserable. But by the third time around, I was beginning to formulate strategies. And by the end of the week, I was breezing through the exam with time to spare and making 100's.

Now it's your turn. But you don't have to go into the exam miserably unprepared like I did at first --- and like most applicants still do because they are too lazy to prepare. All you have to do is follow my simple step-by-step test prep instructions and go ace that baby!

As you probably expect, the new 473 exam is more challenging than the old 470. I definitely find the memorization on the 473 to be more difficult. That is, it was more difficult until I developed some new strategies that make it quite manageable. The detailed tasks that you are required to perform on the 473 are more demanding as well. And, like all Postal tests, the 473 is a rigidly timed exam, so speed is still an issue.

All in all, you will find taking the 473 exam to be similar to taking any other Postal exam. If you are diligent about your test preparation, you will walk away from the exam smiling and planning for your new Postal career while others come away crying. If, on the other hand, you do not take your test preparation seriously – if you are not willing to do the necessary practice work – you will be one of the crybabies.

As many of my customers know, I tend to get a bit dramatic at times. To quote some of my favorite lines ...lines that seem appropriate when discussing Postal exams but that my earlier customers are probably tired of hearing anyway ... *Do not let this opportunity escape for lack of effort! Show the initiative. Muster the effort. Go forth and conquer!*

T. W. Parnell

Table of Contents

How to Use this Guide

This guide is designed to assure 100% effective test preparation while demanding the least possible time and effort. Three elements are needed for successful test preparation ...

- You need to know what's on the exam.
- You need to learn unique test-taking strategies for the various parts of the exam.
- You need a quantity of up-to-date and realistic practice tests for mastering the unfamiliar job-related skills and the speed demanded on this rigidly timed exam.

This guide provides these very elements in the simplest possible fashion. When choosing a study guide, what you look for is realistic practice tests and simple yet effective test-taking strategies. That's what my guides offer, and that's why so many of my customers now work for the Post Office.

For maximum success, just follow these simple steps.	
Depending upon how much practice you personally need, and depending upon how much effort you are willing to give, completing this course can take anywhere from 6 to 12 hours. First you learn about exam content and test-taking strategies. Then you wrap up by taking some practice tests. The best plan is to work an hour or so per day beginning a few weeks before your test date. However, this course is flexible and can be arranged to fit any schedule. If you wait until the last minute, like so many of us do, that's okay too. You can compress all the test prep work down into only a few days if you have to. I do not recommend this route, but many applicants do adequately prepare for their exams over the last few days.	
Step 1	Spend a couple of hours studying the exam content and test-taking tips covered in first 54 pages of the book. The actual amount of time required depends upon your personal reading speed and upon how much you already know about the exam. If you have the Postal Exam Training Course Audio CD, follow along in the first 54 pages as you listen to the CD. If you have the Postal Test Prep CD-ROM, follow along in the first 54 pages as you take the test prep classes on the CD-ROM.
Step 2	Then, beginning on page 55, use the six practice tests in your guide to master the skills, strategies, and speed demanded on the exam. Each practice test takes 60 to 90 minutes. Thus, completing all six tests could require 6 to 9 hours. However, after taking several tests, some people find that they need more practice for some sections and less for others. At this point, these people may begin a more selective form of practice. They may begin to concentrate more on the sections they find harder and less the other sections. If you make a similar determination and end up not taking all six tests in their entirety, your total practice time will be reduced. To receive any real practice value, you must time yourself precisely as you take the tests. The 473 exam is rigidly timed test. In order to master the speed demanded, it is imperative that you time yourself precisely. If you have the Timed Practice Test Audio CD, use it for exact timing and realistic section-by-section instructions as you take the tests. If you have the Postal Test Prep CD-ROM, use the recorded practice test sessions on the CD-ROM for the same exact timing and realistic instructions as you take the tests.

If you do not have the CD-ROM or audio CD's mentioned above, see the order form in the back of the book or our website *www.PostalExam.com* for details on these performance boosting tools.

ABOUT EXAM 473 & 473-C

Exam 473 is used to fill all career Processing, Distribution, Delivery, and Retail positions - over 90% of all fulltime Postal jobs. This exam was launched December 2004 to replace old exam 470. Listed below are the specific entry-level jobs filled from the 473 exam. (See page 48 for job descriptions.) Most upper level jobs are filled from individuals who start in one of these entry-level positions and work their way up.

City Carrier
Mail Handler
Mail Processing Clerk
Sales, Service, and Distribution Associate

According to our contacts within the Postal Service, **the 473 exam can be given under two different names ... Exam 473 and Exam 473-C**. When given to fill *all* the above jobs, it is called Exam 473. When given to fill only City Carrier jobs, it is called Exam 473-C. The "C" in "473-C" stands for "Carrier". The exam is the same; it's just the name that is different. You see, the City Carrier position is the Postal job in highest demand. (See page 51.) Since they need to fill City Carrier jobs more often than other positions, it is not unusual for them to give the exam (473-C) more often to fill just City Carrier jobs and less often (473) to fill all the jobs.

When taking the 473 and/or 473-C exam, you are in essence applying for local jobs. Taking the exam in Atlanta makes you eligible for jobs only in Atlanta. Taking the exam in Atlanta cannot help you get a job anywhere else in the country except Atlanta. If you want to be eligible for jobs in other locations, you must take the exams in those other locations when it is offered there. The only time you can transfer a score from one location to another is when they are actually giving the test in the second location. At that point, you can either (1) transfer your score to the second location - but your name will no longer be on the register at the first location or (2) simply go take the exam again at the second location - this way you will have your name on both registers.

Applicants taking the 473 exam for all the jobs are usually allowed to choose which of the jobs they want to apply for. You can mark one, two, three, or all four jobs. Unless you simply refuse to accept one or more of these jobs, we encourage you to mark all four. This will greatly increase your likelihood of being hired by increasing the number of potential opportunities open to you. However, there are rare cases where you are not allowed to choose the jobs you want to apply for. In these cases, you are told that, by taking the exam, you have applied for any available jobs.

Also when taking the 473 exam for all the jobs, applicants are usually allowed to choose up to three locations where they would like to work. These are nearby locations, not nationwide. When taking the test in Atlanta for instance, you would be able to choose up to three facilities in the Atlanta metro area. Again, we encourage you to mark the maximum of three locations in order to increase your likelihood of being hired by increasing the number of potential opportunities open to you. And, again, there are rare cases where you are not allowed to choose the locations where you want to work. In these cases, you are told that by taking the exam, you have applied for work at any facilities within the local district.

If you end up with a job and/or location that is not exactly your favorite, transfers are quite possible. We know of many individuals who accepted a less than ideal job or location just to get their Postal career started as quickly as possible. Then, they later arranged a transfer to a more preferred position or location. You cannot have a transfer just because you want it. The circumstances must be right. Nonetheless, transfers do happen all the time.

How to Apply & Test Dates

You don't apply for a job - you apply to take an exam. You don't get to fill out an employment application unless you score high enough on the exam. How to apply is easy. Finding out when you can apply is the difficult part. Detailed below are the problems and the solutions...

Erratic Testing Schedules
Exams are given by the many Postal districts and/or sub-districts on an as-needed basis. The result is hundreds of individual testing locations, each giving tests whenever it chooses.

Application Dates
When an exam is to be given, they announce an application period that can be as short as one week or as long as several months. You can only apply during the specified application dates.

Announcement Number
An individual announcement number is assigned for each testing event. You must have a correct and valid announcement number in order to apply.

Test Dates
On the average, applicants are scheduled to take the test about eight weeks after applying. But this can vary greatly. In some cases the test is not given until several months afterwards.

Scheduling Notice
You will receive a scheduling notice by mail about two weeks before your scheduled test date. It is not possible to find out anything about your test date until you receive the scheduling notice.

How to Find Application Dates & Announcement Numbers

If you have not applied yet, your most pressing need is to find application dates and announcement numbers. Described below are ways you can find this critically needed info.

Finding Application Dates & Announcement Numbers Online
The Postal Service now publishes exam application dates and announcement numbers online at *http://uspsapps.hr-services.org/UspsLocate.asp?strExam=*. When visiting this page, select a state from the dropdown window, and all open exams for that state will be displayed. (Note: This address was valid as of this book's publish date. However, future site revisions may render this address invalid. If it does not work for you, go to *www.usps.com* and search for job related links.)

Below is a sample of what you will see on the announcement page followed by explanations.

City/State	Announcement Number	Exam Number	Exam Title	Opening Date	Closing Date
DALLAS, TX	114452	473	Processing, Distribution and Delivery Positions	02/07/2005	02/11/2005
ODESSA, TX	116235	473-C	City Carrier	03/21/2005	03/25/2005

The **City/State** is the location of the key Post Office for the testing event. This Post Office is usually responsible for a larger area surrounding it.

The **Announcement Number** is a link to the online application for its particular exam. The quickest way to apply from this point is to simply click on the announcement number.

The **Exam Number** and **Exam Title** are self-explanatory.

The **Opening Date** is the date that the application period begins for that particular exam.

The **Closing Date** is the date that the application period ends for that particular exam.

The **Test Date** is not given because it is not available until later.

Online announcements greatly simplify the application process. But, **there is a catch - exam info is displayed only during the application period.** If you don't happen to check the online announcement page during the application dates, you will miss out altogether. We suggest that you check at least once a week until the test you want to take is finally announced.

Other Methods to Inquire about Application Dates & Announcement Numbers

Why can't we just call to ask for exam info? Because the Postal Service does not publish their phone numbers, that's why. They may not, but we do! Over 250 numbers for facilities nationwide are listed in our Postal phone directory at the back of this book. About half these numbers, listed as "Exam Office" numbers, connect you to real live human beings who can answer your specific questions. The other half, listed as "Recording" numbers, ring into what the Postal Service calls "Hiring & Testing Hotlines". You can call these numbers 24/7 to hear recorded announcements of employment and testing opportunities.

When an exam is to be given, **notices are posted in the lobbies of local Post Offices.** But, how many of us make a habit of checking out the local Post Office bulletin board?

Sometimes, but certainly not always, they run an ad in the local newspaper. Due to budget limitations, they are rarely able to advertise in the paper.

How to Apply Online and by Phone

Paper application forms are no longer used. You can only apply online or by phone.

To apply online, go to *http://uspsapps.hr-services.org/* or simply click the announcement number on the online announcement page. After entering an announcement number, you are asked for your contact info, social security number, etc. (Note: This address was valid as of this book's publish date. However, future website revisions may render this address invalid. If it not work when you try it, go to *www.usps.com* and search for job related links.)

When applying online, you are asked to answer survey questions dealing with Postal job duties ... are you able to work evening/weekend shifts, to perform certain types of physical labor, etc. If you answer "No" to any questions, you get a message that basically says Postal employment may not be best for you. These questions are more for your benefit than theirs. The questions give you a good idea of job responsibilities so you can decide which jobs are right for you. You can skip most of these questions without harm by simply clicking "Continue".

To apply by phone, call the toll-free application number 1-866-999-8777 with a touch-tone phone. Using the keypad and by speaking slowly and clearly, you will be asked to provide your contact info, social security number, etc. Again, the first thing asked for is an announcement number. (Note: This phone number was valid as of this book's publish date. However, future changes by the Postal Service may render this number invalid. If it does not work when you try it, use the phone directory in this book to call a nearby facility and ask for help.)

WHAT'S ON THE EXAM?

The twin 473 and 473-C exams consist of the below four parts.

Part A – Address Checking has 60 questions. Each question is a pair of items consisting of an address (street/P.O. Box, city, and state) and a ZIP code. You are given 11 minutes to compare the items and answer "A" if they are exactly alike, "B" if they are different and the difference is in the address, "C" if they are different and the difference is in the ZIP code, or "D" if they are different and the difference is in both the address and the ZIP code.

In **Part B – Forms Completion**, you are shown various forms similar to those used by the Postal Service and asked questions about how they should be completed. You are given 15 minutes to answer 30 multiple-choice questions. The answer choices are A, B, C, or D.

Part C – Coding and Memory consists of two sections. For both sections, you are shown a chart of delivery routes (A, B, C, and D) and various address ranges that fit within the delivery routes.

- In the **Coding Section**, you are given 6 minutes to answer 36 questions. Each question is an address, and the answer should be the delivery route (A, B, C, or D) where the chart indicates that the address belongs. In the Coding Section, you are allowed to look at the chart as you answer the questions.
- In the **Memory Section**, you are given 7 minutes to answer 36 similar address questions. Again, the answer is the delivery route (A, B, C, or D) where the chart indicates that the address belongs. But in the Memory Section, you are ***not*** allowed to look at the chart as you answer the questions. Instead, you are given a few minutes to memorize the addresses and delivery routes, and then you must answer the questions from memory.

In **Part D – Personal Characteristics and Experience Inventory** you are given 90 minutes to answer 236 questions. These questions assess your personal characteristics, tendencies, and/or experiences related to performing effectively as a Postal employee. These are psychologically oriented multiple-choice questions. For instance, one question might state something like "I would rather be closely managed than be allowed to manage my own time." For a question like this, the answer choices might be (A) Strongly Agree, (B) Agree, (C) Disagree, or (D) Strongly Disagree. Other questions are statements about actions you take in particular circumstances, and the answer choices might be (A) Very Often, (B) Often, (C) Sometimes, or (D) Rarely.

Answers for all four parts of the exam are marked on an **Answer Sheet**. The answer sheet is broken into four parts, one for each of the above four parts of the exam. For each question, you darken an oval on the answer sheet that contains the proper answer - A, B, C, D, etc. In this book, the answer sheets are necessarily printed with black ink. However, **on real exams, answer sheets are printed in various colors**. Depending upon which exam you take, the answers sheet may be printed with blue ink, green ink, pink ink, etc. This should not present any problems, but we wanted to forewarn you so that you are not taken by surprise. Unexpected surprises can be distracting and may affect your performance.

SCORING FORMULAS & HOW UNANSWERED (BLANK) QUESTIONS AFFECT YOUR SCORE

Each individual part of the exam is scored separately. Then the scores for the individual parts are combined to create the overall exam score. Details follow. (Don't blame me, by the way, for the goofy formulas and the lack of complete information. I'm just quoting Postal policies.)

To score **Part A - Address Checking**, count your correct answers and your wrong answers. Subtract 1/3 of the number of wrong answers from the number of correct answers. The result is your score.

Address Checking Example: Let's say that, out of the 60 Address Checking questions, I answered 58 in the time allowed. And, of the 58 that I answered, 49 were correct, and 9 were wrong. To score myself, I subtract 3 (1/3 of the 9 of wrong answers) from 49 (the number of correct answers). My score is a 46.
Note: When figuring 1/3 of the number of wrong answers, the result will rarely be a whole number ... as in 1/3 of 9 = 3. So, you will frequently need to round off. For instance, if you had 8 wrong answers, 1/3 of 8 = 2.67. In this case, you round 2.67 off to the whole number 3.

For **Part B – Forms Completion**, simply count the number of correct answers, and that's your score.

Forms Completion Example: Let's say that, out of the 30 Forms Completion questions, I answered 29 in the time allowed. And, of the 29 that I answered, 26 were correct, and 3 were wrong. My score is simply a 26 ... the number of correct answers. Wrong answers do not figure into the formula for this section.

Both sections of **Part C – Coding and Memory** are scored just like the Part A - Address Checking. We count the number of correct answers and the number of wrong answers. Then, we subtract 1/3 of the number of wrong answers from the number of correct answers. The result is our score.

Coding Section Example: Let's say that, out of the 36 Coding questions, I answered 34 in the time allowed. And, of the 34 that I answered, 28 were correct, and 6 were wrong. To score myself, I subtract 2 (1/3 of the 6 of wrong answers) from 28 (the number of correct answers). My score is a 26.
Memory Section Example: Let's say that, out of the 36 Memory questions, I answered 35 in the time allowed. And, of the 35 that I answered, 32 were correct, and 3 were wrong. To score myself, I subtract 1 (1/3 of the 3 of wrong answers) from 32 (the number of correct answers). My score is a 31.
Note: As discussed above for Part A - Address Checking, when figuring 1/3 of the number of wrong answers, you will frequently need to round off to a whole number.

Part D – Personal Characteristics and Experience Inventory is scored, but the Postal Service refuses to release any details on how it is scored or how its score affects your overall exam score.

Similarly, the Postal Service refuses to release the formula for calculating the **final overall exam score**. We know how they score at least the first three parts of the exam, but not how they mix the scores for the individual parts together to come up with a final score.

It is important that you **score every practice test you take** in order to measure your progress and to determine how much more effort is needed and/or where it is needed. However, measuring your progress can be difficult if you do not have the proper tools (scoring formulas). Sure, you can score the individual parts of the exam, but if anyone claims they can tell you how the scores for the individual parts convert into an overall exam score, they are telling you an untruth. Our best advice is simply to never be satisfied with any score you make. Score each practice test for the sole purpose of beating that score next time. Always strive to improve your performance on the next practice test. Your goal should be to capture every possible point - to achieve your highest possible score. Applicants are called in for employment on the basis of scores, so your objective is to be as close to the top of the list as you possibly can be!

How do unanswered questions (blank answers) affect your score? Unanswered questions are not mentioned in the scoring formulas. But, do not mistakenly assume that this means they are acceptable. Just the opposite, unanswered questions severely hurt your exam score. Consider this ... There are 162 questions in the first three parts of the exam that we know how they score. (As previously discussed, when it comes to scoring, Part D - Personal Characteristics & Experience Inventory is a big unknown at this time.) Therefore, if you answered each of these 162 questions correctly within the time allowed, you would accumulate 162 points. To make a high score, you need to capture as many of these points as possible. Every point you fail to capture, whether by leaving a question unanswered or by answering it incorrectly, reduces your final score. Obviously, it is to your advantage to correctly answer as many questions as possible and to leave the fewest possible questions blank.

SHOULD YOU GUESS ON THE EXAM?

You should not guess on Part A - Address Checking or Part C - Coding and Memory. Due to their scoring formulas, you are penalized for incorrect answers. Therefore, guesses are more likely to hurt you than help you. Subtracting only 1/3 of the number of wrong answers may not seem like much of a penalty, but when you factor in the odds that your guesses will be wrong three out of four times, the truth becomes obvious. The bottom line is that each guess will likely offset one of your correct answers. Therefore, each guess really costs you two points ... one point for the question you guessed at incorrectly and one point for the question you answered correctly but lost because the incorrect guess offset it.

However, **guesses are acceptable on Part B - Forms Completion** due to its particular scoring formula. On this part of the exam, if you guess and get the correct answer, you picked up an extra point. And if you guessed wrong, you simply missed a point that you were not going to capture anyway. If you do make a guess, go with your first choice - don't sit and debate between two or three possible answers. Psychological tests have shown that your first choice is usually the best one. Obviously, however, guessing in any form should be a last resort.

You should not guess on Part D - Personal Characteristics and Experience Inventory. You should answer honestly and sincerely. There are no right or wrong answers. For each question, you simply select the answer that best reflects your own individual personality, temperament, experience, etc. You absolutely should *not* attempt to manipulate this part of the exam by trying to select answers you think they prefer. There are built-in indicators that will expose any attempt at manipulation. Just imagine what kind of assumptions they will make about you if they catch you trying to manipulate these questions. You may think that you can outsmart them, but you simply cannot. This part of the exam was created by highly trained and skilled professionals whose goal is to identify applicants who should - and applicants who should NOT - be considered for employment. Both ethically and practically, the best and only course is to answer honestly and sincerely.

ARE YOU ALLOWED TO MAKE NOTES DURING THE EXAM?

The written instructions say: **"Unless instructed otherwise for a specific part, you may make notes or write anywhere in the <u>test booklet</u>."** There are only two sections where you are told not to make marks or notes ... during the two memorization segments of the Memory section on Part C - Coding and Memory. This will be detailed further as we discuss strategies for the individual parts of the exam.

This ability to make marks or notes is quite new. Historically, applicants have been forbidden to make marks or notes for the most part. Since this is so new, some Postal examiners are not yet fully aware of it. When taking the exam, if one of the monitors asks you to stop making marks or notes, refer the monitor to the bottom of page one in the test booklet where it states that you are indeed allowed to do so unless specifically instructed otherwise. This should solve the problem. But, if the monitor persists, do what the monitor asks. Getting into an argument with the monitor is a no-win situation. This very situation happened to me the first time I took the 473 exam.

The only marks you are allowed to make on the <u>answer sheet</u>, however, are the actual answer choices that you darken. Absolutely no other marks are allowed on the answer sheet.

Note that the information in the first two paragraphs above relates to the test (question) booklet only, not to the answer sheet. You can make marks or notes in the test (question) booklet unless specifically instructed otherwise, but you can absolutely never make any marks on the answer sheet except for the answer choices you darken.

PREPARATION BEFORE THE EXAM

On this type of exam, **knowledge is of no value without sufficient practice** to develop the skills, strategies, and speed needed for success. This calls for consistent study and practice. Following are several tips for your advance preparation:

- **Study all of the material in this book and take all the practice exams before your test date.** Do not wait until the day before the exam to start studying! On the other hand, do not complete all your practice work months before the exam date either. Natural memory loss will cause you to lose some of the skills and speed that you worked so hard to master.

- It is very important that you **take the practice tests under conditions as similar as possible to the real exam.** Find a quiet setting where you will not be disturbed while taking the practice tests. Timing yourself precisely while taking the practice tests cannot be stressed enough. It is impossible to master the speed required without being precisely timed. To conveniently and precisely time yourself, use either our Timed Practice Test CD or our Test Prep CD-ROM. Visit our website *www.PostalExam.com* or see the order form in the back of the book for details. Use the answer keys in the back of the book to score each practice exercise as you complete it. This will enable you to identify areas of weakness and concentrate more on them.

- A psychological term called the **"practice effect"** applies to all parts of the exam. The practice effect occurs when a person repeatedly takes an exam over and over a number of times during a brief period of time. For most people, exam scores will be higher the more often you take the test because of increasing familiarity with the material. This trend should become evident as you score your practice exams. Your score on the second exam should be higher than on the first, the third should be even higher, and so on.

- As you learn to **pace yourself for speed and accuracy**, your scores should increase. For example, let's say that at first you were only able to finish half the questions on a practice test during the time allowed. This may be discouraging, but at least you answered most of them correctly - you only missed a few. You should be proud of this score, right? No, wrong --- *very wrong!* You are putting far too much emphasis on accuracy and not nearly enough on speed. To solve this, you must push yourself and practice to develop more speed. Or, let's say you finish an entire practice exam within the required time period, but half of your answers are wrong. It should be obvious that you are placing too much emphasis on speed and not enough attention on accuracy. To solve this, simply slow down and check your answers more carefully. The key is to find a happy medium between speed and accuracy.

- This book gives you **simple short-cut strategies** that will greatly enhance your test-taking ability and your score. It is critically important that you understand and master these strategies so that you can make the highest possible score.

SCHEDULING NOTICE

About two weeks before your test date, you will receive a scheduling notice advising when and where to report for the exam.

The scheduling package includes a 15 page booklet and a loose page that is your admission pass for the exam. In addition to the date, time, and location for your test, it contains general information and a few sample questions for each part of the exam. The package instructs you to bring your admission pass (the loose page), a picture ID, and two #2 pencils with you to the exam.

Also included in the scheduling packages are the same survey questions described on page 12 (How to Apply Online). As discussed, these questions are more for your benefit than theirs. They give you a good idea of job duties so you can decide which job(s) are right for you.

The **sample questions in the package** are provided simply to make unprepared applicants aware of exam content. Altogether, these few sample questions do not represent even 10% of a complete practice test, and they provide no real practice value.

Note, however, that **the format of the few sample questions in the package confirms that the exam format in this book is accurate and up-to-date**. Do not be confused by conflicting formats that may be presented in other books.

The scheduling package repeatedly states "You will not be expected to answer all the questions in the time allowed." This is certainly true of most applicants who do nothing to prepare for the exam. But, **this does not mean that failing to answer all the questions is acceptable.** As discussed earlier in the scoring formula section, you need to capture every possible point, and every point you lose - whether by answering incorrectly or by leaving questions unanswered - hurts your final score. After completing this course, you however, will be prepared to achieve your highest possible score. You will have mastered the skills and speed necessary to succeed.

The scheduling package's description of Part C - Coding and Memory can be confusing. The wording may lead you to believe that there are only two segments in Part C, one for the Coding section and one for the Memory section, but this is simply not true. Why they fail to mention the additional various practice and memorization segments is beyond us. But, please be assured that the format presented in this guide for Part C - Coding and Memory is absolutely correct. I have taken the exam enough times to know precisely of what I speak.

TEST DAY

Once your scheduled test date arrives, here are a few pointers that will help out:

- **Get a good night's rest, and have a light, nutritious meal**.
- **Do not drink too many liquids before the test. Do visit the restroom before the test.** This may sound childish, but it may literally make the difference between success and failure. The test will last about 3 ½ hours, and they will not stop for any breaks whatsoever. If you leave the room for any reason, you simply lose the time, the test sections, and/or the questions that were covered in your absence. In some cases, they do not allow applicants to leave the exam room during the test for any reason whatsoever. You surely will not perform well if forced to take the exam under uncomfortable and distracting conditions.

- **Dress in layers so that you can comfortably tolerate extreme temperatures in the exam room.** I have gone to testing events during the heat of summer dressed in light clothing only to freeze due a supercharged air conditioning system. I have gone to testing events during the cold of winter dressed in warm clothing only to be roasted in the exam room due to a supercharged heating system. The exam is usually given in a large rented facility. The Postal employees giving the exam have no more knowledge of the heating and cooling system or ability to control the temperature than you do. Dress so that you can add or remove layers of clothing to accommodate whatever environment is encountered in the exam room.

- **Leave home early**, **and plan to arrive at the test site early**. Allow time for any conceivable delays (auto problems, traffic congestion, etc.) that you can possibly imagine. If your notice says that the test is scheduled for 9:00 AM, the doors will be literally locked at precisely 9:00 AM. It doesn't matter whether you are 30 seconds or 30 minutes late - you are late period, and you will not be admitted. The rules are absolutely rigid on this matter. Also, due to the large number of applicants, there is usually a long line of people at the exam site waiting to be processed and seated. I have witnessed a few cases where there were simply not enough seats to accommodate all the applicants. It is a very good idea to arrive early so that you won't have to stand in line forever and to assure that you don't get turned away.

- Another reason to arrive early is to have a chance to **familiarize yourself with the examination room**. Applicants who have acquainted themselves with their surroundings are more comfortable and tend to perform better.

- **Bring your admission pass (the loose page from the scheduling packet) and a picture I.D.** You will be checked at the door for these items, and you will not be admitted into the test site or allowed to take the exam if you do not have them.

- **Bring pencils** as instructed in your scheduling packet. Usually there are plenty of extra pencils available at the test site, but don't automatically assume that this will be true. If you don't bring your own pencils, and if they don't provide any for you, how can you take the test? For maximum performance, don't bring just any pencils, bring our exclusive *Test Scoring & Speed Marking Pencils*. See page 43 for details.

- **Work diligently on each part of the test until you are instructed to stop**. Every second counts. If you finish before time is called, go back to check your answers in that section, but only in that section. Do not ever open your booklet to a section other than the one where you are supposed to be working at that point. Turning to a section other than the one where you are supposed to be working at that particular moment is grounds for disqualification.

- On a related topic, **do not ever open your test booklets or pick up your pencil until you are instructed to do so.** Likewise, immediately stop working, close your test booklet, and put down your pencil when instructed to do so. Failure to comply may look like an attempt to cheat and may cause you to be disqualified. It would be heartbreaking to be disqualified because you innocently doodled with your pencil or because you absentmindedly opened your test booklet when you were not supposed to. Excellent training tools to help avoid such catastrophes are our Timed Practice Test CD and Postal Test Prep CD-ROM described in the order form at the back of the book and on our website *www.PostalExam.com.* In addition to precisely timing you as you take your practice tests, these CD's review the instructions for you section by section and emphatically direct you exactly when to open or close your booklet and when to pick up or put down your pencil.

- **If you finish all the questions in one section before time is called, can you go back to other sections to finish questions there that you did not have time complete?** No, absolutely not. You will be specifically instructed to open your test booklet only to the section you are taking at that moment, and then to close it immediately when time is called. Opening your booklet to another section is grounds for disqualification.

- **If you finish one section with extra time left over, can you go back to re-darken answers in previous sections that may not appear to be darkened well enough?** No, absolutely not. Again, you will be specifically instructed to mark answers only for the section you are supposed to be taking at that time. Marking answers in another section of the answer sheet may appear to be an attempt to cheat and may lead to your disqualification.

- **I feel compelled to emphasize the possibility of being disqualified.** You can be disqualified for failure to follow instructions or for doing anything that might be interpreted as an attempt to cheat. There are monitors continually walking about the room to assure that applicants follow instructions and do not cheat. If an applicant appears to be doing something unacceptable, he or she can be disqualified without even knowing it. The monitor may silently make a note of the person's name, and then arrange for that person to receive an ineligible (failure) rating. This person might have performed wonderfully and might have deserved a great score, but the record will reflect an ineligible rating due to some type of improper conduct. Or, a person who appears to be acting improperly might be physically escorted from the room and rated ineligible. When taking your test, the exam administrator will stringently discuss actions that can lead to disqualification. I don't want to make you paranoid, but being disqualified is a real possibility. I simply want to impress this possibility upon you to assure that it will not happen to you.

- **Mark your answers clearly.** If you erase, do it completely. The machine scoring your answer sheet is not able to distinguish between intentional marks and accidental marks or changes.

- **Pace yourself.** Find a happy medium between speed and accuracy. Do not spend too much time on any one question.

- **Try not to let other people or noises distract you.** There will be distractions and noises no matter how hard the test administrator and monitors try to avoid it. As a matter of fact, the monitors can create distractions themselves. I have personally experienced situations where two or three monitors stopped for a chat ... right beside me ... and during the test!

EXAM CONTENT AND TEST TAKING STRATEGIES

There are four essential test prep keys - knowledge of exam content, test-taking strategies, realistic practice tests, and commitment. We provide everything you need except the commitment. Thorough and complete test preparation demands dedication and a drive to succeed.

Following are important points of which you should be aware as you begin your preparation:

- When you take the real exam, and likewise when you take the practice tests in your book, in every case **you will be working with two 8½" X 11" booklets** or pages - the very size of this book. One will be the test booklet containing the questions. The other will be the answer sheet booklet where you mark your answers.
- **The questions are all multiple choice, and the answer choices are letters - A, B, C, D, etc.** To mark answers on the answer sheet, darken the oval containing the correct answer or letter.

Success is virtually impossible without effective test-taking strategies. Following are strategies that apply to the test as a whole. Later we will learn about strategies the individual parts.

Exam Strategy #1 We will use the military strategy "**Divide and Conquer**". If we master each part of the exam individually, we cannot help but succeed on the exam as a whole.

Exam Strategy #2 **Check frequently to assure that the number of the question you are answering matches the number on the answer sheet where are marking.** Marking answers in the wrong answer sheet spots can be disastrous. To increase your speed and to avoid getting out of order, **the test booklet and answer sheet should be placed as close together as possible** at all times. If both booklets are fully opened, you are working on at least 11" X 34" of paper spread out on top of your table as pictured in the below illustration. The questions and answer spots are so far apart that errors are likely to happen.

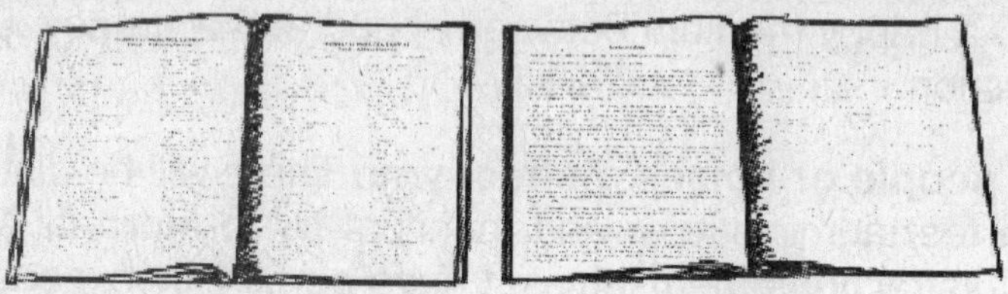

To avoid this problem, **fold the answer sheet booklet in half at the stapled seam so that all you see is the single 8½" X 11" answer sheet page.** This one step can reduce the distance between questions and answers by half. Then, depending on the positions of the questions and answers, you can usually even **lay the folded answer sheet booklet partially on top of the opened test booklet** as illustrated below. Now the questions and answers may be only a few inches apart. These strategies can bring the questions and answer spots very close together indeed for greater speed and accuracy. It would be great if you could fold the test booklet in half at the stapled seam as well, but the test booklet is simply too thick to conveniently fold.

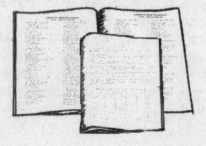

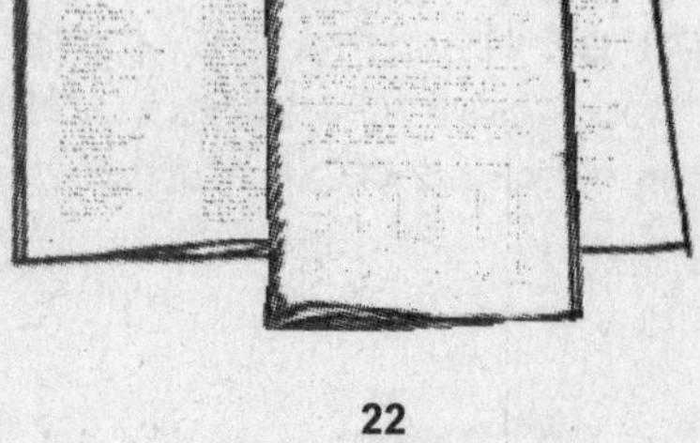

Exam Strategy #3 Another strategy to avoid getting out of order is to **use one of your spare pencils, the side of your hand, or your finger(s) to guide your eyes** back and forth between the test booklet and the answer sheet. In essence, you are using one of these items to mark your spot and track your progress as you race through the test so that you don't get out of order. But, do not use any thing else (like a ruler or piece of paper) for a guide as you practice at home. It may be easier, but you will not have access to these tools when taking the actual test. The only items you are allowed to have with you are the ones you were instructed to bring - which includes only yourself (complete with all parts of your body) and your pencils. Becoming dependent on a tool that will not be available at the real exam can have disastrous results.

Exam Strategy #4 **If you somehow get out of order despite efforts to the contrary, all may not be lost**. The best plan to salvage such a predicament is to skip ahead to the next question and continue - being cautious to mark answers in the correct spot. Then, when you finish, and if sufficient time remains, you can try to find where you got off track and attempt corrections.

Exam Strategy #5 **Each strategy presented offers value in terms of points earned on the test.** Some strategies enable you to capture many points, and others only a few. The sum total is what is important to you. To achieve your highest possible score, you should master all these strategies through practice - do not ignore the ones that may seem less valuable. Any tool that can add any points at all to your score is incredibly valuable.

Exam Strategy #6 The first three parts of the exam are rigidly timed. In each part you are asked to complete more questions in a limited period of time than many people can accomplish without help. This book is your help. Your goals are to (1) learn about exam content; (2) study the test-taking strategies; and (3) master the necessary skills, strategies, and speed as you take the practice exams. **On this type of exam, knowledge is of little value without practicing to master what you have learned.** As previously mentioned, our Timed Practice Test CD and our Test Prep CD-ROM are convenient tools for practicing realistically and for timing yourself precisely to master the needed speed. Visit our website *www.PostalExam.com* or see the order form in the back of the book for details.

Exam Strategy #7 **When marking an answer on the answer sheet, how much of the oval do you have to darken?** Will one tiny mark in the oval be enough? Do you need to scribble around and around in the oval forever trying to assure that every tiny part is darkened? What if your mark strays over into a neighboring oval? These are important questions that the Postal Service has officially answered for the first time in the 473 exam instructions. When taking the actual exam, the written instructions say that, for the scanner to read your answers correctly, you should darken over half of the oval and that you should not let your mark stray over into a neighboring oval. This is great news because many applicants have historically wasted precious time trying to carefully darken 100% of the oval. This slowed them down so much that they were not able to complete nearly enough questions within the limited time allowed. A convenient way to assure that you have darkened at least half of the oval is to concentrate on blacking out the letter. If you darken enough of the oval to cover the letter, you should have darkened at least half of the oval. But, as you practice, check occasionally to make sure that, when blacking out the letter, you have indeed darkened at least half of the oval. Don't waste your time trying to darken every nook and cranny. But, at the same time, you absolutely cannot afford to get so lax that you end up darkening less than half the oval. It would be a terrible shame to perform wonderfully on the exam but then to have the scanner score you badly because you were not diligent enough about darkening your answers.

Exam Strategy #8 **Once you master the necessary level of speed, you will notice that you develop a certain pace** - not unlike a runner competing in a race. What happens to a runner who stumbles or stops in the middle of a race? The runner not only loses time while he/she is stopped, the runner also loses time as he/she strives to regain the original pace - the runner is not moving as rapidly until his/her maximum pace is again achieved. The runner would have performed much better if he/she had not stopped.

The same principle holds true on this rigidly timed exam. As you race through the exam marking answers, **do not stop to make a correction if you suddenly realize that you have answered a question incorrectly**. Like the runner, you would be giving yourself a double whammy - you lose time while you're stopped, plus you work more slowly (answer fewer questions) as you rebuild your pace. Think of the seconds lost as you attempt the following steps to make a correction:

1. Stop writing.
2. Raise your pencil away from the paper.
3. Reverse the position of your pencil so that the eraser is facing the paper.
4. Erase the wrong answer.
5. Raise your pencil away from the paper again.
6. Reverse the position of your pencil again so that the lead is facing the paper.
7. Brush away the bits of rubber that were ground off your eraser as you used it.
8. Invariably, you see that part of the mark remains, so you decide to erase again.
9. So, you raise your pencil away from the paper again.
10. Reverse your pencil again so that the eraser is facing the paper.
11. Erase the remaining marks.
12. Raise your pencil away from the paper again.
13. Reverse the position of your pencil again so that the lead is facing the paper.
14. Brush away the bits of rubber again.
15. Look closely to assure that you really did erase all of the mark this time.
16. Mark the correct answer.
17. Attempt to rebuild you original pace as you answer the next several questions.

Most people go through these 17 counterproductive and time consuming steps every time they stop to make a correction. A better idea would be to pause just long enough to make a tiny dot next to the incorrect answer. Then, when you finish all the questions in that section (and most people are able to do so after completing this course), go back to correct the answers where you made the tiny dots. This strategy enables you to make the best use of the limited time available.

Exam Strategy #9 As you are beginning to see, and will shortly see even more, this exam is not like any other test you've ever taken before. In many cases, the information and strategies presented will be understood better and appreciated more after experiencing a practice test. You are therefore encouraged to **review the instructions and strategies again after completing each of your practice exams.**

Part A – Address Checking

In this section, there are 60 questions that must be answered in 11 minutes. Each question is a pair of items consisting of an address (street/P.O. Box, city, and state) and a ZIP code. In each case, the left half of the pair is in a column labeled "Correct List", and the right half of the pair is in a column labeled "List to be Checked". You are to determine whether the two items are exactly alike in every way (spelling, capitalization, numbers, punctuation, etc.) or if they or different in any way. Then, you mark your answer as follows...

A. If they are completely alike.
B. If they are different and the difference is in the address (street/P.O. Box and city/state) only.
C. If they are different and the difference is in the ZIP code only.
D. If they are different and there are differences in both the address and the ZIP code.

It is most important that you understand what they mean by Address on this part of the test. The Address includes (1) the street or the P.O. Box address *and* (2) the city and state. It includes everything in the column labeled Address. It includes everything but the ZIP code. So, when looking for Address differences, you are looking for differences anywhere except in the ZIP code.

Let's review the below sample questions that are laid out exactly like the real thing.

A. No Errors	B. Address Only	C. ZIP Code Only	D. Both

	Correct List		List to be Checked	
	Address	*ZIP Code*	*Address*	*ZIP Code*
1.	1420 Elgin Pkwy El Dorado, AR	67743-1822	1420 Elgin Pkwy El Dorado, AR	67743-1882
2.	83 SW Ave Ste 3E Anaheim CA	98525	83 SW Ave Ste 3E Anaheim CA	98525
3.	121 Cardona Way El Paso, TX	78934-1331	121 Cardoma Way El Paso, TX	78934-1331
4.	P.O. Box 63114 Washington, DC	26555-3114	P.O. Box 63314 Washington, DC	26655-3114

Sample 1. Looking closely, we find that the addresses (street, city, and state) are identical. But, looking at the ZIP code, we find a difference. The last four numbers on the left are 1822, and on the right they are 1882. The difference is in the ZIP code only, so we would mark answer choice C.

Sample 2. Here we find that everything is alike – the address (street, city, and state) and the ZIP code. So, we should mark answer choice A.

Sample 3. Comparing the addresses, we find that the street names are spelled differently. On the left, "Cardona" is spelled with an "n". On the right, "Cardoma" is spelled with an "m". Everything else, including the ZIP code, is alike. So, we would mark answer choice B.

Sample 4. Close examination shows that the P.O. Box numbers are different (63114 on the left and 63314 on the right) and that the first five numbers in the ZIP codes are different (26555 on the left and 26655 on the right). So, we should mark answer choice D.

The **format of Part A - Address Checking** is not terribly important, but I will describe it so you won't be taken by surprise. They first give you a 2 minute introductory exercise with only a few questions just to show how this part of the exam is structured. Then, they give you a 2 minute exercise with 10 questions so you can experience the real pressure of time. Answers for these two exercises are marked on sample answer sheets in the test booklet, not on the real answer sheet. Neither of these exercises is scored. Finally, they give you the actual 11 minute test with 60 questions, and you mark your answers this time on the actual answer sheet.

This part of the exam is more of a speed test for many people. **Comparing addresses is not terribly difficult, but doing so accurately at the pace demanded can be quite challenging indeed.** Following are the strategies needed to master Part A - Address Checking.

Address Checking Strategy #1 **Push yourself for speed.** Force yourself to practice at pace beyond your level of comfort. When you become comfortable at that faster speed, push yourself yet again to an even faster pace beyond your newly acquired level of comfort. Repeat the cycle over and over as you continually increase your ability and tolerance for speed. All of us learned in school to place most our emphasis on accuracy and little, if any, on speed. The result is that most of us have a speed/accuracy imbalance - at least in terms of this exam. The challenge is, via practice, to learn to place a little more emphasis on speed and a little less on accuracy. This may sound odd, but consider this ... How good a score should you expect if every question you answered was correct, but you were only fast enough to answer half the questions in the time allowed? You will score far better if you answer all the questions within the time allowed, even if you answer a few incorrectly because you were working so fast!

Address Checking Strategy #2 **Distributive Practice** is what athletes do ... consistent practice over a period of time. Considering the speed and eye/hand coordination demanded, the Part A - Address Checking section is similar to an athletic event. Approach your practice as though you were training for the Postal Olympics rather than a Postal exam.

Address Checking Strategy #3 As you begin each exam part, the examiner will briefly explain the instructions, tell you to open your booklets, direct you to pick up your pencil, and finally tell you to begin. Unlike most others, who are hanging on the examiner's every word and therefore have a delayed reaction time, you (1) should have your finger on the edge of your booklet before the examiner says the first word; (2) immediately flip it open as the examiner begins to utter the word "Open"; (3) as the examiner gives further instructions, answer the first few questions in your mind; and (4) when the examiner says to pick up your pencil, immediately mark those first few answers that you did in your mind. You did not cheat, but **you did pick up an advantage of a few points over most other applicants by using your foreknowledge and common sense.**

Address Checking Strategy #4 You cannot eat a pizza whole ... you cut it into manageable pieces. Similarly, **you cannot compare the complete address and ZIP code all at the same time ... you need to break them down into bite-size pieces.** Look at the below sample.

2232 Baltazarr St. Bakersfield, CA	97342-2911	2232 Baltazarr St. Bakersville, CA	97324-2911

Do your comparison step-by-step. Start with the street/P.O. Box, then the city/state, and finally the ZIP code. Comparing our sample step-by-step, we first compare the street addresses and find them to be alike. Then we compare the city/state and find a difference - Bakersfield on the left and Bakersville on the right. Finally, we compare the ZIP codes and find another difference - 97342 on the left and 97324 on the right. So, we would mark the answer D. Breaking the items down into bite-size pieces and comparing them step-by-step dramatically increases speed and accuracy.

Address Checking Strategy #5 **If you find a difference in the street/P.O. Box part of the address, immediately stop and move on to the ZIP code.** Don't waste time comparing the city/state. When comparing addresses, all it takes is one difference to make them different. Finding 100 more differences won't matter at all. Once you find a single difference, you have determined that the addresses are different, so move on to the ZIP codes to see if they are alike or different.

Address Checking Strategy #6 **When you find a difference, make a quick mark where you found the difference.** If you find a difference in the address, make a quick mark there and move on to the ZIP codes. If you find another difference in the ZIP codes, make a quick mark there also. Then, instead of dwelling on the question trying to remember where the differences were, just glance back at your marks. The marks will tell you where the differences are, and you will immediately know whether to mark the answer as B, C, or D. Of course, if there is no mark, you know to mark the answer A. This strategy tremendously increases speed and accuracy.

If you finish with time left to check your answers, **first check the ones without marks - the ones you found to be alike.** Afterward, if you have time, check the ones with marks - the ones you found to have differences. Studies show that most questions marked as different are correct. Most mistakes occur when we miss a subtle difference because we are working so fast, and we incorrectly mark a question as alike when the addresses or ZIP codes were really different.

Important Note: As discussed earlier, the instructions on page one of the actual exam say you may make marks anywhere in the test booklet unless instructed otherwise for a specific part. There are no instructions that prohibit you from making marks in Part A. Therefore, the above strategy of making marks to identify differences is perfectly acceptable. However, also as discussed earlier, this policy of allowing us to make marks is new. Since this is so new, not all Postal examiners are fully aware of it. If, while taking the exam, a monitor asks you to stop making marks, refer the monitor to the bottom of page one where it states that you are allowed to do so. This should solve the problem. But, if the monitor persists, do whatever the monitor asks. Getting into an argument with a monitor is a no-win situation.

Address Checking Strategy #7 **Do not guess on Part A - Address Checking**. As previously discussed, due to the scoring formula, wrong answers count against you. On this section, there is more risk of harm than good when guessing.

Address Checking Strategy #8 One of the most important strategies is to **memorize the answer choices.** You do not have time to look back at the instructions after each question to determine which answer to mark. If you have look back each time, you will never be able to answer all 60 questions within the 11 minutes allowed. The answer choices are copied below for you. *Memorize them right now!* Do not go forward one more inch until you know them by heart.

A. No Errors	**B. Address Only**	**C. ZIP Code Only**	**D. Both**

Address Checking Strategy #9 **Practice is the key to performance.** The only way to master the skills and speed demanded is practice. You cannot practice too much. There are six practice tests in your book. Take all of them, and take them realistically ... meaning time yourself precisely. Our Timed Practice Test Audio CD or our Test Prep CD-ROM are ideal tools for exact and convenient timing. Visit *www.PostalExam.com* or see the order form for details. Experience tells us that six is the ideal number of practice tests. If, however, you feel the need for more practice after taking all the tests in the book, you can simply take them again as many times as you like. After taking six full practice tests, you will have dealt with over 1,300 addresses. The likelihood of your remembering individual addresses at that point is very small indeed.

PART B – FORMS COMPLETION

In Part B - Forms Completion, you are shown various Postal Service forms, and you have 15 minutes to answer 30 questions about how these forms should be completed. More specifically, you are shown 5 different forms, and there are 6 questions about each form, for a total of 30 questions.

As with the previous section, the **format of Part B - Forms Completion** is not terribly important, but I will describe it so you will not be surprised. First they give you a 2 minute introductory exercise with only a few questions. Your answers for this exercise are marked on a sample answer sheet in the test booklet, not on the actual answer sheet. This exercise is not scored. Then, they give you the real test, and you mark your answers for the real test on your actual answer sheet.

For a better understanding of this part of the exam, let's take a look at the below sample form and at the few sample questions about this form on the next page.

Authorization to Hold Mail	
Postmaster - Please hold mail for:	
1. Name(s)	
2. Address	
3a. Begin Holding Mail (Date)	**3b.** Resume Delivery (Date)
4. ☐ **Option A** I will pick up all accumulated mail when I return and understand that mail delivery will not resume until I do. (This is suggested if your return date may change or if no one will be at home to receive mail.)	
5. ☐ **Option B** Please deliver all accumulated mail and resume normal delivery on the ending date shown above.	
6. Customer Signature	
For Post Office Use Only	
7. Date Received	
8a. Clerk	**8b.** Bin Number
9a. Carrier	**9b.** Route Number
Customer Option A Only	
Carrier: Accumulated mail has been picked up. **10a.** Resume delivery on (date) ____________________ **10b.** By: ____________________	

Sample Question 1: Where should you enter the customer's address? A. Box 2 B. Box 6 C. Box 9b D. Line 10b
The customer address is supposed to be entered in Box 2. Answer choice A is Box 2. So, we would darken the answer A for question 1 on our answer sheet.

Sample Question 2: In which box or boxes could 10/12/05 be an acceptable entry? A. Box 3a or Box 3b B. Box 7 C. Line 10a D. Box 3a, Box 3b, Box 7, or Line 10a
This is a trick question. Looking at answers choices A, B, and C, we see that they all call for a date. So, we would mark answer choice D because it includes all the boxes listed for A, B, and C.
You must read a question like this carefully. They are not asking if the date of 10/12/05 could be put in all of these boxes on the very same form. What they are really asking is which boxes call for a date as opposed to a name, an address, a zip code, etc.

This part of the exam is really about common sense. They ask you what information should be entered on a form and/or where it should be entered. You look at the form and find the answer. The form is right there for you to see. You do not have to memorize or remember anything.

Some questions can be tricky, like sample question 2 above. If you looked no farther than answer choice A, you might assume that it is the correct answer. Be sure to consider all the answers before making a decision. Check each answer choice to determine which one is the correct answer.

Don't let the format of the answers confuse you. For a particular question, say question 9, you may look at the form and find that the correct answer for this question is Box 6b, which happens to be answer choice D for question 9. At this point you are working with several numbers and letters ... 6, B, 9, and D ... as in Box 6b, question 9, and answer D. So you rush over to the answer sheet and immediately get confused. Are you supposed to be marking 6B, 9D, 9B, 6D, or what? You're working at maximum speed dealing with what seems like eighty million different numbers, letters, boxes, answer choices, dates, ZIP codes, addresses, etc., etc. etc. It's a wonder that you can get your name straight, much less the answer to question 9. The bottom line is that you must mark your answers carefully making sure that you are marking the proper question number and answer choice (9D), not a box number (6b) that was involved in the question or answer.

Before you begin answering questions, glance over the form briefly ... meaning only a few seconds, not a few minutes. You want to become slightly familiar with the form, not to memorize it. You simply do not have enough time to spend more than a few seconds looking over each form. Plus, reviewing the form does not help you that much anyway. There might be anywhere from 10 to 30 boxes on a form, but they will only ask you 6 questions about each form. Why spend time reviewing 100% of the form when they may only ask you about 20% of the boxes?

As with all parts of the exam, **practice is the key to performance.** Practice is the only way to master the skills, master the speed, and assure a high score. And the practice must be realistic - must be timed exactly - to be of any value. As mentioned before, our Timed Practice Test Audio CD and our Test Prep CD-ROM are ideal tools for realistic practice and precise timing.

PART C – CODING & MEMORY

Part C - Coding & Memory consists of two sections … the Coding Section and the Memory Section. Both sections are scored, so you get two scores from this one exam part. Both sections are broken down further into various segments.

Unlike other parts of the exam, **the format of Part C - Coding & Memory is very important.** We will discuss the format shortly and then later explain why it is so important for the Memory strategies.

First, we need to explore the Coding Guide, the focal point of this part. Below is a realistic sample of what the Coding Guide will look like on your exam.

CODING GUIDE

Address Range	Delivery Route
1200 – 1579 Stargate Dr. 800 – 900 Maple Street 20 – 60 State Rt 63	A
1580 – 1800 Stargate Dr. 61 – 99 State Rt 63	B
10000 – 15000 Bluebell 1 – 20 Hwy 90 901 – 1200 Maple Street	C
All mail that doesn't fall in one of the address ranges listed above	D

The same Coding Guide will be used throughout the whole of Part C - Coding & Memory. All the Address Ranges and Delivery Routes in the guide will remain the same all the way through both the Coding Section and the Memory Section. Notice the below points about the Coding Guide.

- The **Address Range** column of the Coding Guide contains address ranges. These are not addresses, they are address <u>ranges</u>. For instance, the address range 1200 - 1579 Stargate Dr. includes all addresses from 1200 to 1579 on Stargate Dr.
- The **Delivery Route** column contains one-letter codes for delivery routes. Each route serves the address ranges in its row. For instance, Delivery Route A serves addresses 1200 to 1579 on Stargate Dr., addresses 800 to 900 on Maple Street, and addresses 20 to 60 on State Rt 63. Any addresses within those ranges on those streets are served by Delivery Route A.
- Notice that **some street names appear twice.** For instance, Maple Street is served by Route A for addresses 800 - 900 and served by Route C for addresses 901 - 1200.
- Notice also that **Delivery Route D serves all addresses that do not fall into the ranges listed for Routes A, B, and C.** For instance, the address 127 Hwy 90 does not fall into any listed ranges. (The Hwy 90 range ends at 20.) The address 825 W Main St. does not appear in any of the ranges either. (There are no W Main St. addresses listed at all.) So these addresses would be served by Route D.

Sample Questions

Here's how the questions look in both the Coding Section and the Memory Section. Each question is an address. Your job is to find which Delivery Route (A, B, C, or D) serves this address. You do this by first finding which address range on the Coding Guide the address in the question belongs to. Then, for an answer, you select the proper Delivery Route (A, B, C, or D) for that address range. The Coding Guide and address ranges remain the same in both sections.

The only difference between the Coding Section and the Memory Section is that, **during the Coding Section, you can look at the Coding Guide** to find your answers. However, **during the Memory Section, you must answer from memory.** You are given a few minutes to memorize the Coding Guide, and then you must answer questions based upon what you memorized.

The below questions are laid out exactly as you will see them on the real test. Note that the address appears on the left and the Delivery Routes are listed on the right. We cannot figure out why in the world the Delivery Routes are listed this way. You already know that you're supposed to choose a Delivery Route for the answer, and you already know the choices are A, B, C, and D.

I think they list the Delivery Routes beside the question just to confuse us. While taking the exam, I have seen people simply circle their answer choices (A, B, C, or D) in the list of Delivery Routes beside the question. But, this is not how we're supposed to mark our answers. The only acceptable way to mark answers is to darken the appropriate answer choice on our answer sheet. People who think they are marking answers by circling A, B, C or D have unfortunately not really marked any answers at all. Do not get caught in this trap. Ignore the list of Delivery Routes beside the question, and mark your answers on the answer sheet where they are supposed to be.

As we work the below sample questions, refer to the sample Coding Guide on the previous page.

	Address	Delivery Route			
1.	1050 Maple Street	A	B	C	D
2.	12002 Bluebell	A	B	C	D
3.	78 State Rt 36	A	B	C	D
4.	1660 Stargate Dr.	A	B	C	D

1. **1050 Maple Street** – Let's attack this question step-by-step. (1) Looking for Maple Street on the Coding Guide, we quickly find it in the Delivery Route A box. But, the address of 1050 in the question doesn't fit the range of 800-900 for Maple Street in Box A. So, Route A cannot be the answer. (2) We look to see if there is another listing for Maple Street, we find another listing in Box C, and we find that the address of 1050 in the question fits in the Box C range of 901-1200 for Maple Street. (3) So, the answer must be C, and we darken C on the answer sheet.
2. **12002 Bluebell** – Bluebell only appears once in the Coding Guide ... in Route C. And, the address of 12002 in the question falls within the range of 10000 - 15000 for Blubell in Route C. So, the answer is Route C, and we would darken answer choice C on our answer sheet.
3. **78 State Rt 36** – This is a trick question. State RT 63 appears in the coding guide. But, the address in the question is on State RT 36, not State RT 63. However, working at high speed, it is easy to confuse these two addresses. The correct answer is D (Route D) because the address in the question does not appear in any of the address ranges listed for Routes A, B, or C.
4. **1660 Stargate Dr.** – This address fits the Stargate Dr. range in Route B, so the answer is B.

Format of Part C – Coding & Memory

The various sections and segments in Part C can be confusing. It is imperative, however, that you fully understand the format in order to use the strategies discussed later. Below is a breakdown of the format. As we review the format, remember that the Coding Guide and all the address ranges stay the same throughout both sections and all segments. Neither the Coding Guide nor the address ranges change as you work your way through Part C. They always remain the same.

Part C - Coding & Memory	
Coding Section The first section, the Coding Section, is broken down into 3 segments as described below. • **Coding Section - Segment 1** The first segment of the Coding Section is a 2 minute introductory exercise. • **Coding Section - Segment 2** The second segment is a 90 second (1½ minutes) practice exercise. • **Coding Section - Segment 3** This is the actual Coding Section test. You have 6 minutes to answer 36 questions.	**Memory Section** The second section, the Memory Section, is broken down into 4 segments. • **Memory Section - Segment 1** The first segment is a 3 minute study and memorization period. • **Memory Section - Segment 2** The second segment is a 90 second (1½ minutes) practice exercise. • **Memory Section - Segment 3** The third segment is a 5 minute study and memorization period. • **Memory Section - Segment 4** This is the actual Memory Section test. You have 7 minutes to answer 36 questions.

Okay, that's about as clear as mud. For a better understanding, we will pick both sections apart piece-by-piece over the next few pages. First we will get a handle on all the confusing segments, and then we will discuss strategies for mastering this challenging part of the exam.

Coding Section

The first section of Part C - Coding & Memory is the Coding Section. This section is broken down into 3 segments. The Coding Guide is displayed for your use during all 3 segments. Below is a detailed breakdown of the Coding Section.

Coding Section
The Coding Section is broken down into 3 segments as described below. During all 3 segments, the Coding Guide is displayed for your use in finding answers.

- **Coding Section - Segment 1**
  The first segment of the Coding Section is a 2 minute introductory exercise with only a few questions and with the Coding Guide shown. The purpose of the segment is to show unprepared applicants how to answer the questions. You mark answers for this segment on a sample answer sheet in the test booklet, not on the actual answer sheet. This exercise is not scored.
- **Coding Section - Segment 2**
  The second segment is a 90 second (1½ minutes) practice exercise with 8 questions and with the Coding Guide shown. Its purpose is to allow you to experience the very real pressure of time. As with Segment 1, you mark your answers for this exercise on a sample answer sheet in the test booklet, not on the actual answer sheet. And, again, this exercise is not scored.
- **Coding Section - Segment 3**
  This is the actual Coding Section test. You have 6 minutes to answer 36 questions, and the Coding Guide is shown. This is the real test ... you mark your answers on the actual answer sheet ... and this segment is scored.

Note: Pay particular attention to the fact that, in Segments 1 and 2 of the Coding Section above, the Coding Guide is displayed and the exercises are not scored. We will use this to our advantage when discussing our memorization strategies for the Memory Section.

The Coding Section can be challenging, but not nearly as difficult as the Memory Section, the next section. This is because you can use the Coding Chart to look up answers during all segments of the Coding Section. However, **you absolutely do need to practice** the Coding Section to (1) master the skills and speed involved, (2) train yourself to quickly identify where the addresses fit into the Coding Guide, and (3) train yourself to identify the tricky addresses designed to confuse you. And, as always, for any real practice value, you must practice realistically and time yourself precisely.

As discussed before, our Timed Practice Test Audio CD and our Test Prep CD-ROM are ideal tools for precisely timing yourself, for realistic practice, and for convenient practice. See the order form in the back of the book or our website *www.PostalExam.com* for details.

As we continue discussing Part C - Coding & Memory, bear in mind that the Coding Guide and the address ranges in the Coding Guide remain the same throughout both sections and all segments.

Memory Section

This is the *Bad Boy* … the reason why so many people fail! Most people have a horrible time with the memorization. Below is a detailed breakdown of the Memory Section.

> **Memory Section**
> The second section of Part C, the Memory Section, is broken down into 4 segments. Your goal in this section is to memorize the Coding Guide and answer the questions from memory.
>
> - **Memory Section - Segment 1**
>   The first segment of the Memory Section is a 3 minute study period. You are to spend the 3 minutes trying to memorize the Coding Guide which is displayed during this segment.
> - **Memory Section - Segment 2**
>   The second segment is a 90 second (1½ minutes) practice exercise with 8 questions The Coding Guide is not shown. You are supposed to try answering the questions from memory. You mark your answers for this exercise on a sample answer sheet in the test booklet, not on the actual answer sheet, and this exercise is not scored.
> - **Memory Section - Segment 3**
>   The third segment is a 5 minute study period. You are to spend the 5 minutes trying to memorize the Coding Guide which is displayed during this segment.
> - **Memory Section - Segment 4**
>   This is the actual Memory Section test … you have 7 minutes to answer 36 questions… you must answer from memory … the Coding Guide is not shown … you mark answers on the actual answer sheet ... this segment is scored. You will notice on the answer sheet that these questions are numbered 37 - 72 rather than 1 - 36. This is because, of the 72 total questions in Part C, 1 - 36 are from the Coding Section, and 37 - 72 are from the Memory Section.

The Memory Section questions are just like the Coding Section questions - they are addresses for which you are to identify the proper Delivery Route (A, B, C, or D) from the Coding Guide. Except, in the Memory Section, you must do it from memory!

If you had enough time to study and memorize, you could handle it. But, they give you only two brief, broken study periods - a 3 minute period and a 5 minute period. These two broken study periods only serve to break your concentration. The least they could do is give you all 8 minutes (3 minutes + 5 minutes) together in a single study period. But even if they did, the memorization would still be almost impossible without some serious help in the form of strategies.

That's where my guide comes in. **The best part of this guide is the memorization strategies.** My strategies make this inhuman section manageable. In fact, after learning my strategies, many people find the Memory Section to be the easiest part of the test instead of the hardest!

Let's explore these strategies that make the Memory Section manageable…

Memory Strategy #1 The Coding Guide seems to be arranged to make the memorization as hard as possible. So, **we will rearrange the address ranges in our mind to make the memorization easier.** Our sample Coding Guide is copied at the top of the next page. You will need to refer to the Coding Guide as we discuss this strategy. First, though, we will examine the Coding Guide to identify particular features that will be important as we attack the memorization. Then, we will look at the address ranges in the Coding Guide one at a time to find the best way to memorize each. Okay, if you're ready, buckle your seat belts, and we're off…

Address Range	Delivery Route
1200 – 1579 Stargate Dr. 800 – 900 Maple Street 20 – 60 State Rt 63	A
1580 – 1800 Stargate Dr. 61 – 99 State Rt 63	B
10000 – 15000 Bluebell 1 – 20 Hwy 90 901 – 1200 Maple Street	C
All mail that doesn't fall in one of the address ranges listed above	D

- **As we start looking at our strategy, first notice a few points about the address ranges …**
    - **Some of the street names repeat.** For instance, Stargate appears in both Routes A and B, Maple Street in both A and C, and State Rt 63 in A and B. So, we must plan to memorize two different ranges for each of these streets. Notice that when a street name repeats, the addresses increase. The numbers in the second range for a particular street are larger than the numbers in the first range. Notice also that when a street name repeats, the second range for that street usually seems to pick up exactly where the first range stopped.
    - Notice that **the ranges can fit different descriptions.** Some end in a zero like 800-900. But, when the first range for a particular street ends with a zero, then the next range for that same street must begin with "1" number like 901-1200. Other ranges for a particular street end with a "9" like 1200-1579. When the first range ends with a "9", then the next range for the same street will begin with a zero number like 1580-1800. Some ranges have smaller numbers like 1-10 or 61-99, other ranges are large address numbers like 10000-15000, and yet other ranges fit somewhere in the middle.
- Now that we have a pretty good picture of how the ranges are formatted, **let's take a look at how to memorize the first street, Stargate Dr., along with its two address ranges.**
    - The address range for Stargate Dr. in Route A is 1200-1579, but we round off 1579 and memorize 1580 instead like this … 1200-1580. Why? Continue reading to find out.
    - The address range for Stargate Dr. in Route B is 1580-1800. This time we memorize these exact numbers … 1580-1800. Continue reading for the rest of the story.
    - Back to the question of why we memorize 1200-1580 instead of 1200-1579 … Our objective is to make the memorization easier by reducing the amount of material to be memorized. If we memorized 1200-1579 for the first address range and 1580-1800 for the second range, we would have to remember four items: 1200, 1579, 1580, and 1800. When memorizing 1200-1580 and 1580-1800, we only have to remember three items: 1200, 1580, and 1800.
    - Now, we put it all together and memorize the below line by silently repeating it over and over …

Stargate Dr. • 1200-1580-A • 1580-1800-B

- Said out loud, the line “Stargate Dr. • 1200-1580-A • 1580-1800-B” would sound like this …

Stargate Dr. *(pause)* twelve hundred - fifteen eighty - A *(pause)* fifteen eighty - eighteen hundred - B

When reciting this line, there should be a major pause where it says “*pause*”, and there should be a slight pause where we see a dash (-) between items. For instance, when reciting 1200-1580-A, you want to slightly pause between each of these items. You do *not* want to say “1200 **to** 1580 **is** A” because you would be forcing yourself to memorize the extra words “to” and “is”. The pauses serve the same purpose without adding more memorization burden.

- Okay, we’ve memorized the line “Stargate Dr. • 1200-1580-A • 1580-1800-B”. Now, what do we do with it? When taking the test, if a question has a Stargate Dr. address, reciting this line silently will immediately tell us the answer like this …
  - → If the address in the question fits within the 1200-1580 range, the answer is A.
  - → If the address in the question fits within the 1580-1800 range, the answer is B.
  - → If the address in the question doesn’t fit within either of these ranges, the answer is D.
- As explained below, this strategy enables you to quickly and easily identify the Delivery Route for every possible Stargate Dr. address except one - the address 1580 Stargate Dr.
  - → We memorized the line “Stargate Dr. • 1200-1580-A • 1580-1800-B”. Reciting or looking at this line, it is not possible to tell if the address 1580 Stargate Dr. fits into the A range or the B range. The address 1580 Stargate Dr. overlaps both ranges. So, what do we do?
  - → If you happen to remember that the A range really ended with 1579 and the B range started with 1580, then you know that the correct answer for 1580 Stargate Dr. is B.
  - → If you don’t remember this, then you simply choose either A or B as your answer. Don’t let this bother you, though. You see, the odds that you will find this particular address - 1580 Stargate Dr. - in a question are only one chance out of several thousand. The odds are tremendously in your favor. The bottom line is that this strategy is the easiest method to correctly answer over 99% of the possible questions/addresses.
  - → However, after mastering this strategy while taking your first few practice tests, you can experiment with memorizing the actual ranges instead of rounded off ranges if you want to assure the ability to answer 100% of the questions instead of 99%. Referring back to our Stargate example, when memorizing actual ranges, you would use the below line.

    Stargate Dr. • 1200-1579-A • 1580-1800-B

    If you do not find it overly difficult when adding in the extra number (1579) that must be remembered, continue memorizing the actual ranges instead of the rounded off ranges.

- Okay, now that we understand how to rearrange the address ranges for easier memorization, **let’s look at how to memorize the two Maple Street address ranges.**
  - The range for Maple Street in Route A is 800-900, so we will memorize these very numbers.
  - The range for Maple Street in Route C is 901-1200, but as previously explained, we round off 901 to simply 900 and memorize “900-1200” instead.
  - So, here is the line we memorize for Maple Street …

    Maple Street • 800-900-A • 900-1200-C

    As before, when we see a Maple Street address in a question, we silently recite this line and immediately know the answer. If we see the overlapping address 900 Maple Street, we simply choose A or C as our answer (unless we decided to memorize the actual ranges, in which case we know that the correct answer is A).

- **On to the memorizing the next address ranges for State Rt 63.**
  - The State Rt 63 address range in Route A is 20-60, so we memorize these exact numbers.
  - The address range in Route B is 61-99, so we round 61 off to 60 and memorize 60-99.
  - So, here is the line we memorize for State Rt 63 …

    State Rt 63 • 20-60-A • 60-99-B
  - If we see a State Rt 63 address in a question, we silently recite this line and immediately know the answer. If we see the overlapping address 60 State Rt 63, we choose either A or B as our answer (unless we decided to memorize the actual ranges, in which case we know that the correct answer is A).
- **Now it gets a little easier. The remaining two address ranges we must memorize do not repeat** in different Delivery Routes, so we only have to remember one address range for each of the last two streets. We will first work on Bluebell.
  - Since Bluebell appears only once in Route C, we will memorize it with its exact numbers of 10000-15000.
  - So, what we memorize for Bluebell is …

    Blubell • 10000-15000-C
  - If we see a question with any Bluebell address, we know the answer will either be C or D. If the address in the question fits within our memorized range, the answer must be C. If the address in the question does not fit within our memorized range, the answer must be D.
- **Finally, we will work on the Hwy 90 address range in Route C.**
  - Since Hwy 90 appears only once in Route C, we memorize it with its exact numbers of 1-20.
  - So, what we memorize for Hwy 90 is …

    Hwy 90 • 1-20-C
  - If we see a question with any Hwy 90 address, we know the answer will either be C or D. If the address in the question fits within our memorized range, the answer must be C. If the address in the question does not fit within our memorized range, the answer must be D.
- **This strategy significantly reduced the amount of material to be memorized and, more importantly, it rearranged the addresses for an easier memorization job.** This strategy is one of the sweetest features of my study guide. It has enabled us to convert the coding guide into the simple lines repeated in the below chart that are not nearly as hard to memorize.

Stargate Dr. • 1200-1580-A • 1580-1800-B

Maple Street • 800-900-A • 900-1200-C

State Rt 63 • 20-60-A • 60-99-B

Blubell • 10000-15000-C

Hwy 90 • 1-20-C

Memory Strategy #2 **As you use the above strategy to memorize, can you abbreviate the street names to make the memorization easier?** _No! You absolutely cannot!_ As detailed below, they throw in trick questions that that prohibit you from abbreviating.

- They use different, but very similar, street names to trick you. For instance, on one 473 exam I took, the correct street name in the Coding Guide was "Marydale". In a few of the questions, however, they had a street name of "Maryville". You immediately see the difference as I am explaining it. But, what about when you are being forced to race through the questions at 90 miles per hour and you are trying to answer from memory. Catching such a subtle difference under those circumstances in most challenging.
- Obviously, If you tried to abbreviate the street name "Marydale" down to just "Mary" or, worse yet, tried to abbreviate it down to just the initial "M", you would never be able to answer the trick questions correctly.
- On another exam, the street name in the Coding Guide was "County Rd 42". On this test, they had trick questions with names like "County Rd 24" and "County Rd 442". Again, if you did not memorize the full street name, you could not answer these questions correctly.

Memory Strategy #3 Now that we know the best way to memorize, **how would like to have an extra two study periods?** Well, you can. Here's how. Think back to the Coding Section, and remember that the Coding Guide stays the same all the way through both sections.

- **Segment 1 of the Coding Section** is 2 minute introductory exercise where you have the Coding Guide to look at, and the exercise is not scored. Since it's not scored, why should you try to answer the questions correctly? Why not spend the 2 minutes studying for the Memory Section that's about to hit you square in the face? You can, but with one stipulation. Take a couple of seconds to darken some random answers on the sample answer sheet in your test booklet, and then spend the rest of the time studying. You see, there are monitors wandering around the exam room, and one of their jobs is to make sure you understand what's expected of you. The directions for this segment say to mark some answers, and if a monitor sees that you haven't marked any answers, he/she may stop to have a whispered conversation with you about what you're supposed to be doing. To avoid this interruption, spend a few seconds marking random answers, and then spend the rest of the time studying.
- **The same is true of Segment 2 of the Coding Section.** This is a 90 second (1½ minutes) practice exercise that is not scored. So again, why try to answer correctly. Again, take a couple of seconds to darken some random answers on the sample answer sheet in your test booklet, and then spend the rest of the time studying.
- **You just picked up two extra study periods.** Very few, if any, of the other test takers will have this advantage - only those who bought my study guide like you did and who diligently applied themselves to their test preparation like you did!

Memory Strategy #4 **Can we make notes or marks, and will it help us?** As previously discussed, the instructions say that you can make notes anywhere in the test booklet unless instructed otherwise. The instructions for Part C say that you are _not_ allowed to make notes during the two Memory Section study periods, but you _are_ allowed to make notes during are all other Memory Section segments (including the actual Memory test) and during all Coding Section segments (including the actual Coding test). What does the mean to us? Let's discuss the options …

In Memory Strategy #1, we rearranged the addresses to make the memorization easier, but we had to do it all in our mind. Wouldn't be easier if we could write down the rearranged addresses? Yes, it would. But, **do we have the time or ability to do so?** Let's recap all the segments from both sections one at a time to see what we can and cannot do - and what we should and should not do.

- **Coding Section**
  - **Segment 1:** This is a 2 minute exercise where we plan to mark random answers and spend most of the time studying the Coding Guide. We are allowed to make notes or marks during this segment. But, the problem with trying to write down the rearranged addresses during this segment is that, if even you could do the rearranging and then write down the addresses within the 2 minutes allowed, there would be no time left for studying. It might be worth it if we could come back to this segment later to study what we wrote, but we cannot. Once we finish this segment, we move on to the next segments, and **we will never again see this page or anything that we wrote on it.** So, trying to make notes during this section is probably not a good idea.

    However, there are other ways to use this privilege of making marks besides writing down the addresses. Specifically, if it helps you identify, rearrange, and memorize the address ranges, **you can draw shapes, draw arrows, doodle, or make any other kinds of marks**. Some people may draw, say, stars beside the two Stargate ranges in routes A and B on our sample Coding Guide. Or, they may draw arrows connecting the two State Rt 63 ranges in routes A and B. Or, they may draw boxes, circles, etc. around the two Maple Street ranges in routes A and C. On your first few practice tests, try making similar marks to see if it helps you identify and group the like addresses for easier memorization. If it works for you, stay with it. But, if it does not help - or worse, if it proves to be a distraction - stop immediately.
  - **Coding Section - Segment 2:** This is a 90 second (1½ minute) exercise where we again plan to mark random answers and spend most of the time studying the Coding Guide. We are allowed to make notes or marks during this segment. However, this segment is so short that making notes of any kind is simply impossible. You can try drawing shapes or arrows, but there is simply not enough time to write much down.
  - **Coding Section - Segment 3:** This is the actual 6 minute Coding test. We are allowed to make notes or marks during this segment, but this scored test is too important to risk. You need to concentrate on answering questions and capturing points during this segment. However, if you finish answering the questions and checking them with time to spare, then you most certainly should use the extra time to study and memorize. And, if drawing shapes or arrows helps you memorize, go for it.
- **Memory Section**
  - **Memory Section - Segment 1:** We are not allowed to make notes or marks of any kind during this 3 minute study period.
  - **Memory Section - Segment 2:** This is a 90 second (1½ minute) exercise where you must work from memory because the Coding Guide is not shown. According to the instructions, you are allowed to make notes or marks during this segment. But, you would have to make notes from memory, and this segment is so short that making notes is simply impossible.
  - **Memory Section - Segment 3:** We are not allowed to make notes or marks of any kind during this 5 minute study period.

- **Memory Section - Segment 4:** This is the actual 7 minute Memory test. We are allowed to make notes or marks during this segment. But should we? Let's take a look to see.
  - → First, do you have enough time to write down the abbreviated address ranges you memorized? I believe that you will have enough time - if you decide to try it.
  - → In my experience, the strategies we've discussed so far should enable you to correctly answer all the questions with time left over. The first few times I took the 473 exam, before perfecting my strategies, I performed miserably on the Memory section, and no amount of time was enough. However, after developing and applying my strategies, the Memory section became a breeze. I was able to ace it with time left over.
  - → Still on the subject of timing … On the Coding test, where you had to waste precious time going back and forth to the Coding Guide to find the correct answers, they gave you 6 minutes for 36 questions. On this Memory test, they give you 7 minutes instead of 6, and you don't waste time going back and forth to the Coding Guide because you are working from memory. So, you basically have an extra minute to accomplish what takes a lesser amount of time.
  - → So, if you have a little extra time, will making notes benefit you? For me personally, no. I do better without any notes on this segment. But, you are not me, and notes may or may not benefit you. If you want to give it a try, take a few practice tests without making any kind of notes during this section, and then try taking a few practice tests using the strategy I'm about to explain. If it works for you, go for it. If not, drop it like a hot potato.
  - → Here's the deal … As you begin the actual 7 minute Memory test, before trying to answer any questions, you can take a moment to write down the rearranged addresses you memorized. Then, as you go through the questions, try to answer from memory if possible because it's quicker. But, if you get confused, simply look over the rearranged addresses you wrote down to find the correct answer.

Important note on making marks or notes

As discussed earlier, the instructions say "Unless instructed otherwise for a specific part, you may make notes or write anywhere in the test booklet." Therefore, the above strategy is perfectly acceptable. However, also as discussed earlier, this new policy of allowing us to make marks is a radical departure from previous policies. Since this is so new, not all examiners are fully aware of it. If, while taking the exam, a monitor asks you to stop making marks, refer the monitor to the bottom of page one on the actual exam where it states that you are allowed to do so. This should solve the problem. But, if the monitor persists, do whatever the monitor asks. Getting into an argument with a monitor is a no-win situation.

Memory Strategy #5 As always, **practice is the key to performance.** The one and only way to master your memory strategies is to practice extensively. As stated over and over again, you cannot practice too much, and there is no such thing as too much practice.

However, with the Memory Section, you need to complete and stop all your practice work about two days before your test date … at least one day before. If you continue doing memory practice work all the way up to the day before the test, you may go into the exam with the address ranges from the practice tests still floating around in your brain. The memory section is hard enough as it is. Don't make it even harder by confusing yourself this way.

As suggested before, for maximum practice value, check out our Timed Practice Test Audio CD and Test Prep CD-ROM on our website *www.PostalExam.com* or on the order form in the back of the book. Either of these convenient tools assures realistic practice and precise timing.

Part D – Personal Characteristics & Experience Inventory

In **Part D – Personal Characteristics and Experience Inventory** you are given 90 minutes to answer 236 questions. As detailed below, the 236 questions are divided into two groups, and the first group is divided into two segments.

- The first group consists of 160 questions. Each of these questions has four answer choices. The questions in this group are not really questions; they are statements as explained below.

  - In segment one of this group, the four answer choices for all questions are …

    A. Strongly Agree
    B. Agree
    C. Disagree
    D. Strongly Disagree

    A question/statement in this segment might say something like "When assigned a task, I prefer to be told the objective and then to be left alone to accomplish the objective in my own way." Then, you choose the answer that best describes your feelings on this subject.

  - In segment two of this group, the four answer choices for all questions are …

    A. Very often
    B. Often
    C. Sometimes
    D. Rarely

    A question/statement in this segment might say something like "In order to approach my duties in an organized fashion, I maintain a prioritized list of tasks that is updated daily." Again, you choose the answer that best describes how you relate to this statement.

- The second group consists of 76 questions that can have anywhere from four to nine answer choices. A question in this group may ask something like "What type of manager do you prefer?" The answer choices to this question might be something like the below samples. Again, you choose the answer that best describes your personal opinion.

  A. A manager who helps me manage my time very carefully.
  B. A manager who allows me to work at my own pace.
  C. A manager who requires daily progress reports.
  D. A manager who assigns tasks and then never bothers me anymore.
  E. A manager who encourages my suggestions.
  F. A manager who makes up his/her own mind without needing anyone else's opinion.
  G. None of the above.

It is important to understand that you can only mark one answer for each question. There will be some questions where more that one answer choice seems appropriate. But, you must choose the one that seems best and mark it. A number of questions will give you answer choices something like the below examples:

All of the above
None of the above
Two of the above
Two or more of the above

In these cases, read the questions/statements and the answer choices carefully to assure that you choose the most appropriate answer.

You are given 90 minutes to answer these 236 questions. They also say, however, that **if you finish before time is called, you can turn in your tests booklets and quietly leave.** And, most people do indeed finish before the 90 minutes is up and leave early.

On this part of the exam, it is imperative that you answer honestly and sincerely. You may be tempted to choose the answers that seem to make you look best. But, **you absolutely should not attempt to manipulate this part of the exam** by trying to select answers you think they prefer. There are built-in indicators that will expose any attempt at manipulation. Just imagine what kind of assumptions they will make about you if they catch you trying to manipulate these questions. You may think that you can outsmart them, but you simply cannot. This part of the exam was created by highly trained and skilled professionals whose goal is to identify applicants who should - and applicants who should *not* - be considered for employment. Both ethically and practically, the best and only course is to answer honestly and sincerely.

Research on Part D - Personal Characteristics and Experience Inventory suggests that **several different scores, one for each of several different categories, are created based upon your answers.** Comments from the company that assisted the Postal Service in creating this part of the test indicate that the below fields may be included in the categories associated with the 473 exam. Bear in mind that this information was "indicated" to us. This information may not be 100% accurate, and it is not possible to confirm specific details.

Performance & Productivity
Customer Service
Work Ethics & Dependability
Retention (likelihood of long-term employment)
Selling Skills

So far, **the Postal Service refuses to release any information about how this part of the exam is scored.** Similarly, they refuse to discuss if it the score from this part of the exam affects your overall exam score, and if so, how.

We suggest that you check our Postal Exam Newsletter (page 377) occasionally for any new information we can learn about Part D - Personal Characteristics & Experience Inventory and about its scoring formulas.

There are no right and wrong answers on this part of the exam, and speed is not an issue. For each question, you simply select the answer that best reflects your own individual personality, temperament, experience, etc. For this reason, **it is not possible to prepare for this part of the exam.** Therefore, there are no Personal Characteristics & Experience Inventory questions on our practice exams, and the Personal Characteristics & Experience Inventory section on our practice answer sheets have been left blank.

The best preparation anyone can give you for this part of the exam is this advice ...

- ***Answer honestly and sincerely!***
- ***Do not attempt to manipulate the questions!***

Test Scoring & Speed Marking System

Science and common sense combine to create a breakthrough in test taking technology - the "Test Scoring & Speed Marking System." This system's unique strategies and specially designed test taking pencils more than double your marking speed while providing absolute assurance that your answers will register perfectly when scanned.

As you have no doubt discovered by now, speed is a key ingredient on Postal exams. With practice, you should be able to master the tasks required on the exam. But, if you cannot master the speed required as well - if you cannot answer all the questions within the limited time allowed - then you have gained nothing at all.

Even if you manage to answer all the questions correctly within the time allowed, what have you gained if your answers do not register when scanned? Scanning failures can result from not using a #2 pencil, from not making dark enough marks, from not darkening enough of the bubble, etc.

If you want to get paranoid, think about this ... What if your pencil was stamped #2, but it didn't really have a #2 lead? This has actually happened. There have been cases where, even though the applicant did everything right and made absolutely sure that the pencil was stamped #2, the answers did not scan properly. It turned out that the pencil manufacturer had mistakenly stamped a batch of pencils as #2 when they really had a different type of lead.

What if you were offered a magic tool that would more than double your speed at marking answers and provide absolute assurance that your answers would scan properly? Even if this magic tool only enabled you to mark a couple of extra answers per minute, imagine the additional points you could capture on this 3½ hour test! Then imagine the level of success this magic tool would offer if it could assure that every single one of your answers registered perfectly when scanned!

Well, there is such a magic tool - Pathfinder's exclusive *Test Scoring & Speed Marking Pencil.* This pencil was especially designed by Pathfinder to assure success on standardized tests, and it is made exclusively for Pathfinder by one of the most respected pencil manufacturers in the U.S. The *Test Scoring & Speed Marking Pencil* is available only from Pathfinder. No other company or pencil offers all these score enhancing features ...

✎ Oversized #2 lead

The *Test Scoring & Speed Marking Pencil* is a standard size pencil that feels completely natural in your hand and that can be sharpened with any pencil sharpener. But, the #2 lead in this pencil is more than twice the diameter of standard pencil leads. This oversized lead provides a broader marking surface that enables you to easily darken answers more than twice as fast as normal.

✎ Specially formulated core

Included in the proprietary formula for the *Test Scoring & Speed Marking Pencil's* unique #2 core, or lead, are special wax compounds and extra fine graphite. These ingredients provide several features that enhance scanning performance and improve speed ...

- The formula is specifically designed for optimum conductivity and reflectivity to assure excellent electronic scanning. You have 100% assurance that your answers will scan perfectly.
- The extra fine graphite in the formula provides a smoother, darker, and fuller mark for even more assurance of scanning performance.
- In addition to enhanced scanning, the wax compounds in the formula provide another benefit. The wax compounds lubricate while marking to offer even greater test taking speed.

Hexagonal construction

The *Test Scoring & Speed Marking Pencil's* hexagonal (six sided) construction offers two benefits. You've probably noticed that pencils come in two basic shapes - round or hex with six flat sides. A hex pencil has a more ergonomic design that works more comfortably and efficiently with your hand. When taking a really important test, a really important *timed* test to be more specific, a hex pencil offers another extremely valuable benefit ... the hex pencil's six flat sides discourage rollaways. Nothing is more frustrating than chasing roll-away pencils under tables and across floors when you are supposed to be answering questions on a rigidly timed test. Round pencils seem to roll away at every chance. This benefit may sound trivial at first, but it can literally make the difference between success and failure. I'm embarrassed to admit that this rollaway disaster actually happened to me. Years ago, before discovering the benefits of hex pencils, I was taking an exam with regular old-fashioned round pencils. As insurance, I had four pencils with me. In the middle of the exam, I accidentally dropped the pencil I was using. Not only did this pencil roll off the table, in the process it bumped into my spare pencils, and they rolled off as well. So, off I go literally chasing pencils under tables and across floors while everyone else was marking answers. Had I been serious about getting a Postal job, such an incident would have resulted in certain failure. This very incident is what prompted my original pencil research project, which in turn led me to eventually develop the *Test Scoring & Speed Marking Pencil.*

Now that you've been introduced to the *Test Scoring & Speed Marking Pencil*, let's discuss some strategies that will help you achieve maximum benefits from its exclusive features ...

Speed Marking Strategy #1 **Use a dulled pencil.** The scheduling packet sent to you will instruct you to bring two number 2 lead pencils. What condition will you want these pencils to be in? Sharp, of course! Frequently, they have extra pencils available at the test site for applicants who forget their own pencils or for applicants who break the lead on their own pencils. What condition will these extra pencils be in? Sharp, of course! We have always been taught to use a freshly sharpened pencil, and we prefer to use a freshly sharpened pencil. So, we will naturally bring sharp pencils with us to the test. If offered extras at the test site from a box of loose pencils, which will we choose? The sharpest ones we can find, of course.

This is precisely the opposite of what we should do. Picture in your mind a fine point ink pen and a broad tipped marker. If you wanted to darken a large circle in a hurry, which would you use? Which would enable you to darken a given area faster? The broad tipped marker, of course, because of its larger marking surface. It would take forever to darken a large circle with a fine point pen. The same principle holds true for pencils. Picture a freshly sharpened pencil and one with a dulled and blunted lead. Which one has a broader marking surface? Which one will darken a circle quicker? Which one will mark answers faster on your exam? The one with the dulled and blunted lead, of course. This is your first Speed Marking Strategy - **make sure your pencil has a dulled and blunted point.** If offered extras, choose dulled ones. If only sharpened pencils are available, immediately dull them. A sharp pencil is you worst enemy.

Speed Marking Strategy #2 **Use an enhanced pencil position and grasp.** The following two techniques can significantly increase your speed. Most people find these techniques to be lifesavers. With practice, these techniques will become second nature for you.

- **The first strategy is to hold the pencil in a more horizontal than vertical position** as displayed in the below illustration. This dramatically increases your speed by enabling you to use the larger and broader side of the pencil lead, rather than the point, as your marking surface. Experiment with different angles of contact to find which works best for you. Holding your pencil like this will feel awkward and unnatural at first. But stick with it. With sufficient practice, most people eventually feel very comfortable using the pencil in this fashion. (On parts of the exam where speed is not as critical and/or where you use your pencil for more regular type writing, it may be better to change back to a normal writing position and grasp.)

- **The second strategy is to grasp the pencil each time you pick it up so that your thumb (or forefinger) is always touching the side with the printing on it**. Pick it up and hold it the very same way each time so that you consistently use the same broad and flattened edge as your contact surface. When laying the pencil down, always place it with the printed side facing up so that you can more easily grasp it properly when picking it up again. Most people rotate the pencil within their grasp as they write with it, which tends preserve the lead's conical point. In a normal writing situation, this is logical. However, there is nothing normal or logical about this test. By consistently holding the pencil in the same position all the time, you maintain the integrity of the dulled and flattened contact point, and you even improve and broaden the contact surface by constant contact with the paper at the same point.

Speed Marking Strategy #3 **At the very most, use only two or three revolutions of your pencil to darken each answer.** With the *Test Scoring & Speed Marking Pencil*, you should be able to do it in only one or two revolutions. With practice and by using the above strategies, this is indeed possible. What's more - it is necessary in order to answer all the questions within the time allowed. You do not have time to endlessly scribble around and around inside the circle to assure that you have darkened every nook and cranny. Your goal is to darken "over half of the oval" to quote the written 473 exam instructions. Between using the *Test Scoring & Speed Marking Pencil* with its oversized marking surface and using the strategies presented here, darkening "over half" the oval with one to two pencil revolutions should be quite manageable.

Pathfinder's *Test Scoring & Speed Marking System* includes a set of our exclusive *Test Scoring & Speed Marking Pencils* along with a booklet of unique performance boosting strategies. For only $9.95, this package is a tremendous score enhancing value. Check out the order form in the back of the book or visit our website *www.PostalExam.com* to order your *Test Scoring & Speed Marking System*.

HIRING PROCESS & JOBS FILLED FROM EXAM 473/473-C

What happens after the exam?

After the exam is given, the names of all applicants who pass (score 70 or higher) are placed on a local hiring register, which is simply a list of names ranked in order by score. In essence, if you pass the exam, you have automatically applied for the jobs and locations you marked. As job openings become available, the highest names (scores) on the register are called in for interviews. They will use this register to fill both immediate and future job openings until the next exam is given and a new register is created.

Eventually, the hiring register becomes nonfunctional because many of the people listed on it are no longer available. So, they trash the old register, offer the exam again, and build a new register from the results of the new exam. If your name was on the old register but you were never called in for a job, then your name was tossed when they trashed the old register. At this point, if you still want to be considered for a job, you must take the exam again so that your name will be listed on the new hiring register.

Depending upon how the local district operates and their needs, it can be anywhere from six months to several years between testing events. Since exams are offered so infrequently, it is imperative that you apply yourself diligently to your test preparation and that you achieve your highest possible score now while you have the chance. It may be years before you have another opportunity.

There's no way to tell how soon after the exam you may be called for an interview. It depends upon too many variables...

- It depends upon your score, which in turn depends upon how well you prepared.
- It depends upon your ranking on the register. If you're #3, you may get called immediately. If you are halfway down the list, you may never get called in. If you are near the bottom of the list, you will probably never get called in at all. Unfortunately, there's no way to find out your ranking. They will not disclose this information under any circumstances.

  Your ranking on the register, by the way, depends to a large degree upon how many other applicants prepared as well as you did. Most applicants make no effort to prepare at all. The successful applicants are always those who prepared well. If you were the only one who bought this guide and who took the test preparation seriously, you may be #1. However, if a number of other applicants did the same, you have competition.
- It depends upon how many jobs they need to fill both now and in the future. Your district may be expanding, building new facilities, and hiring lots of new employees. Or, they may have a temporary hiring freeze in place due to budget problems.

The bottom line is that, after taking the exam, the only thing you can do is wait and hope. There's absolutely nothing you can do to speed up the process or to improve your chances. If you need a job right away, my advice is to continue searching while waiting to hear from the Postal Service and accept any reasonable offer because you have no guarantee when or if they will call you.

Employment Interview

The most important element of the hiring process is your score. Without a high enough score, nothing else matters. But, there is another important step - the employment interview. As with any other potential employer, you must go through the interviewing process, and **the interview can make you or break you**. There are many publications available about how to present yourself in an interview. You may want to review one in preparation for your interview. Below are points to consider and/or to be prepared for:

- Arrive early. Do not be late!
- Remember - first impressions are lasting.
- Your personal appearance, grooming, attitude, and behavior are being examined.
- Establish eye contact with the interviewer. Failure to do so leaves a poor impression.
- Be attentive and interested. Ask relevant questions.
- Try to relax. Speak clearly and in a normal tone of voice.
- Don't respond too quickly. Pause to think before answering.
- Be prepared to answer honestly about past work experiences and work relationships.
- Do not make excuses for past mistakes. Show that you have learned from them.
- Be prepared to discuss why you want a Postal career and what you can contribute.
- Thank the interviewer for his/her time. Make his/her last impression of you favorable.

There is one question that is frequently asked when interviewing for a City Carrier job. They frequently ask how you would react if faced with a bad dog when attempting a delivery. Several applicants have shared their responses to this question with us, but there is one response that seems to be the best. (Please bear in mind that this is an opinion, and that it is only an opinion.) The best response we have heard is, if the dog is particularly aggressive, to postpone delivery until supervisory advice can be obtained in order to avoid an unnecessary on-the-job injury or incident.

Job Descriptions, Starting Wages & Benefits

There are four entry-level jobs filled from exam 473/473-C. Most upper-level processing, distribution, and delivery career positions (the bulk of all fulltime jobs) are filled by individuals who started in one of these entry-level positions and worked their way up. When you are first hired into one of these entry-level jobs, you start out as a Part-Time Flexible (PTF) employee. This PTF title is discussed on page 50. Below are job descriptions with starting wages for these entry-level jobs. Details on fulltime Postal benefits are provided on the next page.

City Carrier	City Carriers are fulltime career employees that deliver and collect mail on foot or by vehicle providing customer service in a prescribed area. City Carrier applicants must have a current valid state driver's license, a safe driving record, and at least two years of documented driving experience.
Starting Wages	$17.48 per hour as of early 2005

Mail Handler	Mail Handlers are fulltime career employees that load and unload containers of mail. Mail Handlers transport mail and empty containers throughout the building. They also open and empty containers of mail.
Starting Wages	$14.34 per hour as of early 2005

Mail Processing Clerk	Mail Processing Clerks are fulltime career employees that operate and monitor performance of automated mail processing equipment or perform manual sorting of mail. Mail Processing Clerks collate, bundle, and transfer processed mail from one area to another.
Starting Wages	$16.45 per hour as of early 2005

Sales, Service & Distribution Associate	Sales, Service & Distribution Associates are fulltime career employees that provide direct sales and customer support services in a retail environment and perform distribution of mail.
Starting Wages	$16.45 per hour as of early 2005

Fulltime Postal Benefits

The four jobs filled from the 473 exam are entry-level career positions. Like all fulltime Postal jobs, they come with the below complete package of benefits (accurate as of early 2005).

Salary Adjustments
Regular salary increases, overtime pay, night shift differential, and Sunday premium pay.

Health Insurance
Postal employees are eligible for the Federal Employees Health Benefits Program, which provides excellent coverage with most of the cost paid by the Postal Service.

Retirement
Postal employees are eligible for the federal retirement program, which provides a defined benefit annuity at normal retirement age as well as disability coverage.

Thrift Savings Plan
Career Postal employees may contribute to the Thrift Savings Plan, which is similar to 401(k) retirement savings plans.

Life Insurance
Postal employees are eligible for the Federal Employees' Group Life Insurance Program. Basic coverage is paid for by the Postal Service, with the option to purchase additional coverage through payroll deduction.

Flexible Spending Accounts
Career Postal employees are eligible for the Flexible Spending Accounts Program after one year of service. Tax-free FSA contributions can be used to cover most out-of-pocket health care and dependent/day care expenses.

Leave
Career Postal employees are eligible for a generous leave program to that includes vacation leave and sick leave.

Holidays
The Postal Service observes 10 holidays each year.

Explanation of the Part-Time Flexible (PTF) Title

It is absolutely imperative that you understand the Part-Time Flexible (PTF) title. **When you are first hired into one of the four entry-level jobs filled from the 473 exam, you start out as a PTF.** You need to understand that this is the starting position for your fulltime Postal career. This is not merely a part-time job offer that you should view lightly.

I have heard horror stories from applicants who, when told they were being hired as a PTF, refused the offer thinking that it was merely a part-time job. In their ignorance, what these unfortunate applicants really did was turn down the fulltime job they had worked so hard to get. In actuality, the PTF offer is the starting point for your new Postal career.

Postal policy says that PTF's may not work a fixed shift, and they are not guaranteed 40 hours a week. However, according to my past customers, PTF's typically do work regular shifts and get fulltime hours. Perhaps most importantly, PTF's receive fulltime career wages and benefits.

Once you are hired, you may be classified as a PTF for anywhere from a few weeks to several years. When "fulltime" vacancies open up, they are given to PTF's on a seniority basis ... the PTF's who have been there the longest get the first "fulltime" positions.

Another important point is the fact that all **new employees serve a 90 day probationary period.** The Postal Service starts all new employees out in a probationary position so that any who don't seem to be performing adequately can be discharged more easily. We have all heard stories about how difficult it is to fire a career federal civil service employee, and this job security is one of the more attractive aspects of working for the Post Office. Since it is so difficult to discharge a career employee, the Postal Service uses the probationary period to weed out undesirables. However, you should not be overly alarmed. It takes a real disaster to be considered undesirable.

Fulltime Job in Highest Demand

The job in greatest demand is City Carrier. The Postal Service hires more City Carriers than any other job. Consider the below quote from a recent Postal publication:

"The number of delivery points increases by 1.7 million each year. This increase results in … 4,800 new carriers."

Basically, this means that **the Postal Service must hire at least 4,800 new City Carriers each year** just to satisfy expanding demand. And this doesn't include the large number of City Carriers that must be hired each year to replace employees that leave due to normal reasons. The Postal Service experiences more employee turnover in City Carrier positions than in any other jobs. Plus, Postal authorities say that fewer individuals are applying for City Carrier positions in recent years. The bottom line is that, while there is more demand for City Carriers due to expansion and employee turnover, fewer people are applying for these jobs.

As a matter of fact, **many Postal districts have begun testing frequently - as often as twice a year - just to fill City Carrier Positions.** This is amazing in view of the fact that individual districts usually only offer the exam once every few years.

To recruit more applicants for City Carrier jobs, **the Postal Service significantly increased starting wages for this position.** As of early 2005, City Carriers started out at $17.48 per hour … the highest starting wages for any entry-level Processing and Distribution job.

What more could we ask for? Unless you simply refuse to work as a City Carrier, this is the job to apply for. Even if you don't love the idea of being a City Carrier, it could be a great way to get your foot in the door and then transfer to another type position at the first opportunity.

Employment Eligibility Requirements

The employment eligibility requirements are generous. Almost anyone can qualify. Specifics follow.

Education
There is no education requirement. A high school diploma is not even required.

Age
Anyone between the ages of 18 (16 with a high school diploma) and 65 at the time of employment is qualified.

Citizenship
Must be a U.S. citizen or permanent resident alien.

Language
Basic competency in English.

Selective Service Registration
Males born after 12/31/59 must be registered with the Selective Service.

Employment History
Must provide current and 10 year (if applicable) employment history.

Military Service
Veterans must provide Copy 4 of the DD Form 214 and Certificate of Release or Discharge from Active Duty.

Background Check
A local criminal history check is required prior to employment, and a more extensive criminal history check is completed at employment.

Drug Screen
A qualification for employment is to be drug free and is determined through a drug screen.

Medical Assessment
A medical assessment is conducted to provide information about an applicant's ability to physically or mentally perform in a specific position.

Safe Driving Record
A safe driving record is required for employees who drive at work.

Special Hiring & Testing Benefits for Military Veterans

Eligible veterans may qualify for special testing, scoring, and hiring benefits. The following benefits and requirements are quoted from various publications. However, these requirements are revised from time to time, particularly as U.S. military personnel become involved in armed conflicts.

To take advantage of these special benefits, or for additional information, veterans should call the nearest Postal facility listed in the phone directory at the back of this book.

Rather than waiting for the next public exam to be given, honorably discharged veterans may apply within 120 days (before or after) of their discharge date for any exam that was offered to the public during the period they were in the military.

Rather than waiting for the next public exam to be given, eligible 10 point veterans may apply once at any time for any or all exams at any or all installations. In some cases for some jobs, an eligible 10 point veteran must be hired before a non-veteran even if the non-veteran has a higher score.

Eligible veterans may qualify to have 5 or 10 preference points added to their raw test scores. It is possible for an eligible veteran to score over 100 on an exam after adding preference points. The following explanation of preference points was excerpted from a Postal Service publication.

5 Points (Tentative)
May be awarded to a former member of the Armed Forces who was separated with an honorable discharge (or under honorable conditions), is not disabled, and who meets one or more of the following criteria:

- Served active duty in a pre-World War II campaign or during World War II (12/7/41 - 4/28/52).
- Served active duty during the period beginning 4/28/52 and ending 7/1/55.
- Served active duty for more than 180 consecutive days, other than for training, any part of which occurred between 2/1/55 and 10/14/76.
- Began active duty after 10/14/76 and before 9/8/80 and served in a campaign or expedition for which a campaign badge is authorized.
- Enlisted after 9/7/80 or entered on active duty through means other than enlistment after 10/14/82 and completed 24 months of continuous service or the full period for which called to active duty and served in a campaign or expedition for which a campaign badge is authorized.
- Enlisted after 9/7/80 or entered on active duty through means other than enlistment after 10/14/82 and completed 24 months of continuous service or the full period for which called to active duty and served active duty during the period beginning 8/2/90 and ending 1/2/92.
- Served in a campaign or expedition for which a badge is authorized and was discharged early under 10 U.S.C. 1171 or for hardship under 10 U.S.C. 1173.

10 Points - Compensable (Less than 30%)
May be awarded to a former member of the Armed Forces who was separated with an honorable discharge (or under honorable conditions) and has a service-connected disability that is at least 10% but less than 30% compensable.

10 Points - Compensable (30% or More)
May be awarded to a former member of the Armed Forces who was separated with an honorable discharge (or under honorable conditions) and has a service-connected disability that is 30% or more compensable.

10 Points (Other)
May be awarded to:

- Veterans who were awarded the Purple Heart.
- Veterans who receive compensation or pension from the Department of Veterans Affairs or disability retired pay from the Armed Forces.
- Veterans who have a service-connected disability that is not compensable or that is less that 10% compensable.
- The unremarried widow or widower of a honorably separated veteran, provided the deceased veteran served in active duty during a war, or the veteran died while in the Armed Forces.
- Spouses of certain veterans with a service-connected disability.
- Mothers of certain deceased or disabled veterans.

PRACTICE EXAM #1

As detailed below, included in this practice exam are all four parts of the actual exam and an answer sheet.

- **Part A – Address Checking**

Included is a 100% realistic replica of the scored Address Checking test on the actual exam.

- **Part B – Forms Completion**

Included is a 100% realistic replica of the scored Forms Completion test on the actual exam.

- **Part C – Coding & Memory**

Included are 100% realistic replicas of the complete Coding and Memory sections with all seven segments.

- **Part D – Personal Characteristics & Experience Inventory**

As explained in the guide, it is not possible to prepare for this part of the exam. Therefore no Personal Characteristics & Experience Inventory questions are included in the practice test for this part of the exam. However, for realistic formatting, we have included a page in the practice test for this exam part.

- **Answer Sheet**

Included near the back of the book are 100% realistic replicas of the answer sheet from the actual exam. When taking a practice exam, tear out one of these Practice Answer Sheets. Mark your answers to the scored segments of the exam on this answer sheet. As noted above, it is not possible to prepare for Part D. Therefore, bubbles are not included on the answer sheet for Part D. However, for realistic formatting, we have noted where Part D would appear on the answer sheet.

The format of this practice exam is identical to the actual exam, and the instructions are similar to those on the actual exam.

It is imperative that you take this practice exam in as realistic a fashion as possible - meaning that you must time yourself precisely. **Your practice will have no value unless it is done realistically.** Our Timed Practice Test Audio CD and our Test Prep CD-ROM are ideal tools for conveniently having the instructions presented section-by-section and for absolutely precise timing. See the order form in the back of the book or our website *www.PostalExam.com* for details.

Answer keys are provided in the back of your book. It is imperative that you use the formulas given in the book to **score each practice test as you complete it**. Scoring is necessary in order to measure your progress and to identify your individual areas of weakness that may need extra attention.

After completing and scoring each practice exam, move on to the next. **After finishing all six exams, you should be prepared to excel on the actual exam.**

Do not look over the practice exam questions until you are ready to start and to time yourself - usually meaning until you have started either the Timed Practice Test Audio CD or the Postal Test Prep CD-ROM. Similarly, after completing one section of the practice test, do not look over the next one until your are ready to start it. Likewise, stop working and put down your pencil immediately when the allotted period of time has expired. As has been emphasized before but cannot be emphasized enough, your practice is of absolutely no value unless it is done realistically. Also, you must train yourself (1) to not open your test booklet or pick up your pencil until instructed to do so and (2) to close your booklet and put down your pencil immediately upon being so instructed. The Postal Service has zero tolerance on these matters. Any variance may be viewed as cheating and may result in your disqualification.

Turn to the next page when you are ready to begin this Practice Exam.

Important Note about this Practice Exam

The questions, addresses, forms, etc. in this practice exam are very realistic samples, but they are not the actual ones that you will see on the real test. There are hundreds of different versions of this exam, and each version has different questions, addresses, forms, etc. Even if you could get some real questions from one version of the exam, the questions on the version of the exam you take would surely be different.

PRACTICE EXAM #1

Part A – Address Checking

Directions

In Part A consists of 60 questions to be completed in 11 minutes. You are given a **Correct List** of addresses and ZIP codes. A **List to be Checked,** also with addresses and ZIP codes, appears next to the **Correct List**. The **List to be Checked** should be exactly like the **Correct List**, but it may contain errors.

Your task is to compare each row of information in the **Correct List** and the **List to be Checked** to find if there are **No Errors**, an error in the **Address Only**, an error in the **ZIP Code Only**, or an error in **Both** the address and the ZIP code.

After comparing each row of information, select an answer from the below answer choices, and mark your answer on the answer sheet in the section titled Part A - Address Checking.

A. No Errors	**B. Address Only**	**C. ZIP Code Only**	**D. Both**

Turn the page and begin when you are prepared to time yourself for exactly 11 minutes.

Part A – Address Checking

A. No Errors	B. Address Only	C. ZIP Code Only	D. Both

	Correct List Address	Correct List ZIP Code	List to be Checked Address	List to be Checked ZIP Code
1.	8412 Los Alamos Way Agua Dulce, NM	78633	8412 Los Alamos Way Agua Dulce, NM	78363
2.	1212 Holderreith Ste 32 Meyerville, N.Y.	10568-7787	1212 Holderreith Ste 32 Meyerville, N.Y.	10568-7787
3.	19 West Main Street Oldtown, ME	05874-3450	19 West Main Street Oldtown, ME	05874-3450
4.	PO BOX 899 HICKSFIELD MD	36480-0899	PO BOX 899 HICKSFIELD MO	36480-0989
5.	1929 Terminal A Atlanta, GA	56841-8681	1919 Terminal A Atlanta, GA	58641-8681
6.	16300 Old River Rd. VanCleave, Ms	39507	16300 Old River Rd. VanCleave, Mn	39507
7.	2 Red Bluff St Springfield, IL	85001-1234	2 Red Bluff St Springfield, IL	85001-1234
8.	6415 Collette Anchorage, AK	95801	6415 Collette Anchorage, AK	65801
9.	PO Box 2594 Orlando, Flordia	20476	PO Box 2954 Orlando, Flordia	20746
10.	13892 Dillon Dr. Tomball, TX	60372	13892 Dillon Rd. Tomball, TX	60372
11.	Post Office Box 19802 Stockton, CA	39281-9802	Post Office Box 19802 Stockton, CA	39821-9802
12.	811 Boyd St. Tucson, AZ	72103-4402	811 Loyd St. Tucson, AZ	72103-4402
13.	402 Tall Pines Apt. 8J Boise, Idaho	34021	402 Tall Pines Apt. 8J Boise, Idaho	34021
14.	11807 Rue St. New Orleans, LA	60435-1024	11807 Rue St. New Orleans, LA	60435-1024
15.	93 Miller Rd. Queens, New York	09278-4402	93 Millers Rd. Queens, New York	09278-4442

continued on next page

Part A – Address Checking

continued

A. No Errors	B. Address Only	C. ZIP Code Only	D. Both

	Correct List		List to be Checked	
	Address	*ZIP Code*	*Address*	*ZIP Code*
16.	7929 Long Point Raleigh, NC	78420	7929 Long Point Raleigh, ND	78420
17.	1302 20th Street Missoula, MO	89047-6705	1302 20th Street Missoula, MT	89047-6705
18.	3017 LITTLE FORK LINCOLN, NE	67042-5603	3017 LITTLE FORD LINCOLN, NE	67042-5063
19.	12 S Wayside Lexington, Ky	79541	12 N Wayside Lexington, Ky	79541
20.	P.O. 4027 Springfield, MA	10430-4027	P.O. 4027 Springfield, MA	10430-4027
21.	800 Hunt Rd Cedar Rapids, Iowa	77362	800 Hunt Rd Cedar Rapids, Iowa	77362
22.	P.O. BOX 594587 Norfolk, VA	10867-4587	P.O. BOX 595487 Norfolk, VA	10867-4857
23.	29 E 4th St. Waco, TN	57261	29 E 4th St. Waco, TX	57261
24.	8534 Gulf Frwy Sioux Falls, SD	86910-4402	8534 Gulf Frwy Sioux Falls, SD	89610-4402
25.	12 Baker Apt. 9C Johnstown, PA	47402-1397	12 Baker Apt. 9C Johnstown, PA	47420-1397
26.	3120 Decker Dr. Eugene, Oregon	91904-8943	3120 Decker Dr. Eugene, Oregon	99104-8943
27.	407 Willow CT Seattle, WA	87829-4402	407 Willow CT Seattle, WA	87829-4442
28.	1568 San Jacinto Chicago, IL	40567-4402	1568 San Jacinto Chicago, IL	40567-4402
29.	1601 Bob Smith Rd Tampa, Fl.	39042-1078	1601 Bob Smith Dr Tampa, Fl.	39042-1078
30.	1702 S Pecan Dr. Savannah, GA	47021-7593	1702 N Pecan Dr. Savannah, GA	47021-7953

continued on next page

Part A – Address Checking

continued

A. No Errors	B. Address Only	C. ZIP Code Only	D. Both

Correct List / **List to be Checked**

	Address	ZIP Code	Address	ZIP Code
31.	PO Box 322893 Huntsville, AL	36702-2893	PO Box 322893 Huntsville, AL	37602-2893
32.	111 E. CANAL ROAD Los Angeles, CA	91220-3390	1111 E. CANAL ROAD Los Angeles, CA	91220-3390
33.	1306 Apache Tr Fort Wayne, MI	21962-0042	1306 Apache Tr Fort Wayne, MN	21962-0042
34.	1505 Garth Rd Baytown, Georgia	95267-4421	1505 Gard Rd Baytown, Georgia	92567-4421
35.	807 Baker Rd Burwell, LA	77632	807 Baker Rd Burwell, LA	77632
36.	4802 Raccoon Dr. Denver, Colorado	89057-4602	4802 Raccoon Dr. Denver, Colorado	89057-4602
37.	1901 E Texas Ave Bedford Park, Utah	21390	1901 E Texas Ave Bedlord Park, Utah	21390
38.	2202 Eaves DR Dallas, TX	67290-4401	2202 Ewes DR Dallas, TX	67209-4401
39.	210 Begonia Ln Parksdale, ID	57829-3201	210 Bagonia Ln Parksdale, ID	57829-3201
40.	408 Center Tulsa, OK	48628-6672	408 Canter Tulsa, OK	48628-6672
41.	3300 Red Cedar Lakewood, Vermont	02018	3300 Red Cedar Lakewood, Vermont	02108
42.	71 Clear Lake Apt. 12C Midland, Texas	77652-6682	71 Clear Lake Apt. 12C Midland, Texas	77652-6682
43.	2307 KIPLING DRIVE NORFOLK, VA	27017-3892	2307 KIPLING DRIVE NORFOLK, WA	27107-3892
44.	19082 Lions Gate Ct San Juan, PR	00217-4481	19082 Lions Gate Pt San Juan, PR	02217-4481
45.	2290 US HWY 59 CHARLESTON, SC	79024	2290 US HWY 59 CHARLESTON, SC	79024

continued on next page

Part A – Address Checking
continued

A. No Errors	B. Address Only	C. ZIP Code Only	D. Both

Correct List / **List to be Checked**

	Correct List: *Address*	Correct List: *ZIP Code*	List to be Checked: *Address*	List to be Checked: *ZIP Code*
46.	8115 Kirkham Ln Providence, RI	29618	8115 Kirkham Ln Providence, RI	29618
47.	PO Box 9873801 Memphis,TN	69201-3801	PO Box 9873801 Memphis,TN	69211-3801
48.	20614 Auburn Pine Ct Denver, CO	27901-4921	20614 Audubon Pine Ct Denver, CO	27901-4921
49.	12 Pine Madison, WI	90267-3381	12 Pine Madison, WI	90067-3381
50.	2406 Elk Creek Dr. Richmond, VA	40278	2406 Elk Creek Dr. Richmond, WA	40728
51.	1903 Lakeville Dayton, Ohio	74201-3865	1903 Lakeville Dayton, Ohio	74201-3865
52.	1806 Chestnut Grove Royal Oak, MI	39201-1229	1886 Chestnut Grove Royal Oak, MI	39201-1229
53.	2245 Yancy Rd. Syracuse, NY	21907-4429	2245 Yancy Rd. Syracuse, NJ	21907-4429
54.	P.O. Box 1292981 Elizabeth, NJ	16310-2981	P.O. Box 1292981 Elizabeth, NJ	16310-2891
55.	28 Magnolia Green Billings, Montana	72892-4114	28 Magnolia Green Billings, Montana	72892-4114
56.	46782 KATY FRWY HOUSTON, TX.	72108-3210	46782 KATY FRWY HOUSTON, TX.	72108-3210
57.	1412 Bill Ave. Apt. 5H Glendale, CA	63108	1412 Bill Ave. Apt. H Glendale, CA	63180
58.	24 Pleasant Road Fairfield, NC	90217-3201	24 Pleasant Road Fairfield, NC	90217-3201
59.	3819 Cypress N Ripley, WV	32092-4418	3819 Cypress N Ripley, WA	32092-4418
60.	1412 Woodlands Pineleaf, WY	90721	1412 Woodlands Pinetree, WY	90721

End of Part A – Address Checking

PRACTICE EXAM #1

Part B – Forms Completion

Directions

Part B tests your ability to identify information needed to complete various U.S. Postal Service forms. This part of the exam consists of 30 questions to be completed in 15 minutes. You will be shown 5 different forms and be asked to answer 6 questions about each form.

Turn the page and begin when you are prepared to time yourself for exactly 15 minutes.

Part B – Forms Completion

Authorization to Hold Mail Postmaster - Please hold mail for:	
1. Name(s)	
2. Address	
3a. Begin Holding Mail (Date)	**3b.** Resume Delivery (Date)
4. ☐ **Option A** I will pick up all accumulated mail when I return and understand that mail delivery will not resume until I do. (This is suggested if your return date may change or if no one will be at home to receive mail.)	
5. ☐ **Option B** Please deliver all accumulated mail and resume normal delivery on the ending date shown above.	
6. Customer Signature	
For Post Office Use Only	
7. Date Received	
8a. Clerk	**8b.** Bin Number
9a. Carrier	**9b.** Route Number
Customer Option A Only	
Carrier: Accumulated mail has been picked up. **10a.** Resume delivery on (date) ____________________ **10b.** By: ____________________	

continued on next page

Part B – Forms Completion

continued

1. Which of these could be an acceptable entry for Box 5?
   A. 6/17/06
   B. A check mark
   C. 89506-1213
   D. Frank Adams

2. If Box 4 is checked, when should mail delivery be resumed?
   A. The date in Box 3a
   B. The date in Box 3b
   C. The date in Box 7
   D. The date in Box 10a

3. The carrier's name should be put in which box?
   A. Box 1
   B. Box 8a
   C. Box 9a
   D. Box 10b

4. In which box or boxes could the number 4833 be entered?
   A. Box 5
   B. Box 8b
   C. Box 9b
   D. Boxes 8b or 9b

5. Where does the customer sign this form?
   A. Box 1
   B. Box 6
   C. Box 9a
   D. Box 10b

6. Which of these could be an acceptable entry for Box 5?
   A. 6/17/06
   B. Frank Adams
   C. 89506-1213
   D. A check mark

continued on next page

Part B – Forms Completion

continued

EXPRESS MAIL — Mailing Label

ORIGIN (POSTAL USE ONLY)

PO ZIP Code **1a.**	Day of Delivery **1b.** ☐ Next ☐ Second	Flat Rate Envelope **1c.** ☐	
Date In **2a.**	**2b.** ☐ Noon ☐ 3 PM	Postage **2c.** $	
Time In **3a.** ☐ AM ☐ PM	Military **3b.** 2nd Day 3rd Day	Return Receipt Fee **3c.**	
Weight **4a.** lbs. ozs.	Int'l Alpha Country Code **4b.**	COD Fee **4c.**	Insurance Fee **4d.**
No Delivery **5a.** ☐ Wknd ☐ Holiday	Acceptance Clerk Initials **5b.**	Total Postage & Fees **5c.** $	

DELIVERY (POSTAL USE ONLY)

Delivery Attempt **1d.** Mo. Day	Time **1e.** ☐ AM ☐ PM	Employee Signature **1f.**
Delivery Attempt **2d.** Mo. Day	Time **2e.** ☐ AM ☐ PM	Employee Signature **2f.**
Delivery Attempt **3d.** Mo. Day	Time **3e.** ☐ AM ☐ PM	Employee Signature **3f.**

6. ☐ WAIVER OF SIGNATURE

NO DELIVERY ☐ Weekend ☐ Holiday

Customer Signature ____________________

CUSTOMER USE ONLY

Method of Payment

7a. Express Mail corporate Acct. No.

Federal Agency Acct. No. or

7b. Postal Service Acct. No.

8a. FROM: (PLEASE PRINT) PHONE: ____________________

8b. TO: (PLEASE PRINT) PHONE: ____________________

ZIP + 4: ____________________

continued on next page

Part B – Forms Completion

continued

7. The customer requests a waiver of signature (wants to make sure the package is delivered whether or not the addressee is on hand to sign for it) and requests that no delivery attempt should be made on a weekend or holiday. In which box or boxes should this be indicated?
   A. Boxes 1b, 1d, and 6
   B. Box 8a
   C. Box 6
   D. Box 4b

8. Which of these could be a correct entry for Box 7a?
   A. 98565640-12
   B. Edward James
   C. July 18, 2005
   D. Seattle, WA

9. Where would the carrier indicate that a second delivery attempt was at 10:17 on the morning of 11/02/05?
   A. Boxes 1b and 2b
   B. Boxes 2a and 3a
   C. Boxes 1d, 1e, and 1f
   D. Boxes 2d, 2e, and 2f

10. Upon acceptance of a package, the clerk should indicate the anticipated delivery schedule where?
   A. Boxes 1b and 2b
   B. Boxes 2a and 3a
   C. Boxes 1d and 1e
   D. None of the above

11. Where should the total amount paid for postage and requested additional services be entered?
   A. Box 2c
   B. Box 5c
   C. Box 3c
   D. Boxes 4c and 4d

12. Which of these could be an acceptable entry for Box 4c?
   A. Charles Eastwood
   B. Bogaloosa, LA
   C. 10/28/06
   D. $3.50

continued on next page

Part B – Forms Completion
continued

<table>
<tr><td colspan="4">Forwarding Order Change Order</td><td colspan="2">Check One
1. ☐ Entire Family ☐ Individual</td></tr>
<tr><td>2a. Carrier Route No.</td><td>2b. Carrier/Clerk</td><td>2c. Receiving Employee</td><td>2d. Original Order Date</td><td>2e. This Order Date</td><td>2f. Expiraton Date</td></tr>
<tr><td colspan="6">3. Print Last Name or Name of Business/Firm (If more than one last name fill out additional form.)</td></tr>
<tr><td colspan="6">4. Print First Name of Each Individual Covered By This Order (Separate each name by a comma.)</td></tr>
<tr><td rowspan="2">Original Address</td><td>5a. Print Number and Street</td><td>5b. Apt./Suite No.</td><td>5c. P.O. Box No.</td><td>5d. Rural Route No.</td><td>5e. Rural Box No.</td></tr>
<tr><td colspan="2">6a. Print City</td><td>6b. State</td><td colspan="2">6c. ZIP + 4</td></tr>
<tr><td rowspan="2">Cancel Forwarding Order</td><td>7a. Print Number and Street</td><td>7b. Apt./Suite No.</td><td>7c. P.O. Box No.</td><td>7d. Rural Route No.</td><td>7e. Rural Box No.</td></tr>
<tr><td colspan="2">8a. Print City</td><td>8b. State</td><td colspan="2">8c. ZIP + 4</td></tr>
<tr><td rowspan="2">New Forwarding Order</td><td>9a. Print Number and Street</td><td>9b. Apt./Suite No.</td><td>9c. P.O. Box No.</td><td>9d. Rural Route No.</td><td>9e. Rural Box No.</td></tr>
<tr><td colspan="2">10a. Print City</td><td>10b. State</td><td colspan="2">10c. ZIP + 4</td></tr>
<tr><td colspan="3">11a. ☐ Moved no order</td><td colspan="3">11b. ☐ Refuses to pay postage due on ALL 4th class</td></tr>
<tr><td colspan="3">12a. ☐ No such number</td><td colspan="3">12b. ☐ No such street, check forwarding order</td></tr>
<tr><td colspan="2">13a. Post Office</td><td colspan="2">13b. Station/ Branch</td><td colspan="2">13c. By (Route No., Name)</td></tr>
</table>

continued on next page

Part B – Forms Completion
continued

13. Which of these could be an acceptable entry for Box 8b?
    A. Concordia, CA
    B. 93421-8997
    C. CA
    D. A check mark

14. Which of these could be an acceptable entry for Box 11a?
    A. CA
    B. 93421-8997
    C. A check mark
    D. Concordia, CA

15. Which of these could be an acceptable entry for Box 10c?
    A. CA
    B. 93421-8997
    C. A check mark
    D. Concordia, CA

16. Which of these could be entered in Box 13c?
    A. 433, Alton Jones
    B. 433
    C. Alton Jones
    D. None of the above

17. The original address was a Rural Route Box. Where would it be entered?
    A. Boxes 5a, 6a, 6b, and 6c
    B. Boxes 5d, 5e, 6a, 6b, and 6c
    C. Boxes 7d, 7e, 8a, 8b, and 8c
    D. None of the above

18. Which box(es) should contain Postal employee name(s)?
    A. Box 2b
    B. Box 2c
    C. Box 13c
    D. All the above

continued on next page

Part B – Forms Completion
continued

Application for Post Office Box or Caller Service			
Customer: Complete white boxes		Post Office: Complete shaded boxes	
1a. Name(s) to which box number(s) is (are) are assigned			**1b.** Box or Caller Numbers _______ through _______
2a. Name of person applying, Title *(if representing an organization)*, and name of organization *(if different from name in Box 1a above)*			**2b.** Will this box be used for: ☐ Personal use ☐ Business use
3a. Address *(number, street, apt. no., city, state, ZIP code)*. When address changes, cross out address here and put new address on back.			**3b.** Telephone number (include area code)
4a. Date application received	**4b.** Box size needed	**4c.** ID and physical address verified by *(initials)*	**4d.** Dates of service _______ through _______
5a. Two types of identification are required. One must contain a photograph of the addressee(s). Social security cards, credit cards, and birth certificates are unacceptable as identification. Write in identifying information. Subject to verification.		**5b.** Eligibility for Carrier Delivery ☐ City ☐ Rural ☐ HCR ☐ None	**5c.** Service Assigned ☐ Box ☐ Caller ☐ Reserve No.
		6. Name(s) of minors or others receiving mail in individual box.	
WARNING: *The furnishing of false or misleading information on this form or omission of information may result in criminal sanctions (including fines and imprisonment) and/or civil sanctions (including multiple damages and civil penalties).*		**7.** Signature of applicant *(Same as Item 3)*. I agree to comply with all Postal rules regarding Post Office box or caller services.	

continued on next page

19. Which boxes should the customer fill out if applicable?
    A. Boxes 1a, 1b, 2a, 2b, 3a, 3b, 4a, 4b, 6, and 7
    B. Boxes 1a, 2a, 2b, 3a, 3b, 6, and 7
    C. Boxes 1b, 4a, 4b, 4c, 4d, 5a, 5b, and 5c
    D. All the above

20. Where does the Postal representative sign this form?
    A. Box 5a
    B. Box 6
    C. Box 4a
    D. The Postal representative does not sign this form

21. Where does the Postal representative indicate that a box was assigned and the size of the box?
    A. Box 5b
    B. Box 1b
    C. Boxes 4b and 5c
    D. Boxes 1b and 4d

22. Theresa Martinez is applying for a box for her personal use. Where should her name go?
    A. Boxes 1a and 2a
    B. Boxes 1a, 2a, and 6
    C. Boxes 1a, 2a, and 5a
    D. None of the above

23. Thomas Albertson is applying for a box to be used by his small business. How and where would he indicate this?
    A. Boxes 1a, 2a, and 3a
    B. Boxes 2a and 2b
    C. Boxes 1a, 2a, 3a, and 4a
    D. All the above

24. What must be verified by a Postal employee?
    A. ID
    B. Physical address
    C. Business registration
    D. ID and physical address

continued on next page

Part B – Forms Completion

continued

Application to Mail at Nonprofit Standard Mail Rates

Part 1 *(For completion by applicant)*

No application fee is required. All information must be complete and typewritten or printed legibly.

1. Complete name of organization *(If voting registration official, include title.)*

2. Street address of organization *(Include apartment or suite number.)*

3. City, state, ZIP+4 code

4a. Telephone *(Include area code.)*

4b. Name of applicant *(Must represent applying organization.)*

5. Type of organization *(Check only one.)*

☐ Religious ☐ Scientific ☐ Agricultural ☐ Veterans' ☐ Qualified political committee

☐ Educational ☐ Philanthropic ☐ Labor ☐ Fraternal ☐ Voting registration official

6. Is this a for-profit organization or does any of the net income inure to the benefit of any private stockholder or individual? ☐ Yes ☐ No

7a. Is this organization exempt from federal income tax? *(If 'Yes', attach a copy of the exemption issued by the Internal Revenue Service that shows the section of the IRS code under which the organization is exempt.)* ☐ Yes ☐ No

7b. Is an application for exempt status pending with the IRS? *(If 'Yes', attach a copy of the application to this form.)* ☐ Yes ☐ No

8. Has this organization previously mailed at the Nonprofit Standard Mail rates? *(If yes, list the Post Offices where mailings were most recently deposited at these rates?* ☐ Yes ☐ No

7c. Has the IRS denied or revoked the organization's federal tax exempt status? *(If 'Yes', attach a copy of the IRS ruling to this form.)* ☐ Yes ☐ No

9. Has your organization had Nonprofit Standard Mail rate mailing privileges denied or revoked? *(If 'Yes', list the Post Office [city and state] where the application was denied or authorization revoked.)* ☐ Yes ☐ No

10. Post Office (not a station or branch) where authorization requested and bulk mailings will be made *(City, state, ZIP code)*

11. Signature of applicant

12. Title

13. Date

Part 2 *(For completion by Postmaster at originating office where application filed)*

14. Signature of Postmaster *(Or designated representative)*

15. Date application filed with Post Office *(Round stamp)*

continued on next page

Part B – Forms Completion

continued

25. First Baptist Church is applying to mail at nonprofit rates. How and where would they indicate the type of nonprofit organization they are?
    A. Put the name of their religious organization in Box 1
    B. Check "Religious" in box 5
    C. Check the proper items in boxes 7a, 7b, and 7c
    D. All the above

26. Where does the applicant sign?
    A. Box 11
    B. Box 1
    C. Box 2
    D. Box 14

27. Where would the applicant indicate that his/her organization had previously mailed at Nonprofit Standard Mail rates?
    A. Box 6
    B. Boxes 7a, 7b, and/or 7c
    C. Box 8
    D. Box 9

28. For which of these would "1812 W Main St." be an acceptable entry?
    A. Box 2
    B. Box 3
    C. Box 4a
    D. Box 10

29. Into which of these boxes could a date be entered?
    A. Box 12
    B. Box 4b
    C. Box 13
    D. None of the above

30. If box 7a is checked, what must be attached to the form?
    A. Copy of exemption issued by IRS
    B. Copy of IRS application for exemption
    C. Copy of IRS denial or revocation ruling
    D. All the above

End of Part B – Forms Completion

PRACTICE EXAM #1

Part C – Coding & Memory

Part C tests your ability to use codes quickly and accurately both from a Coding Guide and from memory. This part of the exam consists of two sections as detailed below.

- The Coding Section has 36 questions to be answered in 6 minutes. During the Coding section, you will look at a Coding Guide to find answers. The Coding Section is broken down into several segments.
- The Memory Section has 36 questions to be answered in 7 minutes. During the Memory Section, you must answer from memory. The Memory Section is broken down into several segments.

The same Coding Guide will be used throughout both sections of Part C. Four delivery routes (identified by the codes A, B, C, and D) are listed on the Coding Guide. Also listed on the Coding Guide are various address ranges on several streets that are served by these delivery routes.

Each question is an address. To answer each question, you must identify the delivery route that serves the address, and mark as your answer the code (A, B, C, or D) for that delivery route.

Turn the page when you are ready to begin the first section, the Coding Section.

Part C – Coding & Memory

Coding Section

The Coding Section of Part C - Coding & Memory consists of 3 segments as detailed below.

- **Coding Section - Segment 1**
  The first segment is a 2 minute introductory exercise. This segment is not scored.
- **Coding Section - Segment 2**
  The second segment is a 90 second (1½ minutes) practice exercise. This segment is not scored.
- **Coding Section - Segment 3**
  The third segment is the actual Coding Section test. You have 6 minutes to answer 36 questions. This segment is scored.

The Coding Guide is displayed during all 3 segments. You will be instructed to mark answers for the first two unscored segments on sample answer sheets, not the actual answer sheet. You will be instructed to mark answers for the third segment, which is scored, on the actual answer sheet.

Turn to the next page when you are ready to begin Coding Section - Segment 1.

Part C – Coding & Memory

Coding Section – Segment 1

Instructions

Segment 1 of the Coding Section is an introductory exercise to acquaint you with how the questions are to be answered. In this segment, you have 2 minutes to answer 4 questions. The Coding Guide is displayed for your use in answering the questions. This segment is not scored. Mark your answers on the sample answer sheet at the bottom of the question page, not on the actual answer sheet.

Turn the page and begin when you are prepared to time yourself for exactly 2 minutes.

Part C – Coding & Memory

Coding Section – Segment 1

CODING GUIDE	
Address Range	**Delivery Route**
1 – 299 Alpine Way 21 – 90 Los Robles CT 2200 – 2299 County Rd 182	A
300 – 599 Alpine Way 2300 – 2899 County Rd 182	B
8000 – 12000 J F Kennedy Blvd 7300 – 9300 Eldridge St 91 – 300 Los Robles CT	C
All mail that doesn't fall in one of the address ranges listed above	D

Part C – Coding & Memory

Coding Section – Segment 1

continued

QUESTIONS

	Address	Delivery Route			
1.	8643 Eldridge St	A	B	C	D
2.	13040 J F Kennedy Blvd	A	B	C	D
3.	2503 County Rd 182	A	B	C	D
4.	53 Los Robles CT	A	B	C	D

SAMPLE ANSWER SHEET

1 (A)(B)(C)(D)
2 (A)(B)(C)(D)
3 (A)(B)(C)(D)
4 (A)(B)(C)(D)

The correct answers are 1-D, 2-D, 3-B, and 4-A

Part C – Coding & Memory

Coding Section – Segment 2

Instructions

Segment 2 of the Coding Section is a practice exercise designed to expose you to the realistic timing demanded. In this segment, you have 90 seconds to answer 8 questions. The Coding Guide is displayed for your use in answering the questions. This segment is not scored. Mark your answers on the sample answer sheet at the bottom of the question page, not on the actual answer sheet.

Turn the page and begin when you are prepared to time yourself for exactly 90 seconds.

Part C – Coding & Memory

Coding Section – Segment 2

CODING GUIDE	
Address Range	**Delivery Route**
1 – 299 Alpine Way 21 – 90 Los Robles CT 2200 – 2299 County Rd 182	A
300 – 599 Alpine Way 2300 – 2899 County Rd 182	B
8000 – 12000 J F Kennedy Blvd 7300 – 9300 Eldridge St 91 – 300 Los Robles CT	C
All mail that doesn't fall in one of the address ranges listed above	D

Part C – Coding & Memory

Coding Section – Segment 2

continued

QUESTIONS

	Address	Delivery Route			
1.	8496 Eldridge St	A	B	C	D
2.	189 Alpine Way	A	B	C	D
3.	2467 County Rd 182	A	B	C	D
4.	259 Los Robles CT	A	B	C	D
5.	700 Alpine Way	A	B	C	D
6.	2251 County Rd 182	A	B	C	D
7.	9578 J F Kennedy Blvd	A	B	C	D
8.	15 Los Robles CT	A	B	C	D

SAMPLE ANSWER SHEET

1 Ⓐ Ⓑ Ⓒ Ⓓ   5 Ⓐ Ⓑ Ⓒ Ⓓ
2 Ⓐ Ⓑ Ⓒ Ⓓ   6 Ⓐ Ⓑ Ⓒ Ⓓ
3 Ⓐ Ⓑ Ⓒ Ⓓ   7 Ⓐ Ⓑ Ⓒ Ⓓ
4 Ⓐ Ⓑ Ⓒ Ⓓ   8 Ⓐ Ⓑ Ⓒ Ⓓ

The correct answers are 1-C, 2-A, 3-B, 4-C, 5-D, 6-A, 7-C, and 8-D.

Part C – Coding & Memory

Coding Section – Segment 3

Instructions

Segment 3 of the Coding Section is the actual Coding test. You have 6 minutes to answer 36 questions. The Coding Guide is displayed for your use in answering the questions. This segment is scored, and the score from this section does affect your overall Exam 473 score. Mark your answers on the actual answer sheet in the section titled Part C - Coding & Memory - Coding Section.

Turn the page and begin when you are prepared to time yourself for exactly 6 minutes.

Coding Section – Segment 3

CODING GUIDE	
Address Range	**Delivery Route**
1 – 299 Alpine Way 21 – 90 Los Robles CT 2200 – 2299 County Rd 182	A
300 – 599 Alpine Way 2300 – 2899 County Rd 182	B
8000 – 12000 J F Kennedy Blvd 7300 – 9300 Eldridge St 91 – 300 Los Robles CT	C
All mail that doesn't fall in one of the address ranges listed above	D

Coding Section – Segment 3

continued

Questions

	Address	Delivery Route			
1.	1100 Eldridge St	A	B	C	D
2.	584 Alpine Way	A	B	C	D
3.	82 Alpine Way	A	B	C	D
4.	2751 County Rd 182	A	B	C	D
5.	11000 J F Kennedy Blvd	A	B	C	D
6.	2928 Country Rd 182	A	B	C	D
7.	80 Los Robles CT	A	B	C	D
8.	7400 Eldridge St	A	B	C	D
9.	8086 J F Kennedy Blvd	A	B	C	D
10.	2609 County Rd 182	A	B	C	D
11.	100 Alpine Way	A	B	C	D
12.	50 Los Robles CT	A	B	C	D
13.	8967 Eldridge St	A	B	C	D
14.	400 Alpine Way	A	B	C	D
15.	138 Los Robles CT	A	B	C	D
16.	9278 Eldridge St	A	B	C	D
17.	267 Alpine Hwy	A	B	C	D
18.	43 Alpine Way	A	B	C	D

continued on next page

Coding Section – Segment 3

continued

CODING GUIDE	
Address Range	**Delivery Route**
1 – 299 Alpine Way 21 – 90 Los Robles CT 2200 – 2299 County Rd 182	A
300 – 599 Alpine Way 2300 – 2899 County Rd 182	B
8000 – 12000 J F Kennedy Blvd 7300 – 9300 Eldridge St 91 – 300 Los Robles CT	C
All mail that doesn't fall in one of the address ranges listed above	D

Coding Section – Segment 3

continued

Questions

	Address	Delivery Route			
19.	179 Los Robles CT	A	B	C	D
20.	432 Alpine Way	A	B	C	D
21.	9690 J F Kennedy Blvd	A	B	C	D
22.	2259 County Rd 182	A	B	C	D
23.	10 Los Robles CT	A	B	C	D
24.	407 Alpine Way	A	B	C	D
25.	240 Los Robles CT	A	B	C	D
26.	2700 County Rd 182	A	B	C	D
27.	150 West Rd.	A	B	C	D
28.	2270 County Rd 182	A	B	C	D
29.	8000 Eldridge St	A	B	C	D
30.	389 Los Robles CT	A	B	C	D
31.	85 Los Robles CT	A	B	C	D
32.	2200 County Rd 180	A	B	C	D
33.	100 Los Robles CT	A	B	C	D
34.	2290 County Rd 182	A	B	C	D
35.	244 Los Robles CT	A	B	C	D
36.	10250 J F Kennedy Blvd	A	B	C	D

End of Part C – Coding Section – Segment 3

Part C – Coding & Memory

Memory Section

The Memory Section of Part C - Coding & Memory consists of 4 segments as detailed below.

- **Memory Section - Segment 1**
  The first segment is a 3 minute study period during which you try to memorize the Coding Guide.
- **Memory Section - Segment 2**
  The second segment is a 90 second (1½ minutes) practice exercise. This segment is not scored.
- **Memory Section - Segment 3**
  The third segment is a 5 minute study period during which you try to memorize the Coding Guide.
- **Memory Section - Segment 4**
  This fourth segment is the actual Memory Section test. You have 7 minutes to answer 36 questions. This segment is scored.

There are no answers to mark during the first and third segments. You will be instructed to mark answers for the second segment on a sample answer sheet, not the actual answer sheet. You will be instructed to mark answers for the fourth segment, which is scored, on the actual answer sheet.

Turn to the next page when you are ready to begin Memory Section - Segment 1.

Part C – Coding & Memory

Memory Section – Segment 1

Instructions

Memory Section - Segment 1 is a 3 minute study period during which you try to memorize the information in the Coding Guide. There are no answers to mark during this study period.

Turn the page and begin studying when you are prepared to time yourself for exactly 3 minutes.

Part C – Coding & Memory

Memory Section – Segment 1

CODING GUIDE	
Address Range	**Delivery Route**
1 – 299 Alpine Way 21 – 90 Los Robles CT 2200 – 2299 County Rd 182	A
300 – 599 Alpine Way 2300 – 2899 County Rd 182	B
8000 – 12000 J F Kennedy Blvd 7300 – 9300 Eldridge St 91 – 300 Los Robles CT	C
All mail that doesn't fall in one of the address ranges listed above	D

Part C – Coding & Memory

Memory Section – Segment 2

Instructions

Segment 2 of the Memory Section is a practice exercise where you have 90 seconds to answer 8 questions from memory. The Coding Guide is not shown. You must answer from memory. This segment is not scored. Mark your answers on the sample answer sheet at the bottom of the page, not on the actual answer sheet.

Begin when you are prepared to time yourself for exactly 90 seconds.

Part C – Coding & Memory

Memory Section – Segment 2

QUESTIONS

	Address	Delivery Route			
1.	491 Alpine Way	A	B	C	D
2.	17 Los Robles CT	A	B	C	D
3.	7860 Eldridge St	A	B	C	D
4.	529 Alpine Way	A	B	C	D
5.	2263 County Rd 182	A	B	C	D
6.	7200 Eldridge St	A	B	C	D
7.	28 Alpine Way	A	B	C	D
8.	8055 J F Kennedy Blvd	A	B	C	D

SAMPLE ANSWER SHEET

1 Ⓐ Ⓑ Ⓒ Ⓓ 5 Ⓐ Ⓑ Ⓒ Ⓓ
2 Ⓐ Ⓑ Ⓒ Ⓓ 6 Ⓐ Ⓑ Ⓒ Ⓓ
3 Ⓐ Ⓑ Ⓒ Ⓓ 7 Ⓐ Ⓑ Ⓒ Ⓓ
4 Ⓐ Ⓑ Ⓒ Ⓓ 8 Ⓐ Ⓑ Ⓒ Ⓓ

The correct answers are 1-B, 2-D, 3-C, 4-B, 5-A, 6-D, 7-A, and 8-C.

Part C – Coding & Memory

Memory Section – Segment 3

Instructions

Memory Section - Segment 3 is a 5 minute study period during which you try to memorize the information in the Coding Guide. There are no answers to mark during this study period.

Turn the page and begin studying when you are prepared to time yourself for exactly 5 minutes.

Part C – Coding & Memory

Memory Section – Segment 3

CODING GUIDE	
Address Range	**Delivery Route**
1 – 299 Alpine Way 21 – 90 Los Robles CT 2200 – 2299 County Rd 182	A
300 – 599 Alpine Way 2300 – 2899 County Rd 182	B
8000 – 12000 J F Kennedy Blvd 7300 – 9300 Eldridge St 91 – 300 Los Robles CT	C
All mail that doesn't fall in one of the address ranges listed above	D

Part C – Coding & Memory

Memory Section – Segment 4

Instructions

Memory Section - Segment 4 is the actual Memory test. You have 7 minutes to answer 36 questions. You must answer from memory. The Coding Guide is not shown. This segment is scored, and the score from this section does affect your overall Exam 473 score. Mark your answers on the actual answer sheet in the section titled Part C - Coding & Memory - Memory Section.

Turn the page and begin when you are prepared to time yourself for exactly 7 minutes.

Part C – Coding & Memory

Memory Section – Segment 4

Questions

	Address	Delivery Route			
37.	333 Alpine Way	A	B	C	D
38.	11820 J F Kennedy Blvd	A	B	C	D
39.	2868 County Rd 182	A	B	C	D
40.	51 Los Robles CT	A	B	C	D
41.	498 Alpine Way	A	B	C	D
42.	2250 County Rd 128	A	B	C	D
43.	9062 Eldridge St	A	B	C	D
44.	180 Alpine Way	A	B	C	D
45.	2600 County Rd 182	A	B	C	D
46.	9051 Eldridge St	A	B	C	D
47.	721 Alpine Way	A	B	C	D
48.	62 Los Robles CT	A	B	C	D
49.	250 Los Robles CT	A	B	C	D
50.	555 Alpine Way	A	B	C	D
51.	3168 County Rd 182	A	B	C	D
52.	90 Alpine Way	A	B	C	D
53.	90909 J F Kennedy Blvd	A	B	C	D
54.	2279 County Rd 182	A	B	C	D

continued on next page

Part C – Coding & Memory

Memory Section – Segment 4

continued

Questions

	Address	Delivery Route			
55.	227 Los Robles CT	A	B	C	D
56.	2228 County Rd 182	A	B	C	D
57.	70 Los Robles CT	A	B	C	D
58.	9065 J F Kennedy Blvd	A	B	C	D
59.	2268 County Rd 183	A	B	C	D
60.	259 Alpine Way	A	B	C	D
61.	198 Los Robles CT	A	B	C	D
62.	399 Alpine Way	A	B	C	D
63.	13000 J F Kennedy Blvd	A	B	C	D
64.	21 Alpine Way	A	B	C	D
65.	2377 County Rd 182	A	B	C	D
66.	11420 J F Kennedy Blvd	A	B	C	D
67.	2271 County Rd 182	A	B	C	D
68.	8300 Elkridge St	A	B	C	D
69.	166 Los Robles CT	A	B	C	D
70.	45 Los Robles CT	A	B	C	D
71.	2708 County Rd 182	A	B	C	D
72.	9000 Eldridge St	A	B	C	D

End of Part C – Memory Section – Segment 4

Part D – Personal Characteristics & Experience Inventory

As explained in the guide, it is not possible to practice or prepare for Part D. There are no right or wrong answers, and speed is not an issue. For each question, you simply select the answer that best reflects your own individual personality, temperament, experience, etc.

Since it is not possible to practice or prepare for Part D, no Personal Characteristics & Experience Inventory sample questions are included in this practice exam.

PRACTICE EXAM #2

As detailed below, included in this practice exam are all four parts of the actual exam and an answer sheet.

- **Part A – Address Checking**

Included is a 100% realistic replica of the scored Address Checking test on the actual exam.

- **Part B – Forms Completion**

Included is a 100% realistic replica of the scored Forms Completion test on the actual exam.

- **Part C – Coding & Memory**

Included are 100% realistic replicas of the complete Coding and Memory sections with all seven segments.

- **Part D – Personal Characteristics & Experience Inventory**

As explained in the guide, it is not possible to prepare for this part of the exam. Therefore no Personal Characteristics & Experience Inventory questions are included in the practice test for this part of the exam. However, for realistic formatting, we have included a page in the practice test for this exam part.

- **Answer Sheet**

Included near the back of the book are 100% realistic replicas of the answer sheet from the actual exam. When taking a practice exam, tear out one of these Practice Answer Sheets. Mark your answers to the scored segments of the exam on this answer sheet. As noted above, it is not possible to prepare for Part D. Therefore, bubbles are not included on the answer sheet for Part D. However, for realistic formatting, we have noted where Part D would appear on the answer sheet.

The format of this practice exam is identical to the actual exam, and the instructions are similar to those on the actual exam.

It is imperative that you take this practice exam in as realistic a fashion as possible - meaning that you must time yourself precisely. **Your practice will have no value unless it is done realistically.** Our Timed Practice Test Audio CD and our Test Prep CD-ROM are ideal tools for conveniently having the instructions presented section-by-section and for absolutely precise timing. See the order form in the back of the book or our website *www.PostalExam.com* for details.

Answer keys are provided in the back of your book. It is imperative that you use the formulas given in the book to **score each practice test as you complete it**. Scoring is necessary in order to measure your progress and to identify your individual areas of weakness that may need extra attention.

After completing and scoring each practice exam, move on to the next. **After finishing all six exams, you should be prepared to excel on the actual exam.**

Do not look over the practice exam questions until you are ready to start and to time yourself - usually meaning until you have started either the Timed Practice Test Audio CD or the Postal Test Prep CD-ROM. Similarly, after completing one section of the practice test, do not look over the next one until your are ready to start it. Likewise, stop working and put down your pencil immediately when the allotted period of time has expired. As has been emphasized before but cannot be emphasized enough, your practice is of absolutely no value unless it is done realistically. Also, you must train yourself (1) to not open your test booklet or pick up your pencil until instructed to do so and (2) to close your booklet and put down your pencil immediately upon being so instructed. The Postal Service has zero tolerance on these matters. Any variance may be viewed as cheating and may result in your disqualification.

Turn to the next page when you are ready to begin this Practice Exam.

Important Note about this Practice Exam

The questions, addresses, forms, etc. in this practice exam are very realistic samples, but they are not the actual ones that you will see on the real test. There are hundreds of different versions of this exam, and each version has different questions, addresses, forms, etc. Even if you could get some real questions from one version of the exam, the questions on the version of the exam you take would surely be different.

PRACTICE EXAM #2

Important Note about this Practice Exam

PRACTICE EXAM #2

Part A – Address Checking

Directions

In Part A consists of 60 questions to be completed in 11 minutes. You are given a **Correct List** of addresses and ZIP codes. A **List to be Checked,** also with addresses and ZIP codes, appears next to the **Correct List**. The **List to be Checked** should be exactly like the **Correct List**, but it may contain errors.

Your task is to compare each row of information in the **Correct List** and the **List to be Checked** to find if there are **No Errors**, an error in the **Address Only**, an error in the **ZIP Code Only**, or an error in **Both** the address and the ZIP code.

After comparing each row of information, select an answer from the below answer choices, and mark your answer on the answer sheet in the section titled Part A - Address Checking.

A. No Errors	**B. Address Only**	**C. ZIP Code Only**	**D. Both**

Turn the page and begin when you are prepared to time yourself for exactly 11 minutes.

Part A – Address Checking

A. No Errors	B. Address Only	C. ZIP Code Only	D. Both

	Correct List		List to be Checked	
	Address	*ZIP Code*	*Address*	*ZIP Code*
1.	5724 Westheimer St. Louis, Missouri	37017-2891	5724 Westhiemer St. Louis, Missouri	37011-2891
2.	12 St. Luke's Way Beaver Dam, WI	21562	12 St. Luke's Way Beaver Dam, WI	21562
3.	5627 Hillcroft Dr. Baton Rouge, LA	37810-4792	5627 Hillcroft Dr. Baton Rouge, LA	37180-4792
4.	Post Office Box 125768 Bangor, Maine	08210-5768	Post Office Box 125768 Bangor, Maine	08210-5678
5.	489 Stella St. Greensboro, N.C.	67390-4127	489 Stella St. Greensboro, N.C.	67390-4172
6.	1567 W. Main El Paso, Texas	79107-4289	4567 W. Main El Paso, Texas	79107-4289
7.	11203 Airline Green Bay, WI	34231-8321	11203 Airline Green Bay, WI	34231-8321
8.	1589 Holland Tacoma, WA.	83210-5120	1589 Holland Tacoma, VA.	83210-5120
9.	2189 SPENCER WICHITA, KANSAS	54189	2819 SPENCER WICHITA, KANSAS	54819
10.	84390 El Mar St. Detroit, MI	10023-2981	84390 El Mar St. Detroit, MI	10023-2881
11.	927 3rd St St Paul, MN	72197-4210	927 3rd St St Paul, MN	72197-4210
12.	219 Uptown Park Ave. Fayetteville, N.C.	81120	219 Uptown Park Ave. Fayetteville, N.C.	81120
13.	55 Allen Pkwy Apt. 112 Bristol, VA	28919-3378	55 Allen Pkwy Apt. 12 Bristol, VA	28919-3378
14.	568 Jensen Dr. Bakertown, New York	47219-3910	568 Jensen Dr. Bakertown, New York	47219-3910
15.	1768 Force Place Buffalo, N.Y.	93201-3291	1768 Farce Place Buffalo, N.Y.	93201-2391

continued on next page

Part A – Address Checking
continued

A. No Errors	B. Address Only	C. ZIP Code Only	D. Both

Correct List / **List to be Checked**

	Address	ZIP Code	Address	ZIP Code
16.	1412 Memorial Ave. Albuquerque, NM	73190-4219	1412 Memorial Ave. Albuquerque, NM	73109-4219
17.	2110 SHAVER DALLAS,TEXAS	70322-7389	2110 SHAVER DALLAS,TEXAS	70322-7389
18.	10 Carriage Hill Bellmawr, N.J.	11290-4289	10 Cabbage Hill Bellmawr, N.J.	11290-4289
19.	2190 North Loop West Shreveport, LA	39037	2190 North Loop West Shreveport, IA	39037
20.	13313 Memorial Hwy Charleston, SC	57690-2890	13333 Memorial Hwy Charleston, SC	57960-2890
21.	PO Box 4653219, Corpus Christi, Texas	77389-3219	PO Box 4653219 Corpus Christi, Texas	77389-3219
22.	678 Pine Street Green Bay, WI	57892-6732	678 Bine Street Green Bay, WI	57892-6732
23.	34 Clear Lake Richmond, V.A.	29231-3489	34 Clear Lake Richmond, V.A.	29221-3489
24.	24 Timbergreen Dr. Tomball, TX	77362	24 Timbergreen Dr. Tomball, TX	73362
25.	709 E. Humble Av Chicago, IL	45893-5312	709 E. Tumble Av Chicago, IL	45893-5312
26.	1405 CATCUS DR CEDAR RAPIDS, IOWA	47320-4428	1405 CATCUS DR CEDAR RAPIDS, IOWA	47320-4428
27.	77 Wright Rd. Apt. 7B Peoria, IL	67210-4321	77 Wright Rd. Apt. 17B Peoria, IL	67210-4221
28.	103 Sue Lane Macon, Georgia	21567-4478	103 Sue Lane Macon, Georgia	21567-4478
29.	406 E Jack Miami, Florida	21208-4287	406 Jack Miami, Florida	21208-4287
30.	307 Sycamore Dr. Rockford, CA	92109	307 Sycamore Dr. Rockford, CA	92109

continued on next page

Part A – Address Checking
continued

A. No Errors	B. Address Only	C. ZIP Code Only	D. Both

Correct List / **List to be Checked**

	Address	ZIP Code	Address	ZIP Code
31.	4101 Elmwood Orlando, FL	39021-6738	4101 Elmhood Orlando, FL	39021-6738
32.	5311 East FM 1960 Houston, TX.	77319-3120	5311 East FM 1690 Houston, TX.	73319-3120
33.	1939 Wilderness Dr. Laramie, Wyoming	83480	1939 Wilderness Dr. Laramie, Wyoming	84380
34.	21 Humble Place Reno, NV	61947-3287	21 Humble Place Reno, NV	61997-3287
35.	42 Links Side Ct. San Bernardino, CA.	98321-4428	42 Links Side Ct. San Bernardino, CA.	98321-4428
36.	702 Misty Hills Ln. Fort Myers, Florida	31096-3891	702 Musty Hills Ln. Fort Myers, Florida	31096-3891
37.	6907 WILD VIOLET ANCHORAGE, AK	93890-3219	6907 WILD VIOLET ANCHORAGE, AL	93980-3219
38.	104 Clover Path St. Honolulu, Hawaii	92890-5437	104 Clover Bath St. Honolulu, Hawaii	92890-5437
39.	890423 67th Ave. San Mateo, CA	98219-4389	890243 67th Ave. San Mateo, CA	98219-4839
40.	24 Spring Way Glendale, AZ	42190-2389	24 Spring Way Gundale, AZ	41290-2389
41.	7926 Greens Apt. 10G Hatten, SC	73026	7926 Greens Apt. 10G Hatten, SC	73026
42.	15433 Country W Dr. Canton, OH	39809-3289	15433 Country W Dr. Canton, OH	39809-3289
43.	4334 Brian Walk Rd Knoxville, TN	50214-3278	4334 Brian Walk Rd Knoxville, TN	50214-3278
44.	59 E 56th St. Fresno, CA	73289-3218	59 E 56th St. Fresno, CA	73289-3218
45.	456 Scenic Shore Dr Seattle, WA	82147-4328	456 Scenic Shore Dr Seattle, WA	82417-4328

continued on next page

Part A – Address Checking
continued

A. No Errors	B. Address Only	C. ZIP Code Only	D. Both

	Correct List		List to be Checked	
	Address	*ZIP Code*	*Address*	*ZIP Code*
46.	2256 Loop 494 Birmingham, AL	37391	2256 Loop 494 W Birmingham, AL	33791
47.	9901 Orange Grove Biloxi, MS.	39501-6732	9901 Orange Grove Biloxi, MS.	39501-6372
48.	1544 Old Oak Lane Bedford Park, IL	33219-3428	1544 Old Oak Lane Breadford Park, IL	33219-3428
49.	16 Desert Star Drive Manchester, NH	08923-4428	16 Desert Star Drive Mancaster, NH	08923-4428
50.	1906 Crystal Springs Duluth, MN	63790-3219	1906 Crystal Springs Duluth, MN	63970-3219
51.	727 Ford Road White Plains, New York	06328	727 Lord Road White Plains, New York	03628
52.	88 Beach Blvd. Gulf Breeze, FL	23289-3278	88 Beach Blvd. Gulf Breeze, FL	23289-3278
53.	3202 S Federal Hwy Seaford, DE	12890-3487	3222 S Federal Hwy Seaford, DE	12290-3487
54.	55 SW College Rd. Knoxville, TN	48902-4367	55 SW College Rd. Knoxville, TN	48920-4367
55.	785 Dedeaux Ave. Gautier, MI	37390-4378	785 Dedeaux Ave. Gautier, MS	37390-4378
56.	43 EXPRESS DR. LAMAR, MISSOURI	69801	43 EXPRESS DR. LAMAR, MISSOURI	69801
57.	815 S Wheatley Newport, RI	53890-2387	815 S Whitely Newport, RI	53890-2387
58.	1566 W Main St. Du Bois, PA	22360-4301	1556 W Main St. Du Bois, PA	22360-3401
59.	400 Locust Apt. 8G Stillwater, OK	78320-3478	400 Locust Apt. 8G Stillwater, OK	78320-3478
60.	925 S Mill Redmond, Oregon	93278	925 S Miller Redmond, Oregon	93278

End of Part A – Address Checking

PRACTICE EXAM #2

Part B – Forms Completion

Directions

Part B tests your ability to identify information needed to complete various U.S. Postal Service forms. This part of the exam consists of 30 questions to be completed in 15 minutes. You will be shown 5 different forms and be asked to answer 6 questions about each form.

Turn the page and begin when you are prepared to time yourself for exactly 15 minutes.

Part B – Forms Completion

RETURN RECEIPT FOR MERCHANDISE		
Postage	1.	5. Postmark Here
Return Receipt for Merchandise Fee	2.	
Special Handling Fee	3.	
Total Postage & Fees	4.	
6.	Waiver of Signature ☐ YES ☐ NO	
7. Recipient's Name *(Please print clearly)*		
8. Street, Apt. No.; or P.O. Box		
9. City, State, ZIP + 4		

continued on next page

Part B – Forms Completion

continued

1. You could enter a dollar amount in each of the following boxes EXCEPT
   A. Box 2
   B. Box 3
   C. Box 4
   D. Box 7

2. Which of these would be a correct entry for Box 8?
   A. Chicago, Illinois 60435-1234
   B. 3:00 PM
   C. James Tibbits
   D. 910 E. 24th St.

3. Where would a check mark be appropriate?
   A. Box 1
   B. Box 6
   C. Box 8
   D. Box 9

4. The total postage and fees were $25.89. Where would you indicate this?
   A. Box 1
   B. Box 2
   C. Box 3
   D. Box 4

5. Where would the entry James Tibbits be appropriate?
   A. Box 5
   B. Box 6
   C. Box 7
   D. Box 9

6. Which box would the postmark be put into?
   A. Box 5
   B. Box 6
   C. Box 7
   D. Box 8

continued on next page

Part B – Forms Completion
continued

Customs Declaration			
1a. ☐ Gift ☐ Commercial Sample ☐ Documents ☐ Other			I, the undersigned, whose name and address are given on the item, certify that the particulars given in this declaration are correct and that this item does not contain any dangerous article or articles prohibited by legislation or by Postal or customs regulations. This copy will remain at the Post Office for 30 days.
2a. Quantity and detailed description of contents	**2b.** Weight lb. oz.	**2c.** Value US Dollars	**2d.** Sender's Name & Address
3a. For commercial items only (If known, HS tariff number and country of origin)	**3b.** Total Weight	**3c.** Total Value	**3d.** Addressee's Name & Address
4a. Date and sender's signature			**4b.** Date and sender's signature

continued on next page

Part B – Forms Completion

continued

7. How would you indicate that a commercial sample is being mailed?
   A. Write "Sample" in Box 3a
   B. Write "Sample" as a description in Box 2a
   C. Check "Commercial Sample" in Box 1a
   D. None of the above

8. Jack White is the sender. Where should his name and address be written?
   A. Box 2b
   B. Box 2c
   C. Box 2d
   D. Box 4b

9. Which of these would be an acceptable entry for Box 2c?
   A. A check mark
   B. 12/8/05
   C. 8953 W. Gail Dr.
   D. $25.00

10. Mrs. Anna Grafton is the addressee. Where should her name and address be written?
    A. Box 2d
    B. Box 3d
    C. Box 4a
    D. Box 4b

11. In which of these would a check mark be an appropriate entry?
    A. Box 1a
    B. Box 2a
    C. Box 2b
    D. Box 4b

12. The total value of all contents is $109.56. Where should this be entered?
    A. Box 2b
    B. Box 2c
    C. Box 3b
    D. Box 3c

continued on next page

Part B – Forms Completion

continued

Certificate of Bulk Mailing

Fee for Certificate		1. Meter stamp or postage (uncancelled) stamps in payment of fee to be affized here and cancelled by postmarking, including date.
Up to 1,000 pieces	Use Current Rate Chart	
For each additional 1,000 pieces, or fraction		
Duplicate Copy		

2a. Number of identical pieces	2b. Class of mail	2c. Postage on each	2d. Number of pieces per lb.	2e. Total number of pounds	2f. Total postage paid	2g. Fee paid

3a. Mailed for	3b. Mailed by

Postmaster's Certificate

It is hereby certified that the above-described mailing has been received and number of pieces and postage verified.

4. ______________________________

(Postmaster or Designee)

continued on next page

Part B – Forms Completion
continued

13. Which of these would be an acceptable entry for Box 2e?
    A. Tabbi Still
    B. 3 lbs.
    C. 2:00 PM
    D. $15.89

14. Where would you indicate number of identical pieces?
    A. Box 2a
    B. Box 2c
    C. Box 2f
    D. Box 2g

15. The fee paid is $24.00. Where would you indicate this?
    A. Box 2d
    B. Box 2e
    C. Box 2f
    D. Box 2g

16. Where should the Postmaster sign this form?
    A. Box 3a
    B. Box 3b
    C. Line 4
    D. Box 1

17. Where should you indicate that the mailing will be via first class mail?
    A. Box 2a
    B. Box 2b
    C. Box 2d
    D. Box 2f

18. Which of these could be an acceptable entry for Box 2c?
    A. 115 lb. 6 oz.
    B. 4,500
    C. 4/1/05
    D. $0.18

continued on next page

Part B – Forms Completion

continued

<table>
<tr><th colspan="3">INSURED MAIL RECEIPT</th></tr>
<tr><td>Postage</td><td>1.</td><td>1a. ☐ Fragile ☐ Liquid
☐ Perishable</td></tr>
<tr><td>Insurance Fees</td><td>2a.</td><td>2b. Insurance Coverage</td></tr>
<tr><td>Restricted Delivery Fee</td><td>3.</td><td rowspan="4">7. Postmark Here</td></tr>
<tr><td>Special Handling Fee</td><td>4.</td></tr>
<tr><td>Return Receipt Fee</td><td>5.</td></tr>
<tr><td>Total Postage & Fees</td><td>6.</td></tr>
<tr><td colspan="3">8. Sent to:</td></tr>
<tr><td colspan="3">9. Street, Apt. No.; or P.O. Box</td></tr>
<tr><td colspan="3">10. City, State, ZIP + 4, Country</td></tr>
</table>

continued on next page

Part B – Forms Completion

continued

19. For which of these could $23.80 be an appropriate entry?
    A. Box 1
    B. Box 2a
    C. Boxes 3, 4, 5, and 6
    D. All the above

20. Where should a Postal representative's signature go on this from?
    A. Box 10
    B. Box 2b
    C. Box 7
    D. A Postal representative does not sign this form.

21. The sender is shipping a fragile item and has purchased $200.00 worth of insurance on this item. Where would these facts be indicated?
    A. Boxes 1 and 7
    B. Boxes 1a and 2b
    C. Box 2a
    D. Box 6

22. The fees applicable to a particular shipment include postage - $14.85, insurance - $2.50, and return receipt - $1.50 for a total of $18.85. Where would the total of $18.85 be entered?
    A. Boxes 5 and 6
    B. Box 2a
    C. Box 4
    D. None of the above

23. For which of these could "1819 El Dorado Street" be an appropriate entry?
    A. Box 8
    B. Box 9
    C. Box 10
    D. None of the above

24. A Postal representative should stamp a postmark where on this form?
    A. Box 7
    B. Beside his or her signature
    C. On the back of the form
    D. A postmark should not be stamped on this form.

continued on next page

Domestic Claim or Registered Mail Inquiry

Mailer Information

1a. Name

1b. Business Name

1c. Address

1d. City, State, ZIP+4

1e. Telephone (include area code)

Addressee Information

2a. Name

2b. Business Name

2c. Address

2d. City, State, ZIP+4

2e. Telephone (include area code)

Payment Assignment
Alternate Payment Address

3a. Who is to receive payment? (Check one)
☐ Mailer ☐ Addressee

3b. Address

3c. City, State, ZIP+4

Description of Lost or Damaged Article(s)
Add extra sheets as needed

Item	Description	Code	Value	Purchase Date
A	**4a.**			
B	**4b.**			
C	**4c.**			

5a. COD amount to be remitted to sender
(For business mailer COD claims only) $

5b. Total amount claimed
for all articles $

Certification and signature

6a. Customer submitting claim
☐ Mailer ☐ Addressee

6b. Customer signature

6c. Date signed

continued on next page

Part B – Forms Completion

continued

25. How should it be indicated that the addressee will receive payment for a claim?
    A. Make a note in Box 2a
    B. Check "Addressee" in Box 3a
    C. Check "Addressee" in Box 6a
    D. Have the addressee sign Box 6b

26. Which of these would "Dallas, TX 77356-1123" be an acceptable entry for?
    A. Box 1d
    B. Box 2d
    C. Box 3c
    D. All the above

27. Which of these would "$87.23" be an acceptable entry for?
    A. Boxes 3a and 4a
    B. Boxes 3b and 4b
    C. Boxes 5a and 5b
    D. Boxes 6a and 6b

28. If the mailer is to receive payment, where should the mailer's address and contact information be entered?
    A. Boxes 1b, 1c, 1d, 1e, 3b, and 3c
    B. Boxes 1b, 1c, 1d, 1e, 2b, 2c, 2d, and 2e
    C. Boxes 2b, 2c, 2d, 2e, 3b, and 3c
    D. All the above

29. Where does a Postal representative's signature go on this form?
    A. A Postal representative's signature is not called for on this form.
    B. Box 6b
    C. Box 2a
    D. Boxes 2a and 6b

30. If a COD amount of $37.90 is to be remitted to the sender, where should this be entered on the form?
    A. Box 4a
    B. Box 5a
    C. Box 5b
    D. None of the above

End of Part B – Forms Completion

PRACTICE EXAM #2

Part C – Coding & Memory

Part C tests your ability to use codes quickly and accurately both from a Coding Guide and from memory. This part of the exam consists of two sections as detailed below.

- The Coding Section has 36 questions to be answered in 6 minutes. During the Coding section, you will look at a Coding Guide to find answers. The Coding Section is broken down into several segments.
- The Memory Section has 36 questions to be answered in 7 minutes. During the Memory Section, you must answer from memory. The Memory Section is broken down into several segments.

The same Coding Guide will be used throughout both sections of Part C. Four delivery routes (identified by the codes A, B, C, and D) are listed on the Coding Guide. Also listed on the Coding Guide are various address ranges on several streets that are served by these delivery routes.

Each question is an address. To answer each question, you must identify the delivery route that serves the address, and mark as your answer the code (A, B, C, or D) for that delivery route.

Turn the page when you are ready to begin the first section, the Coding Section.

Part C – Coding & Memory

Coding Section

The Coding Section of Part C - Coding & Memory consists of 3 segments as detailed below.

- **Coding Section - Segment 1**
  The first segment is a 2 minute introductory exercise. This segment is not scored.
- **Coding Section - Segment 2**
  The second segment is a 90 second (1½ minutes) practice exercise. This segment is not scored.
- **Coding Section - Segment 3**
  The third segment is the actual Coding Section test. You have 6 minutes to answer 36 questions. This segment is scored.

The Coding Guide is displayed during all 3 segments. You will be instructed to mark answers for the first two unscored segments on sample answer sheets, not the actual answer sheet. You will be instructed to mark answers for the third segment, which is scored, on the actual answer sheet.

Turn to the next page when you are ready to begin Coding Section - Segment 1.

Part C – Coding & Memory

Coding Section – Segment 1

Instructions

Segment 1 of the Coding Section is an introductory exercise to acquaint you with how the questions are to be answered. In this segment, you have 2 minutes to answer 4 questions. The Coding Guide is displayed for your use in answering the questions. This segment is not scored. Mark your answers on the sample answer sheet at the bottom of the question page, not on the actual answer sheet.

Turn the page and begin when you are prepared to time yourself for exactly 2 minutes.

Part C – Coding & Memory

Coding Section – Segment 1

CODING GUIDE	
Address Range	**Delivery Route**
2500 – 3399 Elwood Pkwy 501 – 700 Beltway 86 W 161 – 250 Allendale Road	A
3400 – 3650 Elwood Pkwy 251 – 310 Allendale Road	B
850 – 949 University PL 21000 – 23500 US 61 S 701 – 900 Beltway 86 W	C
All mail that doesn't fall in one of the address ranges listed above	D

Part C – Coding & Memory

Coding Section – Segment 1

continued

QUESTIONS

	Address	Delivery Route			
1.	3560 Elwood Pkwy	A	B	C	D
2.	400 Beltway 86 W	A	B	C	D
3.	924 University PL	A	B	C	D
4.	170 Allendale Road	A	B	C	D

SAMPLE ANSWER SHEET

1 (A) (B) (C) (D)
2 (A) (B) (C) (D)
3 (A) (B) (C) (D)
4 (A) (B) (C) (D)

The correct answers are 1-B, 2-D, 3-C, and 4-A.

Part C – Coding & Memory

Coding Section – Segment 2

Instructions

Segment 2 of the Coding Section is a practice exercise designed to expose you to the realistic timing demanded. In this segment, you have 90 seconds to answer 8 questions. The Coding Guide is displayed for your use in answering the questions. This segment is not scored. Mark your answers on the sample answer sheet at the bottom of the question page, not on the actual answer sheet.

Turn the page and begin when you are prepared to time yourself for exactly 90 seconds.

Part C – Coding & Memory

Coding Section – Segment 2

CODING GUIDE	
Address Range	**Delivery Route**
2500 – 3399 Elwood Pkwy 501 – 700 Beltway 86 W 161 – 250 Allendale Road	A
3400 – 3650 Elwood Pkwy 251 – 310 Allendale Road	B
850 – 949 University PL 21000 – 23500 US 61 S 701 – 900 Beltway 86 W	C
All mail that doesn't fall in one of the address ranges listed above	D

Part C – Coding & Memory

Coding Section – Segment 2

continued

QUESTIONS

	Address	Delivery Route			
1.	3480 Elwood Pkwy	A	B	C	D
2.	2550 Elwood Pkwy	A	B	C	D
3.	24500 US 61 S	A	B	C	D
4.	260 Allendale Road	A	B	C	D
5.	22050 US 61 S	A	B	C	D
6.	502 Beltway 86 W	A	B	C	D
7.	951 University PL	A	B	C	D
8.	2163 US 61 W	A	B	C	D

SAMPLE ANSWER SHEET

1	Ⓐ	Ⓑ	Ⓒ	Ⓓ	5	Ⓐ	Ⓑ	Ⓒ	Ⓓ
2	Ⓐ	Ⓑ	Ⓒ	Ⓓ	6	Ⓐ	Ⓑ	Ⓒ	Ⓓ
3	Ⓐ	Ⓑ	Ⓒ	Ⓓ	7	Ⓐ	Ⓑ	Ⓒ	Ⓓ
4	Ⓐ	Ⓑ	Ⓒ	Ⓓ	8	Ⓐ	Ⓑ	Ⓒ	Ⓓ

The correct answers are 1-B, 2-A, 3-D, 4-B, 5-C, 6-A, 7-D, and 8-D.

Part C – Coding & Memory

Coding Section – Segment 3

Instructions

Segment 3 of the Coding Section is the actual Coding test. You have 6 minutes to answer 36 questions. The Coding Guide is displayed for your use in answering the questions. This segment is scored, and the score from this section does affect your overall Exam 473 score. Mark your answers on the actual answer sheet in the section titled Part C - Coding & Memory - Coding Section.

Turn the page and begin when you are prepared to time yourself for exactly 6 minutes.

Coding Section – Segment 3

CODING GUIDE	
Address Range	**Delivery Route**
2500 – 3399 Elwood Pkwy 501 – 700 Beltway 86 W 161 – 250 Allendale Road	A
3400 – 3650 Elwood Pkwy 251 – 310 Allendale Road	B
850 – 949 University PL 21000 – 23500 US 61 S 701 – 900 Beltway 86 W	C
All mail that doesn't fall in one of the address ranges listed above	D

Coding Section – Segment 3

continued

Questions

	Address	Delivery Route			
1.	600 Beltway 86 W	A	B	C	D
2.	270 Allendale Road	A	B	C	D
3.	180 Allendale Road	A	B	C	D
4.	23400 US 61 S	A	B	C	D
5.	2900 Elwood Pkwy	A	B	C	D
6.	800 Beltway 86 W	A	B	C	D
7.	3630 Elwood Pkwy	A	B	C	D
8.	22090 US 61 S	A	B	C	D
9.	550 Beltway 86 W	A	B	C	D
10.	23482 US 61 W	A	B	C	D
11.	790 Beltway 86 W	A	B	C	D
12.	3620 Elwood Pkwy	A	B	C	D
13.	290 Allendale Road	A	B	C	D
14.	867 Beltway 86 W	A	B	C	D
15.	2700 Elwood Pkwy	A	B	C	D
16.	3700 Elwood Pkwy	A	B	C	D
17.	770 Beltway 86 W	A	B	C	D
18.	195 Allendale Road	A	B	C	D

continued on next page

Coding Section – Segment 3

continued

CODING GUIDE	
Address Range	**Delivery Route**
2500 – 3399 Elwood Pkwy 501 – 700 Beltway 86 W 161 – 250 Allendale Road	A
3400 – 3650 Elwood Pkwy 251 – 310 Allendale Road	B
850 – 949 University PL 21000 – 23500 US 61 S 701 – 900 Beltway 86 W	C
All mail that doesn't fall in one of the address ranges listed above	D

Coding Section – Segment 3

continued

Questions

	Address	Delivery Route			
19.	225 Allendale Road	A	B	C	D
20.	3490 Elwood Pkwy	A	B	C	D
21.	880 University PL	A	B	C	D
22.	670 Beltway 86 W	A	B	C	D
23.	22000 US 61 S	A	B	C	D
24.	3500 Elwood Pkwy	A	B	C	D
25.	940 Universal Road	A	B	C	D
26.	3300 Elwood Pkwy	A	B	C	D
27.	276 Allendale Road	A	B	C	D
28.	171 Allendale Road	A	B	C	D
29.	860 University PL	A	B	C	D
30.	592 Beltway 68 N	A	B	C	D
31.	288 Allendale Road	A	B	C	D
32.	21015 US 61 S	A	B	C	D
33.	2900 Elwood Pkwy	A	B	C	D
34.	870 University PL	A	B	C	D
35.	630 Beltway 86 W	A	B	C	D
36.	330 Allendale Road	A	B	C	D

End of Part C – Coding Section – Segment 3

Part C – Coding & Memory

Memory Section

The Memory Section of Part C - Coding & Memory consists of 4 segments as detailed below.

- **Memory Section - Segment 1**
  The first segment is a 3 minute study period during which you try to memorize the Coding Guide.
- **Memory Section - Segment 2**
  The second segment is a 90 second (1½ minutes) practice exercise. This segment is not scored.
- **Memory Section - Segment 3**
  The third segment is a 5 minute study period during which you try to memorize the Coding Guide.
- **Memory Section - Segment 4**
  This fourth segment is the actual Memory Section test. You have 7 minutes to answer 36 questions. This segment is scored.

There are no answers to mark during the first and third segments. You will be instructed to mark answers for the second segment on a sample answer sheet, not the actual answer sheet. You will be instructed to mark answers for the fourth segment, which is scored, on the actual answer sheet.

Turn to the next page when you are ready to begin Memory Section - Segment 1.

Part C – Coding & Memory

Memory Section – Segment 1

Instructions

Memory Section - Segment 1 is a 3 minute study period during which you try to memorize the information in the Coding Guide. There are no answers to mark during this study period.

Turn the page and begin studying when you are prepared to time yourself for exactly 3 minutes.

Part C – Coding & Memory

Memory Section – Segment 1

CODING GUIDE	
Address Range	**Delivery Route**
2500 – 3399 Elwood Pkwy 501 – 700 Beltway 86 W 161 – 250 Allendale Road	A
3400 – 3650 Elwood Pkwy 251 – 310 Allendale Road	B
850 – 949 University PL 21000 – 23500 US 61 S 701 – 900 Beltway 86 W	C
All mail that doesn't fall in one of the address ranges listed above	D

Part C – Coding & Memory

Memory Section – Segment 2

Instructions

Segment 2 of the Memory Section is a practice exercise where you have 90 seconds to answer 8 questions from memory. The Coding Guide is not shown. You must answer from memory. This segment is not scored. Mark your answers on the sample answer sheet at the bottom of the page, not on the actual answer sheet.

Begin when you are prepared to time yourself for exactly 90 seconds.

Part C – Coding & Memory

Memory Section – Segment 2

QUESTIONS

	Address	Delivery Route			
1.	880 Beltway 86 W	A	B	C	D
2.	3420 Elwood Pkwy	A	B	C	D
3.	228 Allendale Road	A	B	C	D
4.	2400 Elwood Pkwy	A	B	C	D
5.	742 Beltway 86 W	A	B	C	D
6.	1000 Beltway 86 W	A	B	C	D
7.	21500 US 61 S	A	B	C	D
8.	174 Allendale Road	A	B	C	D

SAMPLE ANSWER SHEET

1 Ⓐ Ⓑ Ⓒ Ⓓ   5 Ⓐ Ⓑ Ⓒ Ⓓ
2 Ⓐ Ⓑ Ⓒ Ⓓ   6 Ⓐ Ⓑ Ⓒ Ⓓ
3 Ⓐ Ⓑ Ⓒ Ⓓ   7 Ⓐ Ⓑ Ⓒ Ⓓ
4 Ⓐ Ⓑ Ⓒ Ⓓ   8 Ⓐ Ⓑ Ⓒ Ⓓ

The correct answers are 1-C, 2-B, 3-A, 4-D, 5-C, 6-D, 7-C, and 8-A.

Part C – Coding & Memory

Memory Section – Segment 3

Instructions

Memory Section - Segment 3 is a 5 minute study period during which you try to memorize the information in the Coding Guide. There are no answers to mark during this study period.

Turn the page and begin studying when you are prepared to time yourself for exactly 5 minutes.

Part C – Coding & Memory

Memory Section – Segment 3

CODING GUIDE	
Address Range	**Delivery Route**
2500 – 3399 Elwood Pkwy 501 – 700 Beltway 86 W 161 – 250 Allendale Road	A
3400 – 3650 Elwood Pkwy 251 – 310 Allendale Road	B
850 – 949 University PL 21000 – 23500 US 61 S 701 – 900 Beltway 86 W	C
All mail that doesn't fall in one of the address ranges listed above	D

Part C – Coding & Memory

Memory Section – Segment 4

Instructions

Memory Section - Segment 4 is the actual Memory test. You have 7 minutes to answer 36 questions. You must answer from memory. The Coding Guide is not shown. This segment is scored, and the score from this section does affect your overall Exam 473 score. Mark your answers on the actual answer sheet in the section titled Part C - Coding & Memory - Memory Section.

Turn the page and begin when you are prepared to time yourself for exactly 7 minutes.

Part C – Coding & Memory

Memory Section – Segment 4

Questions

	Address	Delivery Route			
37.	308 Allenville Road	A	B	C	D
38.	520 Beltway 86 W	A	B	C	D
39.	3389 Elwood Pkwy	A	B	C	D
40.	280 Allendale Road	A	B	C	D
41.	623 Beltway 86 W	A	B	C	D
42.	904 University PL	A	B	C	D
43.	3600 Elwood Pkwy	A	B	C	D
44.	200 Allendale Road	A	B	C	D
45.	875 University PL	A	B	C	D
46.	22500 US 61 S	A	B	C	D
47.	680 Beltway 86 W	A	B	C	D
48.	765 Beltway 86 W	A	B	C	D
49.	800 University PL	A	B	C	D
50.	2805 Elwood Pkwy	A	B	C	D
51.	294 Allendale Road	A	B	C	D
52.	650 Beltway 86 W	A	B	C	D
53.	3530 Elwood Pkwy	A	B	C	D
54.	168 Allendale Road	A	B	C	D

continued on next page

Part C – Coding & Memory

Memory Section – Segment 4

continued

Questions

	Address	Delivery Route			
55.	300 Allendale Road	A	B	C	D
56.	855 University PL	A	B	C	D
57.	23000 US 61 S	A	B	C	D
58.	2600 Elwood Pkwy	A	B	C	D
59.	216 Allendale Road	A	B	C	D
60.	3450 Elwood Pkwy	A	B	C	D
61.	21111 US 61 S	A	B	C	D
62.	845 Beltway 86 W	A	B	C	D
63.	450 Beltway 86 W	A	B	C	D
64.	3405 Ellawood DR	A	B	C	D
65.	865 University PL	A	B	C	D
66.	23041 Timothy LN	A	B	C	D
67.	746 Beltway 86 W	A	B	C	D
68.	3200 Elwood Pkwy	A	B	C	D
69.	306 Allendale Road	A	B	C	D
70.	240 Allendale Road	A	B	C	D
71.	3401 Elwood Pkwy	A	B	C	D
72.	706 Beltway 86 W	A	B	C	D

End of Part C – Memory Section – Segment 4

Part D – Personal Characteristics & Experience Inventory

As explained in the guide, it is not possible to practice or prepare for Part D. There are no right or wrong answers, and speed is not an issue. For each question, you simply select the answer that best reflects your own individual personality, temperament, experience, etc.

Since it is not possible to practice or prepare for Part D, no Personal Characteristics & Experience Inventory sample questions are included in this practice exam.

PRACTICE EXAM #3

As detailed below, included in this practice exam are all four parts of the actual exam and an answer sheet.

- **Part A – Address Checking**

Included is a 100% realistic replica of the scored Address Checking test on the actual exam.

- **Part B – Forms Completion**

Included is a 100% realistic replica of the scored Forms Completion test on the actual exam.

- **Part C – Coding & Memory**

Included are 100% realistic replicas of the complete Coding and Memory sections with all seven segments.

- **Part D – Personal Characteristics & Experience Inventory**

As explained in the guide, it is not possible to prepare for this part of the exam. Therefore no Personal Characteristics & Experience Inventory questions are included in the practice test for this part of the exam. However, for realistic formatting, we have included a page in the practice test for this exam part.

- **Answer Sheet**

Included near the back of the book are 100% realistic replicas of the answer sheet from the actual exam. When taking a practice exam, tear out one of these Practice Answer Sheets. Mark your answers to the scored segments of the exam on this answer sheet. As noted above, it is not possible to prepare for Part D. Therefore, bubbles are not included on the answer sheet for Part D. However, for realistic formatting, we have noted where Part D would appear on the answer sheet.

The format of this practice exam is identical to the actual exam, and the instructions are similar to those on the actual exam.

It is imperative that you take this practice exam in as realistic a fashion as possible - meaning that you must time yourself precisely. **Your practice will have no value unless it is done realistically.** Our Timed Practice Test Audio CD and our Test Prep CD-ROM are ideal tools for conveniently having the instructions presented section-by-section and for absolutely precise timing. See the order form in the back of the book or our website *www.PostalExam.com* for details.

Answer keys are provided in the back of your book. It is imperative that you use the formulas given in the book to **score each practice test as you complete it**. Scoring is necessary in order to measure your progress and to identify your individual areas of weakness that may need extra attention.

After completing and scoring each practice exam, move on to the next. **After finishing all six exams, you should be prepared to excel on the actual exam.**

Do not look over the practice exam questions until you are ready to start and to time yourself - usually meaning until you have started either the Timed Practice Test Audio CD or the Postal Test Prep CD-ROM. Similarly, after completing one section of the practice test, do not look over the next one until your are ready to start it. Likewise, stop working and put down your pencil immediately when the allotted period of time has expired. As has been emphasized before but cannot be emphasized enough, your practice is of absolutely no value unless it is done realistically. Also, you must train yourself (1) to not open your test booklet or pick up your pencil until instructed to do so and (2) to close your booklet and put down your pencil immediately upon being so instructed. The Postal Service has zero tolerance on these matters. Any variance may be viewed as cheating and may result in your disqualification.

Turn to the next page when you are ready to begin this Practice Exam.

Important Note about this Practice Exam

The questions, addresses, forms, etc. in this practice exam are very realistic samples, but they are not the actual ones that you will see on the real test. There are hundreds of different versions of this exam, and each version has different questions, addresses, forms, etc. Even if you could get some real questions from one version of the exam, the questions on the version of the exam you take would surely be different.

PRACTICE EXAM #3

Part A – Address Checking

Directions

In Part A consists of 60 questions to be completed in 11 minutes. You are given a **Correct List** of addresses and ZIP codes. A **List to be Checked,** also with addresses and ZIP codes, appears next to the **Correct List**. The **List to be Checked** should be exactly like the **Correct List**, but it may contain errors.

Your task is to compare each row of information in the **Correct List** and the **List to be Checked** to find if there are **No Errors**, an error in the **Address Only**, an error in the **ZIP Code Only**, or an error in **Both** the address and the ZIP code.

After comparing each row of information, select an answer from the below answer choices, and mark your answer on the answer sheet in the section titled Part A - Address Checking.

A. No Errors	**B. Address Only**	**C. ZIP Code Only**	**D. Both**

Turn the page and begin when you are prepared to time yourself for exactly 11 minutes.

Part A – Address Checking

A. No Errors	B. Address Only	C. ZIP Code Only	D. Both

	Correct List: Address	Correct List: ZIP Code	List to be Checked: Address	List to be Checked: ZIP Code
1.	18994 Ferne Dr. Junction City, KS	58910	18994 Ferner Dr. Junction City, KS	58910
2.	7 McClellan Cir Waterville, ME	78156-4786	7 McClellan Cir Waterville, ME	78156-4786
3.	24925 Plantation Ln Stanford, Kentucky	24876-5126	24952 Plantation Ln Stanford, Kentucky	24876-5226
4.	190 Atascocita Shores Butler, PA	47963	190 Attasosita Shores Butler, PA	47963
5.	3354 Prairie Drive Newport, Oregon	97812-8432	3354 Prairie Drive Newport, Oregon	97182-8432
6.	954 W Sunset Apt. 1B Colville, WA	91278-5478	954 W Sunset Apt. 1B Colville, WA	91778-5478
7.	8103 Trophy Pl Woonsocket, RI	17890	8103 Brophy Pl Woonsocket, RI	17890
8.	1918 Sage Tree Ulvalde, TX	79120-4573	1918 Sage Tree Ulvalde, TX	79120-4573
9.	P.O. Box 4424587 Spencer, WV	20364-4587	P.O. Box 4424587 Spencer, WV	20364-4587
10.	220 COMMUNITY LN ROCK SPRINGS, WY	84123-4450	220 COMMUNITY LN ROCK SPRINGS, WY	84123-4450
11.	92A Meyer Rd. Great Falls, Montana	84578-1002	928 Meyer Rd. Great Falls, Montana	84578-1002
12.	874 Brazos Bend Tr Rutland, VT	10256-7812	874 Brazos Bark Tr Rutland, VT	10256-7812
13.	2207 Poplar Park Dr. Cranberry, PA	27812	2207 Poplar Park Dr. Cranberry, PA	28712
14.	518 Moonshine Hill Rochester, NH	11102-7819	518 Moonshine Hill Rochester, NV	11112-7819
15.	801 E. Higgins Av Bakersfield, CA	94579-1173	801 E. Higgins Av Bakersville, CA	94579-1773

continued on next page

Part A – Address Checking
continued

A. No Errors	B. Address Only	C. ZIP Code Only	D. Both

	Correct List		List to be Checked	
	Address	*ZIP Code*	*Address*	*ZIP Code*
16.	923 Timber Cove Carol Stream, IL	52213-7863	923 Timber Caves Carol Stream, IL	52213-7863
17.	1315 Falling Leaf Ln New Orleans, LA	71158-4593	1315 Falling Leaf Ln New Orleans, LA	71558-4593
18.	748 W. POWERS CLEVELAND, OHIO	81456	748 W. POWDER CLEVELAND, OHIO	81466
19.	5425 Thistle Drive Richmond, VA	67453-1157	5425 Thistle Drive Richmond, VA	67453-1157
20.	PO Box 63524761 Spring, TX	74183-4761	PO Box 63524761 Spring, TX	74183-4761
21.	900 Henderson Princeton, NJ	14580-8430	900 Hendersonville Princeton, NJ	14580-8430
22.	2211 E FM 517 Rd Medina, Ohio	24589-1056	2211 E FM 715 Rd Medina, Ohio	24859-1056
23.	110 W 8th St. Portales, New Mexico	70489-7510	110 W 8th St. Portales, New Mexico	70489-7510
24.	18419 Point Lookout Moses Lake, WA	99721	18419 Point Lookout Moses Lake, WA	97921
25.	56 Lazy Ln. Rockingham, NC	50041-7826	56 Lazy Ln. Rockingpan, NC	50441-7826
26.	5060 Lechenger Celina, OH	60487-7826	5060 Lechenger Celina, NH	60487-7826
27.	601 Enterprise Ave. Warsaw, N.Y.	10560-7812	601 Enterprise Ave. Warsaw, N.Y.	10560-7812
28.	2104 Balsam Lk Ln Toms River, NJ	80045-7830	2104 Balsam Lk Ln Toms River, NJ	80045-7830
29.	3214 Park Ave. Apt. 29 Abilene, Texas	77632-1458	3214 Park Ave. Apt. 29 Abilene, Texas	77622-1458
30.	5387 Hidden Brook Ln Chattanooga, TN	66145	5387 Hidden Book Ln Chattanooga, TN	66145

continued on next page

Part A – Address Checking
continued

A. No Errors	B. Address Only	C. ZIP Code Only	D. Both

	Correct List		List to be Checked	
	Address	*ZIP Code*	*Address*	*ZIP Code*
31.	1590 Walnut Grove Shelby, NC	58790-7821	1590 Walnut Grove Shells, NC	58790-7821
32.	1302 County Rd 55 Bryan, N.D.	82890-4903	1302 County Rd 55 Bryan, N.D.	82890-4933
33.	1506 Hummingbird LN Joliet, IL	60612	1506 Hummingbird LN Joliet, IL	60612
34.	2918 Marlin Apt. 7G Rutland, Vermont	57902-1209	2918 Marlin Apt. 17G Rutland, Vermont	57902-1029
35.	23 Dickerson St. Oak Harbor, WA	90082-7793	23 Dickinson St. Oak Harbor, WA	90082-7793
36.	401 Brightfield Ave. Hobbs, New Mexico	77032	401 Brightville Ave. Hobbs, New Mexico	77332
37.	3213 Ivory Pointe Dr. St. Helens, OR	90321-8421	3213 Ivory Pointe Dr. Mt. St. Helens, OR	90321-8421
38.	550 29th Street Gillette, W.Y.	80421-4321	550 29th Street Gillette, W.V.	80421-4221
39.	1215 Courthouse Rd. Marysville, GA	52179-1123	1215 Courthouse Rd. Marysville, GA	52179-1123
40.	11 SAVANNAH LN. GULFPORT, M.S.	39506-4521	11 SAVANNAH LN. GULFPORT, M.S.	39506-4521
41.	4607 Nasa Rd. 1 Bay City, Texas	77280	4607 Nassau Rd. Bay City, Texas	77280
42.	525 Sandy Meadow St. Santa Clarita, CA	92213-8901	525 Sandy Meadow St. Santa Clarita, VA	92213-8901
43.	16827 N Hwy 3 Bedford Park, IL	21897-5621	16287 N Hwy 3 Bedford Park, IL	21879-5621
44.	711 4th St. Springfield, M.A.	68210-5541	771 4th St. Springfield, M.A.	68210-5441
45.	2723 Pilgrims Point Cranston, RI	10269-1469	2723 Pilgrims Point Cranston, RI	10269-1469

continued on next page

Part A – Address Checking

continued

A. No Errors	B. Address Only	C. ZIP Code Only	D. Both

	Correct List		List to be Checked	
	Address	*ZIP Code*	*Address*	*ZIP Code*
46.	PO Box 768633 Lubbock, TX	74012-8633	PO Box 768633 Lubbock, TX	74012-8633
47.	1337 Shrub Oak Ln. St. George, Utah	86518-2459	1337 Scrub Oak Ln. St. George, Utah	86518-2459
48.	15 SAM DRIVE LAUREL, MS	30231-8112	15 SAM DRIVE LAUREL, MA	30231-8112
49.	721 Whitecap St. Norfolk, VA	22650	721 Whitecap St. Norfolk, VA	22650
50.	780 Bee Cave Dr. Dickson, TN	40213-8214	780 Bee Cove Dr. Dickson, TN	40213-8214
51.	5011 Chappel Hill Ste 1 Rapid City, S.D.	62189-4792	501 Chappel Hill Ste 1 Rapid City, S.D.	62199-4792
52.	3106 Hawks Apt. 34 Green Bay, WI	82459-3514	3106 Hawks Apt. 34 Green Bay, WI	82459-5314
53.	2503 W. Main Casper, WY	90235-4792	2503 W. Main Casper, WY	92035-4792
54.	2401 Foothill Blvd. Shawnee, OK	79512-5709	2401 Foothill Blvd. Shawnee, OR	79512-5709
55.	619 S Esplande Ln South Point, OH	21569-1036	619 S Esplande Ln South Point, OH	21569-1036
56.	3218 Carmel Valley Wayne, W.V.	58690-8457	3218 Carmel Valley Wayne, W.V.	58960-8457
57.	5507 Victoria Ct. Ponce, P.R.	02578-8439	5507 Victory Ct. Ponce, P.R.	02578-8439
58.	19 SARAH COURT BETHEL, AK	98213	19 SARAH COURT BETHEL, AK	98213
59.	572 Pelican Ave. Union, SC	25698-4586	572 Pelican Ave. Union, SD	25668-4586
60.	28510 Champion Oaks Minot, N.D.	41568-8912	28510 Champion Oaks Mineral, N.D.	41168-8912

End of Part A – Address Checking

PRACTICE EXAM #3

Part B – Forms Completion

Directions

Part B tests your ability to identify information needed to complete various U.S. Postal Service forms. This part of the exam consists of 30 questions to be completed in 15 minutes. You will be shown 5 different forms and be asked to answer 6 questions about each form.

Turn the page and begin when you are prepared to time yourself for exactly 15 minutes.

Part B – Forms Completion

RETURN RECEIPT FOR MERCHANDISE		
Postage	1.	5. Postmark Here
Return Receipt for Merchandise Fee	2.	
Special Handling Fee	3.	
Total Postage & Fees	4.	
6. Waiver of Signature ☐ YES ☐ NO		
7. Recipient's Name *(Please print clearly)*		
8. Street, Apt. No.; or P.O. Box		
9. City, State, ZIP + 4		

continued on next page

Part B – Forms Completion

continued

1. How would a customer indicate that he wants a waiver of signature?
   A. Check "YES" in Box 6
   B. Check "NO" in Box 6
   C. Sign his name beside "Waiver of Signature" in Box 6
   D. None of the above

2. If the postage is $3.55, where would this amount be entered?
   A. Box 1
   B. Box 5
   C. Box 7
   D. Box 8

3. The special handling fee is $5.66. In which box should this amount be entered?
   A. Box 3
   B. Box 4
   C. Box 5
   D. Box 9

4. In which of these would "Viola, MS 38501-1455" be an acceptable entry?
   A. Box 5
   B. Box 6
   C. Box 8
   D. Box 9

5. Which of these could be a correct entry for Box 3?
   A. 9lbs. 4ozs.
   B. 2:30 p.m.
   C. $3.45
   D. A check mark

6. Where would a $4.85 Return Receipt for Merchandise Fee be entered?
   A. Box 1
   B. Box 2
   C. Box 3
   D. Box 6

continued on next page

Part B – Forms Completion
continued

Customs Declaration			
1a. ☐ Gift ☐ Documents ☐ Commercial Sample ☐ Other			I, the undersigned, whose name and address are given on the item, certify that the particulars given in this declaration are correct and that this item does not contain any dangerous article or articles prohibited by legislation or by Postal or customs regulations. This copy will remain at the Post Office for 30 days.
2a. Quantity and detailed description of contents	2b. Weight lb. oz.	2c. Value US Dollars	2d. Sender's Name & Address
3a. For commercial items only (If known, HS tariff number and country of origin)	3b. Total Weight	3c. Total Value	3d. Addressee's Name & Address
4a. Date and sender's signature			4b. Date and sender's signature

continued on next page

Part B – Forms Completion

continued

7. Which of these would be an acceptable entry for Box 2a?
   A. $59.40
   B. 12 - Postal Exam Study Guide (books)
   C. 18lbs. 6ozs
   D. Susie McVey

8. Which of these could be an acceptable entry for Box 1a?
   A. A check mark
   B. Donald Struthers
   C. 6/22/05
   D. $12.35

9. Which of these would be an acceptable entry for Box 3b?
   A. 8 lbs. 2 oz.
   B. A check mark
   C. 10/28/04
   D. Alicia Farmer

10. The total weight is 15 lb. 6 oz. Where should this be written?
    A. Box 2b
    B. Box 2c
    C. Box 3b
    D. Box 3c

11. Louise O'Neal is the sender. Francis Carlson is the addressee. Where should Francis Carlson sign this form?
    A. Box 4a
    B. Box 4b
    C. Box 4a & 4b
    D. Francis Carlson is not supposed to sign this form.

12. Where would you indicate that a gift is being sent?
    A. Box 2a
    B. Box 1a
    C. Box 2b
    D. Box 3d

continued on next page

Part B – Forms Completion
continued

Forwarding Order Change Order

Check One
1. ☐ Entire Family ☐ Individual

2a. Carrier Route No.	**2b.** Carrier/Clerk	**2c.** Receiving Employee	**2d.** Original Order Date	**2e.** This Order Date	**2f.** Expiraton Date

3. *Print* Last Name or Name of Business/Firm *(If more than one last name fill out additional form.)*

4. *Print* First Name of Each Individual Covered By This Order *(Separate each name by a comma.)*

Original Address	**5a.** *Print* Number and Street	**5b.** Apt./Suite No.	**5c.** P.O. Box No.	**5d.** Rural Route No.	**5e.** Rural Box No.
	6a. *Print* City		**6b.** State	**6c.** ZIP + 4	
Cancel Forwarding Order	**7a.** *Print* Number and Street	**7b.** Apt./Suite No.	**7c.** P.O. Box No.	**7d.** Rural Route No.	**7e.** Rural Box No.
	8a. *Print* City		**8b.** State	**8c.** ZIP + 4	
New Forwarding Order	**9a.** *Print* Number and Street	**9b.** Apt./Suite No.	**9c.** P.O. Box No.	**9d.** Rural Route No.	**9e.** Rural Box No.
	10a. *Print* City		**10b.** State	**10c.** ZIP + 4	

11a. ☐ Moved no order **11b.** ☐ Refuses to pay postage due on ALL 4th class

12a. ☐ No such number **12b.** ☐ No such street, check forwarding order

13a. Post Office	**13b.** Station/ Branch	**13c.** By *(Route No., Name)*

continued on next page

Part B – Forms Completion

continued

13. Where should the expiration date for this Forwarding Order Change Order be entered?
    A. Box 2d
    B. Box 2e
    C. Box 2f
    D. None of the above

14. Where should the original Forwarding Order date be entered?
    A. Box 2d
    B. Box 2e
    C. Box 2f
    D. None of the above

15. Where should the date for this Forwarding Order Change Order be entered?
    A. Box 2d
    B. Box 2e
    C. Box 2f
    D. None of the above

16. What would be a correct entry for Box 10b?
    A. TX
    B. 77375
    C. 837 W Main St.
    D. A check mark

17. What would be a correct entry for Box 8a?
    A. 237 Center St., Cheyenne, WY 80572-1932
    B. 80572-1932
    C. 237 Center St
    D. Cheyenne

18. What would be a correct entry for Box 1?
    A. Eldridge, Richard
    B. Yes
    C. 99302
    D. A check mark

continued on next page

<table>
<tr><th colspan="4">Application for Post Office Box or Caller Service</th></tr>
<tr><td colspan="2">Customer: Complete white boxes</td><td colspan="2">Post Office: Complete shaded boxes</td></tr>
<tr><td colspan="3">1a. Name(s) to which box number(s) is (are) are assigned</td><td>1b. Box or Caller Numbers

_____ through _____</td></tr>
<tr><td colspan="3">2a. Name of person applying, Title (if representing an organization), and name of organization (if different from name in Box 1a above)</td><td>2b. Will this box be used for:
Personal use
☐ Business use</td></tr>
<tr><td colspan="3">3a. Address (number, street, apt. no., city, state, ZIP code). When address changes, cross out address here and put new address on back.</td><td>3b. Telephone number (include area code)</td></tr>
<tr><td>4a. Date application received</td><td>4b. Box size needed</td><td>4c. ID and physical address verified by (initials)</td><td>4d. Dates of service

_____ through _____</td></tr>
<tr><td colspan="2" rowspan="2">5a. Two types of identification are required. One must contain a photograph of the addressee(s). Social security cards, credit cards, and birth certificates are unacceptable as identification. Write in identifying information. Subject to verification.</td><td>5b. Eligibility for Carrier Delivery
☐ City ☐ Rural
☐ HCR ☐ None</td><td>5c. Service Assigned
☐ Box
☐ Caller
☐ Reserve No.</td></tr>
<tr><td colspan="2">6. Name(s) of minors or others receiving mail in individual box.</td></tr>
<tr><td colspan="2">WARNING: The furnishing of false or misleading information on this form or omission of information may result in criminal sanctions (including fines and imprisonment) and/or civil sanctions (including multiple damages and civil penalties).</td><td colspan="2">7. Signature of applicant (Same as Item 3). I agree to comply with all Postal rules regarding Post Office box or caller services.</td></tr>
</table>

continued on next page

Part B – Forms Completion

continued

19. What would be a correct entry for Box 4a?
    A. Baltimore, MD
    B. 8/3/05
    C. Nicolas Barnwell
    D. N. B.

20. What would be a correct entry for Box 4c?
    A. Baltimore, MD
    B. 8/3/05
    C. Nicolas Barnwell
    D. N. B.

21. In which box would the entry 3" X 5" be acceptable?
    A. Box 1b
    B. Box 4d
    C. Box 4a
    D. Box 4b

22. Which of these could be an acceptable entry for Box 5c?
    A. A check mark
    B. 8/3/05
    C. Baltimore, MD
    D. Nicolas Barnwell

23. What would be a correct entry for Box 6?
    A. 237 Center St., Cheyenne, WY 80572-1932
    B. 80572-1932
    C. Larry Taylor, Anna Taylor
    D. 12/18/05

24. What would be a correct entry for Box 3b?
    A. Eldridge, Richard
    B. (555) 713-6782
    C. 99302
    D. A check mark

continued on next page

Part B – Forms Completion
continued

Application to Mail at Nonprofit Standard Mail Rates

Part 1 *(For completion by applicant)*

No application fee is required. All information must be complete and typewritten or printed legibly.

1. Complete name of organization *(If voting registration official, include title.)*

2. Street address of organization *(Include apartment or suite number.)*

3. City, state, ZIP+4 code

4a. Telephone *(Include area code.)*

4b. Name of applicant *(Must represent applying organization.)*

5. Type of organization *(Check only one.)*

- ☐ Religious
- ☐ Educational
- ☐ Scientific
- ☐ Philanthropic
- ☐ Agricultural
- ☐ Labor
- ☐ Veterans'
- ☐ Fraternal
- ☐ Qualified political committee
- ☐ Voting registration official

6. Is this a for-profit organization or does any of the net income inure to the benefit of any private stockholder or individual? ☐ Yes ☐ No

7a. Is this organization exempt from federal income tax? *(If 'Yes', attach a copy of the exemption issued by the Internal Revenue Service that shows the section of the IRS code under which the organization is exempt.)* ☐ Yes ☐ No

7b. Is an application for exempt status pending with the IRS? *(If 'Yes', attach a copy of the application to this form.)* ☐ Yes ☐ No

8. Has this organization previously mailed at the Nonprofit Standard Mail rates? *(If yes, list the Post Offices where mailings were most recently deposited at these rates?* ☐ Yes ☐ No

7c. Has the IRS denied or revoked the organization's federal tax exempt status? *(If 'Yes', attach a copy of the IRS ruling to this form.)* ☐ Yes ☐ No

9. Has your organization had Nonprofit Standard Mail rate mailing privileges denied or revoked? *(If 'Yes', list the Post Office [city and state] where the application was denied or authorization revoked.)* ☐ Yes ☐ No

10. Post Office (not a station or branch) where authorization requested and bulk mailings will be made *(City, state, ZIP code)*

11. Signature of applicant

12. Title

13. Date

Part 2 *(For completion by Postmaster at originating office where application filed)*

14. Signature of Postmaster *(Or designated representative)*

15. Date application filed with Post Office *(Round stamp)*

continued on next page

Part B – Forms Completion

continued

25. What would be a correct entry for Box 2?
    A. Boston, MA
    B. 185 Corporate Dr.
    C. 20245-8643
    D. 185 Corporate Dr., Boston, MA 20245-8643

26. What would be a correct entry for Box 4b?
    A. A check mark
    B. Lawrence Ward
    C. (555) 469-9327
    D. Boston, MA 20245-8643

27. What would be a correct entry for Box 4a?
    A. A check mark
    B. Lawrence Ward
    C. (555) 469-9327
    D. Boston, MA 20245-8643

28. If the entry in Box 1 is "Carl Amos, Voter Registrar, Harris County, TX", which choice should be checked in Box 5?
    A. Voting registration official
    B. Qualified political committee
    C. Fraternal
    D. Veterans'

29. What would be a correct entry for Box 3?
    A. Boston, MA
    B. 185 Corporate Dr.
    C. 20245-8643
    D. Boston, MA 20245-8643

30. What would be a correct entry for Box 6?
    A. A check mark
    B. Lawrence Ward
    C. (555) 469-9327
    D. Boston, MA 20245-8643

End of Part B – Forms Completion

PRACTICE EXAM #3

Part C – Coding & Memory

Part C tests your ability to use codes quickly and accurately both from a Coding Guide and from memory. This part of the exam consists of two sections as detailed below.

- The Coding Section has 36 questions to be answered in 6 minutes. During the Coding section, you will look at a Coding Guide to find answers. The Coding Section is broken down into several segments.
- The Memory Section has 36 questions to be answered in 7 minutes. During the Memory Section, you must answer from memory. The Memory Section is broken down into several segments.

The same Coding Guide will be used throughout both sections of Part C. Four delivery routes (identified by the codes A, B, C, and D) are listed on the Coding Guide. Also listed on the Coding Guide are various address ranges on several streets that are served by these delivery routes.

Each question is an address. To answer each question, you must identify the delivery route that serves the address, and mark as your answer the code (A, B, C, or D) for that delivery route.

Turn the page when you are ready to begin the first section, the Coding Section.

Part C – Coding & Memory

Coding Section

The Coding Section of Part C - Coding & Memory consists of 3 segments as detailed below.

- **Coding Section - Segment 1**
  The first segment is a 2 minute introductory exercise. This segment is not scored.
- **Coding Section - Segment 2**
  The second segment is a 90 second (1½ minutes) practice exercise. This segment is not scored.
- **Coding Section - Segment 3**
  The third segment is the actual Coding Section test. You have 6 minutes to answer 36 questions. This segment is scored.

The Coding Guide is displayed during all 3 segments. You will be instructed to mark answers for the first two unscored segments on sample answer sheets, not the actual answer sheet. You will be instructed to mark answers for the third segment, which is scored, on the actual answer sheet.

Turn to the next page when you are ready to begin Coding Section - Segment 1.

Part C – Coding & Memory

Coding Section – Segment 1

Instructions

Segment 1 of the Coding Section is an introductory exercise to acquaint you with how the questions are to be answered. In this segment, you have 2 minutes to answer 4 questions. The Coding Guide is displayed for your use in answering the questions. This segment is not scored. Mark your answers on the sample answer sheet at the bottom of the question page, not on the actual answer sheet.

Turn the page and begin when you are prepared to time yourself for exactly 2 minutes.

Part C – Coding & Memory

Coding Section – Segment 1

CODING GUIDE	
Address Range	**Delivery Route**
1991 – 3200 La Place Hwy 15 – 30 Farmerville LN 100 – 399 Chattanooga Dr.	A
3201 – 3900 La Place Hwy 400 – 699 Chattanooga Dr.	B
830 – 900 CR 228 9000 – 15000 Alta Vista Ave. 31 – 60 Farmerville LN	C
All mail that doesn't fall in one of the address ranges listed above	D

Part C – Coding & Memory

Coding Section – Segment 1

continued

QUESTIONS

	Address	Delivery Route			
1.	850 CR 228	A	B	C	D
2.	70 Farmerville LN	A	B	C	D
3.	20 Farmerville LN	A	B	C	D
4.	420 Chattanooga Dr.	A	B	C	D

SAMPLE ANSWER SHEET

1 Ⓐ Ⓑ Ⓒ Ⓓ
2 Ⓐ Ⓑ Ⓒ Ⓓ
3 Ⓐ Ⓑ Ⓒ Ⓓ
4 Ⓐ Ⓑ Ⓒ Ⓓ

The correct answers are 1-C, 2-D, 3-A, and 4-B.

Part C – Coding & Memory

Coding Section – Segment 2

Instructions

Segment 2 of the Coding Section is a practice exercise designed to expose you to the realistic timing demanded. In this segment, you have 90 seconds to answer 8 questions. The Coding Guide is displayed for your use in answering the questions. This segment is not scored. Mark your answers on the sample answer sheet at the bottom of the question page, not on the actual answer sheet.

Turn the page and begin when you are prepared to time yourself for exactly 90 seconds.

Part C – Coding & Memory

Coding Section – Segment 2

CODING GUIDE	
Address Range	**Delivery Route**
1991 – 3200 La Place Hwy 15 – 30 Farmerville LN 100 – 399 Chattanooga Dr.	A
3201 – 3900 La Place Hwy 400 – 699 Chattanooga Dr.	B
830 – 900 CR 228 9000 – 15000 Alta Vista Ave. 31 – 60 Farmerville LN	C
All mail that doesn't fall in one of the address ranges listed above	D

Part C – Coding & Memory

Coding Section – Segment 2

continued

QUESTIONS

	Address	Delivery Route			
1.	9050 Alta Vista Ave.	A	B	C	D
2.	800 Chattanooga Dr.	A	B	C	D
3.	1998 La Place Hwy	A	B	C	D
4.	3408 La Place Hwy	A	B	C	D
5.	41 Farmerville LN	A	B	C	D
6.	12000 Alta Vista Ave.	A	B	C	D
7.	4000 La Place Hwy	A	B	C	D
8.	201 Chattanooga Dr.	A	B	C	D

SAMPLE ANSWER SHEET

1	Ⓐ Ⓑ Ⓒ Ⓓ	5	Ⓐ Ⓑ Ⓒ Ⓓ
2	Ⓐ Ⓑ Ⓒ Ⓓ	6	Ⓐ Ⓑ Ⓒ Ⓓ
3	Ⓐ Ⓑ Ⓒ Ⓓ	7	Ⓐ Ⓑ Ⓒ Ⓓ
4	Ⓐ Ⓑ Ⓒ Ⓓ	8	Ⓐ Ⓑ Ⓒ Ⓓ

The correct answers are 1-C, 2-D, 3-A, 4-B, 5-C, 6-C, 7-D, and 8-A.

Part C – Coding & Memory

Coding Section – Segment 3

Instructions

Segment 3 of the Coding Section is the actual Coding test. You have 6 minutes to answer 36 questions. The Coding Guide is displayed for your use in answering the questions. This segment is scored, and the score from this section does affect your overall Exam 473 score. Mark your answers on the actual answer sheet in the section titled Part C - Coding & Memory - Coding Section.

Turn the page and begin when you are prepared to time yourself for exactly 6 minutes.

Coding Section – Segment 3

CODING GUIDE	
Address Range	**Delivery Route**
1991 – 3200 La Place Hwy 15 – 30 Farmerville LN 100 – 399 Chattanooga Dr.	A
3201 – 3900 La Place Hwy 400 – 699 Chattanooga Dr.	B
830 – 900 CR 228 9000 – 15000 Alta Vista Ave. 31 – 60 Farmerville LN	C
All mail that doesn't fall in one of the address ranges listed above	D

Coding Section – Segment 3

continued

Questions

	Address	Delivery Route			
1.	3600 La Place Hwy	A	B	C	D
2.	12450 Alta Vista Ave.	A	B	C	D
3.	2100 La Place Hwy	A	B	C	D
4.	13000 Alta Vista Ave.	A	B	C	D
5.	440 Chattanooga Dr.	A	B	C	D
6.	36 Farmerville LN	A	B	C	D
7.	24 Farmerville LN	A	B	C	D
8.	840 CR 228	A	B	C	D
9.	9225 Malta Crista Dr.	A	B	C	D
10.	44 Farmerville LN	A	B	C	D
11.	330 Chattanooga Dr.	A	B	C	D
12.	3403 La Place Hwy	A	B	C	D
13.	863 CR 228	A	B	C	D
14.	26 Farmerville LN	A	B	C	D
15.	16000 Alta Vista Ave.	A	B	C	D
16.	550 Chattanooga Dr.	A	B	C	D
17.	895 Broad St.	A	B	C	D
18.	3700 La Place Hwy	A	B	C	D

continued on next page

Coding Section – Segment 3

continued

CODING GUIDE	
Address Range	**Delivery Route**
1991 – 3200 La Place Hwy 15 – 30 Farmerville LN 100 – 399 Chattanooga Dr.	A
3201 – 3900 La Place Hwy 400 – 699 Chattanooga Dr.	B
830 – 900 CR 228 9000 – 15000 Alta Vista Ave. 31 – 60 Farmerville LN	C
All mail that doesn't fall in one of the address ranges listed above	D

Coding Section – Segment 3

continued

Questions

	Address	Delivery Route			
19.	22 Farmerville LN	A	B	C	D
20.	250 Chattanooga Dr.	A	B	C	D
21.	838 CR 282	A	B	C	D
22.	52 Farmerville LN	A	B	C	D
23.	3178 La Place Hwy	A	B	C	D
24.	11000 Alta Vista Ave.	A	B	C	D
25.	1891 La Place Hwy	A	B	C	D
26.	17 Farmerville LN	A	B	C	D
27.	420 Chattanooga Dr.	A	B	C	D
28.	39 Farmerville LN	A	B	C	D
29.	581 Chattanooga Dr.	A	B	C	D
30.	2050 La Place Hwy	A	B	C	D
31.	9084 Alta Vista Ave.	A	B	C	D
32.	842 CR 228	A	B	C	D
33.	13 Farmerville LN	A	B	C	D
34.	844 CR 228	A	B	C	D
35.	80 Farmerville LN	A	B	C	D
36.	150 Chattanooga Dr.	A	B	C	D

End of Part C – Coding Section – Segment 3

Part C – Coding & Memory

Memory Section – Segment 1

Instructions

Memory Section - Segment 1 is a 3 minute study period during which you try to memorize the information in the Coding Guide. There are no answers to mark during this study period.

Turn the page and begin studying when you are prepared to time yourself for exactly 3 minutes.

Part C – Coding & Memory

Memory Section – Segment 1

CODING GUIDE	
Address Range	**Delivery Route**
1991 – 3200 La Place Hwy 15 – 30 Farmerville LN 100 – 399 Chattanooga Dr.	A
3201 – 3900 La Place Hwy 400 – 699 Chattanooga Dr.	B
830 – 900 CR 228 9000 – 15000 Alta Vista Ave. 31 – 60 Farmerville LN	C
All mail that doesn't fall in one of the address ranges listed above	D

Part C – Coding & Memory

Memory Section – Segment 2

Instructions

Segment 2 of the Memory Section is a practice exercise where you have 90 seconds to answer 8 questions from memory. The Coding Guide is not shown. You must answer from memory. This segment is not scored. Mark your answers on the sample answer sheet at the bottom of the page, not on the actual answer sheet.

Begin when you are prepared to time yourself for exactly 90 seconds.

Part C – Coding & Memory

Memory Section – Segment 2

QUESTIONS

	Address	Delivery Route			
1.	27 Farmerville LN	A	B	C	D
2.	425 Chattanooga Dr.	A	B	C	D
3.	700 CR 228	A	B	C	D
4.	40 Farmerville LN	A	B	C	D
5.	3401 La Place Hwy	A	B	C	D
6.	240 Chattanooga Dr.	A	B	C	D
7.	12500 Alta Vista Ave.	A	B	C	D
8.	90 Chattanooga Dr.	A	B	C	D

SAMPLE ANSWER SHEET

1 Ⓐ Ⓑ Ⓒ Ⓓ
2 Ⓐ Ⓑ Ⓒ Ⓓ
3 Ⓐ Ⓑ Ⓒ Ⓓ
4 Ⓐ Ⓑ Ⓒ Ⓓ
5 Ⓐ Ⓑ Ⓒ Ⓓ
6 Ⓐ Ⓑ Ⓒ Ⓓ
7 Ⓐ Ⓑ Ⓒ Ⓓ
8 Ⓐ Ⓑ Ⓒ Ⓓ

The correct answers are 1-A, 2-B, 3-D, 4-C, 5-B, 6-A, 7-C, and 8-D.

Part C – Coding & Memory

Memory Section – Segment 3

Instructions

Memory Section - Segment 3 is a 5 minute study period during which you try to memorize the information in the Coding Guide. There are no answers to mark during this study period.

Turn the page and begin studying when you are prepared to time yourself for exactly 5 minutes.

Part C – Coding & Memory

Memory Section – Segment 3

CODING GUIDE	
Address Range	**Delivery Route**
1991 – 3200 La Place Hwy 15 – 30 Farmerville LN 100 – 399 Chattanooga Dr.	A
3201 – 3900 La Place Hwy 400 – 699 Chattanooga Dr.	B
830 – 900 CR 228 9000 – 15000 Alta Vista Ave. 31 – 60 Farmerville LN	C
All mail that doesn't fall in one of the address ranges listed above	D

Part C – Coding & Memory

Memory Section – Segment 4

Instructions

Memory Section - Segment 4 is the actual Memory test. You have 7 minutes to answer 36 questions. You must answer from memory. The Coding Guide is not shown. This segment is scored, and the score from this section does affect your overall Exam 473 score. Mark your answers on the actual answer sheet in the section titled Part C - Coding & Memory - Memory Section.

Turn the page and begin when you are prepared to time yourself for exactly 7 minutes.

Part C – Coding & Memory

Memory Section – Segment 4

Questions

	Address	Delivery Route			
37.	15 Farmerville LN	A	B	C	D
38.	660 Chattanooga Dr.	A	B	C	D
39.	831 CR 228	A	B	C	D
40.	2000 La Place Hwy	A	B	C	D
41.	13840 Alta Vista Ave.	A	B	C	D
42.	270 Chattanooga Dr.	A	B	C	D
43.	55 Farmerville LN	A	B	C	D
44.	624 Chattanooga Dr.	A	B	C	D
45.	8000 Alta Vista Ave.	A	B	C	D
46.	42 Farmerville LN	A	B	C	D
47.	3790 La Place Hwy	A	B	C	D
48.	872 CR 228	A	B	C	D
49.	120 Chattanooga Dr.	A	B	C	D
50.	3642 La Place Hwy	A	B	C	D
51.	14100 Alta Vista Ave.	A	B	C	D
52.	3000 La Place Hwy	A	B	C	D
53.	29 Farmerville LN	A	B	C	D
54.	720 Chattanooga Dr.	A	B	C	D

continued on next page

Part C – Coding & Memory

Memory Section – Segment 4

continued

Questions

	Address	Delivery Route			
55.	1400 Alta Vista Ave.	A	B	C	D
56.	380 Chattanooga Dr.	A	B	C	D
57.	14000 Alta Vista Ave.	A	B	C	D
58.	46 Farmerville LN	A	B	C	D
59.	3150 La Place Hwy	A	B	C	D
60.	600 Chattanooga Dr.	A	B	C	D
61.	890 CR 228	A	B	C	D
62.	16 Farmerville LN	A	B	C	D
63.	500 Chattanooga Dr.	A	B	C	D
64.	3800 La Place Parkwy	A	B	C	D
65.	888 CR 228	A	B	C	D
66.	9542 Alta Vista Ave.	A	B	C	D
67.	1800 La Place Hwy	A	B	C	D
68.	28 Farmerville LN	A	B	C	D
69.	3600 La Place Hwy	A	B	C	D
70.	388 Chattanooga Dr.	A	B	C	D
71.	25 Farmerdale LN	A	B	C	D
72.	2890 La Place Hwy	A	B	C	D

End of Part C – Memory Section – Segment 4

Part D – Personal Characteristics & Experience Inventory

As explained in the guide, it is not possible to practice or prepare for Part D. There are no right or wrong answers, and speed is not an issue. For each question, you simply select the answer that best reflects your own individual personality, temperament, experience, etc.

Since it is not possible to practice or prepare for Part D, no Personal Characteristics & Experience Inventory sample questions are included in this practice exam.

PRACTICE EXAM #4

As detailed below, included in this practice exam are all four parts of the actual exam and an answer sheet.

- **Part A – Address Checking**

Included is a 100% realistic replica of the scored Address Checking test on the actual exam.

- **Part B – Forms Completion**

Included is a 100% realistic replica of the scored Forms Completion test on the actual exam.

- **Part C – Coding & Memory**

Included are 100% realistic replicas of the complete Coding and Memory sections with all seven segments.

- **Part D – Personal Characteristics & Experience Inventory**

As explained in the guide, it is not possible to prepare for this part of the exam. Therefore no Personal Characteristics & Experience Inventory questions are included in the practice test for this part of the exam. However, for realistic formatting, we have included a page in the practice test for this exam part.

- **Answer Sheet**

Included near the back of the book are 100% realistic replicas of the answer sheet from the actual exam. When taking a practice exam, tear out one of these Practice Answer Sheets. Mark your answers to the scored segments of the exam on this answer sheet. As noted above, it is not possible to prepare for Part D. Therefore, bubbles are not included on the answer sheet for Part D. However, for realistic formatting, we have noted where Part D would appear on the answer sheet.

The format of this practice exam is identical to the actual exam, and the instructions are similar to those on the actual exam.

It is imperative that you take this practice exam in as realistic a fashion as possible - meaning that you must time yourself precisely. **Your practice will have no value unless it is done realistically.** Our Timed Practice Test Audio CD and our Test Prep CD-ROM are ideal tools for conveniently having the instructions presented section-by-section and for absolutely precise timing. See the order form in the back of the book or our website *www.PostalExam.com* for details.

Answer keys are provided in the back of your book. It is imperative that you use the formulas given in the book to **score each practice test as you complete it**. Scoring is necessary in order to measure your progress and to identify your individual areas of weakness that may need extra attention.

After completing and scoring each practice exam, move on to the next. **After finishing all six exams, you should be prepared to excel on the actual exam.**

Do not look over the practice exam questions until you are ready to start and to time yourself - usually meaning until you have started either the Timed Practice Test Audio CD or the Postal Test Prep CD-ROM. Similarly, after completing one section of the practice test, do not look over the next one until your are ready to start it. Likewise, stop working and put down your pencil immediately when the allotted period of time has expired. As has been emphasized before but cannot be emphasized enough, your practice is of absolutely no value unless it is done realistically. Also, you must train yourself (1) to not open your test booklet or pick up your pencil until instructed to do so and (2) to close your booklet and put down your pencil immediately upon being so instructed. The Postal Service has zero tolerance on these matters. Any variance may be viewed as cheating and may result in your disqualification.

Turn to the next page when you are ready to begin this Practice Exam.

Important Note about this Practice Exam

The questions, addresses, forms, etc. in this practice exam are very realistic samples, but they are not the actual ones that you will see on the real test. There are hundreds of different versions of this exam, and each version has different questions, addresses, forms, etc. Even if you could get some real questions from one version of the exam, the questions on the version of the exam you take would surely be different.

PRACTICE EXAM #4

Part A – Address Checking

Directions

In Part A consists of 60 questions to be completed in 11 minutes. You are given a **Correct List** of addresses and ZIP codes. A **List to be Checked,** also with addresses and ZIP codes, appears next to the **Correct List**. The **List to be Checked** should be exactly like the **Correct List**, but it may contain errors.

Your task is to compare each row of information in the **Correct List** and the **List to be Checked** to find if there are **No Errors**, an error in the **Address Only**, an error in the **ZIP Code Only**, or an error in **Both** the address and the ZIP code.

After comparing each row of information, select an answer from the below answer choices, and mark your answer on the answer sheet in the section titled Part A - Address Checking.

A. No Errors	B. Address Only	C. ZIP Code Only	D. Both

Turn the page and begin when you are prepared to time yourself for exactly 11 minutes.

Part A – Address Checking

A. No Errors	B. Address Only	C. ZIP Code Only	D. Both

Correct List

	Address	ZIP Code
1.	17082 Memorial Oaks Grants, New Mexico	74369-5421
2.	9415 Stockport Apt. O Pennsville, N.J.	22598-5489
3.	109 Autumn Mist Cove Warsaw, NY	04120
4.	Post Office Box 238411 Kenner, LA	45780-8411
5.	3201 Turtle Dove Ln Johnson City, T.N.	89102-8411
6.	903 Circle Bend Chattanooga, TN	21589-1002
7.	3625 Golden Tee Dr. Taos, N.M.	62101-4512
8.	19 48th Street Teana, MS	50493-4406
9.	306 Edwards Blvd. Macon, GA	70612-8512
10.	P.O. Box 3387 Cedar Rapids, IA	32210
11.	17083 MISTY CREEK Derry, N.H.	10034-8513
12.	81 MAXEY LN Biloxi, MS	39437
13.	27440 Kuykendalh Spring, Texas	77252-2561
14.	1221 Graham St. Scotland, M. O.	81046-7321
15.	25 Old Hempstead Rd. Mobile, AL	40698-4582

List to be Checked

Address	ZIP Code
17082 Memorial Oaks Gramps, New Mexico	74369-5421
9414 Stockport Apt. O Pennsville, N.J.	22597-5489
109 Autumn Mist Cove Warsaw, NY	04120
Post Office Box 238411 Kenner, LA	45790-8411
3201 Turtle Dove Ln Johnson City, T.N.	89102-8411
903 Circle Bend Chattanooga, TN	21598-1002
3625 Golden Tea Dr. Taos, N.M.	62101-4510
19 48th Street Teana, MS	50493-4406
306 Edward Blvd. Macon, GA	70612-8512
P.O. Box 3387 Cedar Rapids, LA	32120
17083 MISTY CREEK Derry, N.H.	10034-5813
81 MAXEY LN Biloxi, MS	39437
27440 Kuykendallar Spring, Texas	77252-2561
1221 Graham St. Scotland, M. O.	80146-7321
25 Old Hempstead Rd. Mobile, AK	40698-4592

continued on next page

Part A – Address Checking
continued

A. No Errors	B. Address Only	C. ZIP Code Only	D. Both

Correct List / **List to be Checked**

	Address	*ZIP Code*	*Address*	*ZIP Code*
16.	1678 Virginia Place Augusta, S.C.	92146-1002	1678 Vartuba Place Augusta, S.C.	92146-1002
17.	PO Box 6214 Ardmore, Oklahoma	48793-6214	PO Box 6114 Ardmore, Oklahoma	48793-6124
18.	1600 FM 2920 Spring, TX	31250-3246	1600 FM 2920 Spring, TX	31250-3246
19.	81 FORREST DR. GRAND HAVEN, MI	62108-4231	81 FORREST DR. GRAND HAVEN, MI	62108-4312
20.	1910 Susie Ct. Great Falls, M.O.	73280	1910 Susie Rd. Great Falls, M.O.	73280
21.	30725 Vining Road Franklin, KY	82241-6123	30725 Vining Road Franklin, KY	82241-6123
22.	23 Jesse James Dodge City, Kansas	50371-2891	23 Jassup James Dodge City, Kansas	50371-2897
23.	22811 Industry Ln Tuscaloosa, AL	42130-6782	22811 Industry Ln Tusgulooas, AL	42130-6782
24.	Hwy 105 W Phoenix, A.Z.	15468-6541	Hwy 105 W Phoenix, A.Z.	15468-6541
25.	111352 Clover Dr. Anchorage, AK	92584-2973	111352 Clover Dr. Anchorage, AK	82584-2973
26.	8923 Farr St Kissimmee, Florida	80910-5493	8923 Farr St Kissimmee, PR	80919-5493
27.	208 Tyler Ct. Apt. J Bristol, T. N.	67912	208 Tolar Ct. Apt. J Bristol, T. N.	67921
28.	12319 OAK PARK CT MADISON, W.V.	39756-7826	1239 OAK PARK CT MADISON, W.V.	39756-7826
29.	511 Magnolia Blvd. Green River, WY	50026-7512	511 Magnolia Blvd. Green River, WY	50026-7512
30.	57Juniper Circle Redmond, OR	70328-3912	57Juniper Circle Redman, OR	70328-3972

continued on next page

Part A – Address Checking

continued

A. No Errors	B. Address Only	C. ZIP Code Only	D. Both

	Correct List		List to be Checked	
	Address	*ZIP Code*	*Address*	*ZIP Code*
31.	29 STILL PL TOMBALL, TEXAS	77631-1289	29 STILL PL TOMBALL, TEXAS	77631-1289
32.	18110 Copper Bean St. Alamogorda, NM	35879-1873	18110 Cooper Bane St. Alamogorda, NM	35879-1873
33.	519 Goodson Loop Modesto, C.A.	92760-4592	519 Goodson Look Modesto, C.A.	92760-4590
34.	4199 Winding Road El Dorado, AR	49245-6479	4199 Winding Road El Dorado, AR	49245-6479
35.	#9 Autumn Hills Fort Worth, GA	29430-7812	#8 Autumn Hills Fort Worth, GA	29430-7812
36.	704 Grant St. Apt. 6E Dodgeville, W,I.	70126	704 Grant St. Apt. 6F Dodgeville, W.I.	70126
37.	P.O. Box 32214 Pierre, South Dakota	30729-2214	P.O. Box 32214 Pierre, South Dakota	30729-2214
38.	29 47th St. Memphis, TN	52073-9410	29 47th St. Memphis, TN	52073-9440
39.	202 FOSTER WIGGINS, M. S.	94421-3245	2022 FOSTER WIGGINS, M. S.	94421-3245
40.	11654 Southwest Frwy Houston, TX	77210	11654 Southwest Frwy Houston, TX	79210
41.	110 W Southmore St. Fort Wayne, IN	52762-7441	110 W Southmore St. Fort Wayne, IN	52762-7441
42.	PO Box 53541 Stockton, C.A.	95812-3541	PO Box 53541 Stockton, G.A.	95812-5341
43.	24 Star Light Ave. Providence, R.I.	42130-2214	24 Star Light Ave. Providence, R.I.	41130-2214
44.	921 Shadow Wood Merrifield, VA	21864	921 Shallow Woods Merrifield, VA	21864
45.	7112 WEST PARK ST. TACOMA, W.A.	91200-3751	7112 WEST PARK ST. TACOMA, W.A.	91200-3751

continued on next page

Part A – Address Checking
continued

A. No Errors	B. Address Only	C. ZIP Code Only	D. Both

Correct List / **List to be Checked**

	Address	*ZIP Code*	*Address*	*ZIP Code*
46.	1330 Blue Bell Ave. Huntsville, AL	62210-5412	1330 Blue Bell Ave. Huntsville, AL	62310-5412
47.	1800 West Loop South Lake Mary, F.L.	72116-3124	1800 West Loop North Lake Mary, F.L.	72116-3124
48.	7500 San Felipe Lubbock, Texas	80291-3014	7500 San Felipe Lubbock, Texas	80291-3014
49.	1000 Louisiana Av. Bangor, Maine	43015-8742	1000 Louisiana Av. Bangor, Maine	43015-8742
50.	9227 Clay Rd. Apt. 2D Fayetteville, N.C.	56210-8421	9227 Clay Rd. Apt. 20 Fayetteville, N.C.	56120-8421
51.	555 ROYAL ST. Albany, NY	91238	555 ROYAL ST. Albany, NY	91236
52.	Post Office Box 8945 Reno, NV	36201-8945	Post Office Box 8954 Reno, NV	36201-8954
53.	543 Pine Walk Trail Grants, N.M.	62130-8451	543 Pine Walk Trail Grants, N.M.	62130-8451
54.	725 Town & Country Av Lehigh Valley, PA	71061-5411	725 Town & Country Av Lehigh Valley, PA	71061-5411
55.	9600 BELLAIRE BLVD SAN JUAN, PR	20541-5896	9600 BALLARD BLVD SAN JUAN, PR	20541-9896
56.	1234 Tall Forrest St. Madison, W.I.	69975	1234 Tall Forrest St. Madison, W.I.	69970
57.	78 W 57th Ave. Denver, CO	49822-3462	78 N 57th Ave. Denver, CO	49802-3462
58.	8321 Broadway Rochester, NY	82145-9612	8321 Broadway Rochester, NY	82145-9612
59.	1545 S MASON ST. BOSTON, M.A.	42698-1334	1545 S MASON ST. BOSTON, M.A.	42698-1334
60.	2601 Cartwright Billings, MO	77376	2801 Cartwright Billings, MO	77376

End of Part A – Address Checking

PRACTICE EXAM #4

Part B – Forms Completion

Directions

Part B tests your ability to identify information needed to complete various U.S. Postal Service forms. This part of the exam consists of 30 questions to be completed in 15 minutes. You will be shown 5 different forms and be asked to answer 6 questions about each form.

Turn the page and begin when you are prepared to time yourself for exactly 15 minutes.

Part B – Forms Completion

Authorization to Hold Mail

Postmaster - Please hold mail for:

1. Name(s)

2. Address

3a. Begin Holding Mail (Date)	**3b.** Resume Delivery (Date)

4. ☐ **Option A**
I will pick up all accumulated mail when I return and understand that mail delivery will not resume until I do. (This is suggested if your return date may change or if no one will be at home to receive mail.)

5. ☐ **Option B**
Please deliver all accumulated mail and resume normal delivery on the ending date shown above.

6. Customer Signature

For Post Office Use Only

7. Date Received

8a. Clerk	**8b.** Bin Number
9a. Carrier	**9b.** Route Number

Customer Option A Only

Carrier: Accumulated mail has been picked up.

10a. Resume delivery on (date) ______________________________

10b. By: ______________________________

continued on next page

Part B – Forms Completion

continued

1. Which of these could be a correct entry for Box 8b?
   - A. Hector Moeller
   - B. November 10, 2005
   - C. 773
   - D. 18 Gulf St, Iona, LA 37552

2. Which of these could be a correct entry for Box 2?
   - A. Hector Moeller
   - B. November 10, 2005
   - C. 773
   - D. 18 Gulf St, Iona, LA 37552

3. Into which of these should a name be entered?
   - A. Box 1
   - B. Boxes 8a and 9a
   - C. Line 10b
   - D. All the above

4. Which of these could be a correct entry for Box 1?
   - A. Hector Moeller
   - B. November 10, 2005
   - C. 773
   - D. 18 Gulf St, Iona, LA 37552

5. Which of these can indicate to the carrier the date to resume delivery?
   - A. Box 3b
   - B. Box 5
   - C. Line 10a
   - D. All the above

6. Which of these should be completed only by a Postal representative?
   - A. Boxes 1, 2, 3a, 3b, 4, 5, and 6
   - B. Lines 10a and 10b and Boxes 7, 8a, 8b, 9a, and 9b
   - C. Boxes 7, 8a, 8b, 9a, and 9b
   - D. Lines 10a and 10b

continued on next page

Part B – Forms Completion
continued

EXPRESS MAIL **Mailing Label**

ORIGIN (POSTAL USE ONLY)

PO ZIP Code 1a.	Day of Delivery 1b. ☐Next ☐Second	Flat Rate Envelope 1c. ☐	
Date In 2a.	2b. ☐Noon ☐3 PM	Postage 2c. $	
Time In 3a. ☐AM ☐PM	Military 3b. 2nd Day 3rd Day	Return Receipt Fee 3c.	
Weight 4a. lbs. ozs.	Int'l Alpha Country Code 4b.	COD Fee 4c.	Insurance Fee 4d.
No Delivery 5a. ☐Wknd ☐Holiday	Acceptance Clerk Initials 5b.	Total Postage & Fees 5c. $	

DELIVERY (POSTAL USE ONLY)

Delivery Attempt 1d. Mo. Day	Time 1e. ☐AM ☐PM	Employee Signature 1f.
Delivery Attempt 2d. Mo. Day	Time 2e. ☐AM ☐PM	Employee Signature 2f.
Delivery Attempt 3d. Mo. Day	Time 3e. ☐AM ☐PM	Employee Signature 3f.

6. ☐ WAIVER OF SIGNATURE

NO DELVERY ☐Weekend ☐Holiday

Customer Signature ______________________

CUSTOMER USE ONLY

Method of Payment 7a. Express Mail corporate Acct. No.	Federal Agency Acct. No. or 7b. Postal Service Acct. No.
8a. FROM: (PLEASE PRINT) PHONE: ______________	8b. TO: (PLEASE PRINT) PHONE: ______________ ZIP + 4: ______________

continued on next page

Part B – Forms Completion

continued

7. Into which boxes should a ZIP code be entered?
   A. Box 1a
   B. Box 8a
   C. Box 8b
   D. All the above

8. Into which of these boxes could a full date like 3/8/05 be entered?
   A. Box 1b
   B. Box 2a
   C. Boxes 1d, 2d, and 3d
   D. All the above

9. Where should the sender's name and address be entered?
   A. Box 6
   B. Box 8a
   C. Box 8b
   D. None of the above

10. An entry of a number only would be acceptable in each of the following boxes except which?
    A. Box 4b
    B. Box 1a
    C. Box 7a
    D. Box 7b

11. The second delivery attempt would be documented in which box or boxes?
    A. Box 2d
    B. Box 2e
    C. Box 2f
    D. All the above

12. Which of these could be a correct entry for box 3d?
    A. 2 lb. 3 oz.
    B. 11/13
    C. 11/13/05
    D. $17.65

continued on next page

Part B – Forms Completion
continued

<table>
<tr><td colspan="7">Certificate of Bulk Mailing</td></tr>
<tr><td colspan="2">Fee for Certificate</td><td rowspan="4">Use Current Rate Chart</td><td colspan="4" rowspan="4">1. Meter stamp or postage (uncancelled) stamps in payment of fee to be affixed here and cancelled by postmarking, including date.</td></tr>
<tr><td colspan="2">Up to 1,000 pieces</td></tr>
<tr><td colspan="2">For each additional 1,000 pieces, or fraction</td></tr>
<tr><td colspan="2">Duplicate Copy</td></tr>
<tr><td>2a. Number of identical pieces</td><td>2b. Class of mail</td><td>2c. Postage on each</td><td>2d. Number of pieces per lb.</td><td>2e. Total number of pounds</td><td>2f. Total postage paid</td><td>2g. Fee paid</td></tr>
<tr><td colspan="2">3a. Mailed for</td><td colspan="5">3b. Mailed by</td></tr>
<tr><td colspan="7">Postmaster's Certificate</td></tr>
<tr><td colspan="7">It is hereby certified that the above-described mailing has been received and number of pieces and postage verified.

4. ______________________________
(Postmaster or Designee)</td></tr>
</table>

continued on next page

Part B – Forms Completion

continued

13. Which of these would be an acceptable entry for Box 3b?
    A. 52431-4412
    B. 620 Dawn Drive
    C. 3/9/06
    D. Acme Mass Mailing Services

14. The postage on each item is $0.22. Where would this amount be indicated?
    A. Box 2c
    B. Box 2e
    C. Box 2g
    D. Box 4

15. There are 35 pieces per pound in this mailing. Where would this be entered?
    A. Box 2a
    B. Box 2b
    C. Box 2c
    D. Box 2d

16. The meter stamp should be in which box?
    A. Box 1
    B. Box 2d
    C. Box 2f
    D. Box 4

17. This mailing was mailed for Crescent City Products by Acme Mass Mailing Services. Where would "Crescent City Products" be entered?
    A. Box 2a
    B. Box 2d
    C. Box 3a
    D. Box 3b

18. Which of these would be an acceptable entry for Box 2f?
    A. 56890-2248
    B. $59.76
    C. Diane Gonzales
    D. 250 lbs.

continued on next page

Part B – Forms Completion

continued

INSURED MAIL RECEIPT

Postage	**1.**	**1a.** ☐ Fragile ☐ Liquid ☐ Perishable
Insurance Fees	**2a.**	**2b.** Insurance Coverage
Restricted Delivery Fee	**3.**	
Special Handling Fee	**4.**	**7.** Postmark Here
Return Receipt Fee	**5.**	
Total Postage & Fees	**6.**	
8. Sent to:		
9. Street, Apt. No.; or P.O. Box		
10. City, State, ZIP + 4, Country		

continued on next page

Part B – Forms Completion

continued

19. How should it be indicated on this form that a shipment consists of perishable produce and should be treated accordingly?
    A. Check "Perishable" in Box 1a
    B. Write "Perishable" in Box 6
    C. Check "Perishable" in Box 1a and include a note on the back of the form
    D. Postmark the form with a "Perishable" stamp

20. An insured package containing sensitive computer equipment is being mailed to Charles Goodwin, 354 Elmwood Drive, Lucas, NM 84536-1202 USA. Where should "Charles Goodwin" be entered?
    A. Box 8
    B. Box 9
    C. Box 10
    D. None of the above

21. An insured package containing sensitive computer equipment is being mailed to Charles Goodwin, 354 Elmwood Drive, Lucas, NM 84536-1202, USA. Where should "Lucas, NM 84536-1202 USA" be entered?
    A. Box 8
    B. Box 9
    C. Box 10
    D. None of the above

22. An insured package containing sensitive computer equipment is being mailed to Charles Goodwin, 354 Elmwood Drive, Lucas, NM 84536-1202. Where should "sensitive computer equipment" be entered?
    A. Box 8
    B. Box 9
    C. Box 10
    D. None of the above

23. If the charges for a particular shipment are $11.35 for postage, $3.00 for insurance, and $1.50 return receipt fee, what entry should go in Box 2a?
    A. $11.35
    B. $3.00
    C. $1.50
    D. None of the above

24. If the charges for a particular shipment are $11.35 for postage, $3.00 for insurance, and $1.50 return receipt fee, what entry should go in Box 6?
    A. $11.35
    B. $3.00
    C. $1.50
    D. None of the above

continued on next page

Domestic Claim or Registered Mail Inquiry

Mailer Information	Addressee Information
1a. Name	**2a.** Name
1b. Business Name	**2b.** Business Name
1c. Address	**2c.** Address
1d. City, State, ZIP+4	**2d.** City, State, ZIP+4
1e. Telephone (include area code)	**2e.** Telephone (include area code)

Payment Assignment Alternate Payment Address	**Description of Lost or Damaged Article(s)** Add extra sheets as needed				
3a. Who is to receive payment? (Check one) ☐ Mailer ☐ Addressee	Item	Description	Code	Value	Purchase Date
3b. Address	A	**4a.**			
	B	**4b.**			
3c. City, State, ZIP+4	C	**4c.**			
5a. COD amount to be remitted to sender (For business mailer COD claims only) $	**5b.** Total amount claimed for all articles $				

Certification and signature		
6a. Customer submitting claim ☐ Mailer ☐ Addressee	**6b.** Customer signature	**6c.** Date signed

continued on next page

Part B – Forms Completion

continued

25. The addressee, Anne Lowry, is to receive payment for this claim. How should this be indicated?
    A. Have Ms Lowry sign the form.
    B. Check "Mailer" in Box 3a
    C. Check "Addressee" in Box 3a
    D. None of the above

26. On the same claim where the addressee, Anne Lowry, is to receive payment, where should her address be written?
    A. Boxes 1c and 3b
    B. Boxes 1c and 2c
    C. Boxes 2c and 3b
    D. All the above

27. On the same claim where the addressee, Anne Lowry, is to receive payment, Mr. Joseph West is the mailer. Where should Mr. West's address be entered on this form?
    A. Box 1c
    B. Box 2c
    C. Box 3b
    D. None of the above

28. Joseph West submitted this claim. Whose signature should be in Box 6b?
    A. Joseph West
    B. Anne Lowry
    C. A Postal representative
    D. None of the above

29. The mailer, Joseph West, submitted this claim. What should be checked in Box 6a?
    A. Addressee
    B. Mailer
    C. Both Addressee and Mailer
    D. None of the above

30. This claim is for four items. Where should descriptions of the four items be given?
    A. Boxes 4a, 4b, 4c, and 5b
    B. Three descriptions in Boxes 4a, 4b, and 4c and the fourth description on the back of the form
    C. Three descriptions in Boxes 4a, 4b, and 4c and the fourth description on an attached extra sheet of paper
    D. Three descriptions in Boxes 4a, 4b, and 4c and the fourth description on a separate Domestic Claim or Registered Mail Inquiry form

End of Part B – Forms Completion

PRACTICE EXAM #4

Part C – Coding & Memory

Part C tests your ability to use codes quickly and accurately both from a Coding Guide and from memory. This part of the exam consists of two sections as detailed below.

- The Coding Section has 36 questions to be answered in 6 minutes. During the Coding section, you will look at a Coding Guide to find answers. The Coding Section is broken down into several segments.
- The Memory Section has 36 questions to be answered in 7 minutes. During the Memory Section, you must answer from memory. The Memory Section is broken down into several segments.

The same Coding Guide will be used throughout both sections of Part C. Four delivery routes (identified by the codes A, B, C, and D) are listed on the Coding Guide. Also listed on the Coding Guide are various address ranges on several streets that are served by these delivery routes.

Each question is an address. To answer each question, you must identify the delivery route that serves the address, and mark as your answer the code (A, B, C, or D) for that delivery route.

Turn the page when you are ready to begin the first section, the Coding Section.

Part C – Coding & Memory

Coding Section

The Coding Section of Part C - Coding & Memory consists of 3 segments as detailed below.

- **Coding Section - Segment 1**
  The first segment is a 2 minute introductory exercise. This segment is not scored.
- **Coding Section - Segment 2**
  The second segment is a 90 second (1½ minutes) practice exercise. This segment is not scored.
- **Coding Section - Segment 3**
  The third segment is the actual Coding Section test. You have 6 minutes to answer 36 questions. This segment is scored.

The Coding Guide is displayed during all 3 segments. You will be instructed to mark answers for the first two unscored segments on sample answer sheets, not the actual answer sheet. You will be instructed to mark answers for the third segment, which is scored, on the actual answer sheet.

Turn to the next page when you are ready to begin Coding Section - Segment 1.

Part C – Coding & Memory

Coding Section – Segment 1

Instructions

Segment 1 of the Coding Section is an introductory exercise to acquaint you with how the questions are to be answered. In this segment, you have 2 minutes to answer 4 questions. The Coding Guide is displayed for your use in answering the questions. This segment is not scored. Mark your answers on the sample answer sheet at the bottom of the question page, not on the actual answer sheet.

Turn the page and begin when you are prepared to time yourself for exactly 2 minutes.

Part C – Coding & Memory

Coding Section – Segment 1

CODING GUIDE

Address Range	Delivery Route
1701 – 2700 Lapalco Blvd. 950 – 1349 Beach Blvd. 8600 – 9399 Elkhorn Dr.	A
2701 – 3700 Lapalco Blvd. 9400 – 9899 Elkhorn Dr.	B
11000 – 17000 RR 148 19 – 60 Raceway Rd. 1350 – 1949 Beach Blvd.	C
All mail that doesn't fall in one of the address ranges listed above	D

Part C – Coding & Memory

Coding Section – Segment 1

continued

QUESTIONS

	Address	Delivery Route			
1.	12000 RR 148	A	B	C	D
2.	3000 Lapalco Blvd.	A	B	C	D
3.	1600 Lapalco Blvd.	A	B	C	D
4.	8700 Elkhorn Dr.	A	B	C	D

SAMPLE ANSWER SHEET

1 Ⓐ Ⓑ Ⓒ Ⓓ
2 Ⓐ Ⓑ Ⓒ Ⓓ
3 Ⓐ Ⓑ Ⓒ Ⓓ
4 Ⓐ Ⓑ Ⓒ Ⓓ

The correct answers are 1-C, 2-B, 3-D, and 4-A.

Part C – Coding & Memory

Coding Section – Segment 2

Instructions

Segment 2 of the Coding Section is a practice exercise designed to expose you to the realistic timing demanded. In this segment, you have 90 seconds to answer 8 questions. The Coding Guide is displayed for your use in answering the questions. This segment is not scored. Mark your answers on the sample answer sheet at the bottom of the question page, not on the actual answer sheet.

Turn the page and begin when you are prepared to time yourself for exactly 90 seconds.

Part C – Coding & Memory

Coding Section – Segment 2

CODING GUIDE	
Address Range	**Delivery Route**
1701 – 2700 Lapalco Blvd. 950 – 1349 Beach Blvd. 8600 – 9399 Elkhorn Dr.	A
2701 – 3700 Lapalco Blvd. 9400 – 9899 Elkhorn Dr.	B
11000 – 17000 RR 148 19 – 60 Raceway Rd. 1350 – 1949 Beach Blvd.	C
All mail that doesn't fall in one of the address ranges listed above	D

Part C – Coding & Memory

Coding Section – Segment 2

continued

QUESTIONS

	Address	Delivery Route			
1.	2800 Lapalco Blvd.	A	B	C	D
2.	1960 Beach Blvd.	A	B	C	D
3.	28 Raceway Rd.	A	B	C	D
4.	1790 Lapalco Blvd.	A	B	C	D
5.	1489 Beach Blvd.	A	B	C	D
6.	9700 Elkhorn Dr.	A	B	C	D
7.	3800 Lapalco Blvd.	A	B	C	D
8.	13000 RR 148	A	B	C	D

SAMPLE ANSWER SHEET

1 Ⓐ Ⓑ Ⓒ Ⓓ
2 Ⓐ Ⓑ Ⓒ Ⓓ
3 Ⓐ Ⓑ Ⓒ Ⓓ
4 Ⓐ Ⓑ Ⓒ Ⓓ
5 Ⓐ Ⓑ Ⓒ Ⓓ
6 Ⓐ Ⓑ Ⓒ Ⓓ
7 Ⓐ Ⓑ Ⓒ Ⓓ
8 Ⓐ Ⓑ Ⓒ Ⓓ

The correct answers are 1-B, 2-D, 3-C, 4-A, 5-C, 6-B, 8-D, and 9-C.

Part C – Coding & Memory

Coding Section – Segment 3

Instructions

Segment 3 of the Coding Section is the actual Coding test. You have 6 minutes to answer 36 questions. The Coding Guide is displayed for your use in answering the questions. This segment is scored, and the score from this section does affect your overall Exam 473 score. Mark your answers on the actual answer sheet in the section titled Part C - Coding & Memory - Coding Section.

Turn the page and begin when you are prepared to time yourself for exactly 6 minutes.

Coding Section – Segment 3

CODING GUIDE	
Address Range	**Delivery Route**
1701 – 2700 Lapalco Blvd. 950 – 1349 Beach Blvd. 8600 – 9399 Elkhorn Dr.	A
2701 – 3700 Lapalco Blvd. 9400 – 9899 Elkhorn Dr.	B
11000 – 17000 RR 148 19 – 60 Raceway Rd. 1350 – 1949 Beach Blvd.	C
All mail that doesn't fall in one of the address ranges listed above	D

Coding Section – Segment 3

continued

Questions

	Address	Delivery Route			
1.	9950 Elkhorn Dr.	A	B	C	D
2.	2100 Lapalco Blvd.	A	B	C	D
3.	3649 Lapalco Blvd.	A	B	C	D
4.	42 Raceway Rd.	A	B	C	D
5.	940 Beach Blvd.	A	B	C	D
6.	1254 Beach Blvd.	A	B	C	D
7.	9842 Elkhorn Dr.	A	B	C	D
8.	1600 Beach Blvd.	A	B	C	D
9.	8905 Elkhorn Dr.	A	B	C	D
10.	1849 Beach Blvd.	A	B	C	D
11.	14480 RR 148	A	B	C	D
12.	3842 Lapalco Blvd.	A	B	C	D
13.	980 Beach Blvd.	A	B	C	D
14.	58 Raceway Rd.	A	B	C	D
15.	3363 Lapalco Blvd.	A	B	C	D
16.	9799 Elkhorn Dr.	A	B	C	D
17.	2567 Lapalco Blvd.	A	B	C	D
18.	15018 RR 148	A	B	C	D

continued on next page

Coding Section – Segment 3

continued

CODING GUIDE	
Address Range	**Delivery Route**
1701 – 2700 Lapalco Blvd. 950 – 1349 Beach Blvd. 8600 – 9399 Elkhorn Dr.	A
2701 – 3700 Lapalco Blvd. 9400 – 9899 Elkhorn Dr.	B
11000 – 17000 RR 148 19 – 60 Raceway Rd. 1350 – 1949 Beach Blvd.	C
All mail that doesn't fall in one of the address ranges listed above	D

Coding Section – Segment 3

continued

Questions

	Address	Delivery Route			
19.	25 Raceway Rd.	A	B	C	D
20.	2901 Lapalco Blvd.	A	B	C	D
21.	9583 Elkhorn Dr.	A	B	C	D
22.	11080 RR 148	A	B	C	D
23.	1172 Beech St.	A	B	C	D
24.	16670 RR 148	A	B	C	D
25.	2000 Lapalco Blvd.	A	B	C	D
26.	32 Raceway Rd.	A	B	C	D
27.	70 Raceway Rd.	A	B	C	D
28.	3500 Lapalco Blvd.	A	B	C	D
29.	12786 RR 148	A	B	C	D
30.	959 Beach Blvd.	A	B	C	D
31.	40 Raceway Rd.	A	B	C	D
32.	16240 Railroad	A	B	C	D
33.	9600 Elkhorn Dr.	A	B	C	D
34.	36 Raceway Rd.	A	B	C	D
35.	2351 Lapalco Blvd.	A	B	C	D
36.	12398 RR 146	A	B	C	D

End of Part C – Coding Section – Segment 3

Part C – Coding & Memory

Memory Section

The Memory Section of Part C - Coding & Memory consists of 4 segments as detailed below.

- **Memory Section - Segment 1**
  The first segment is a 3 minute study period during which you try to memorize the Coding Guide.
- **Memory Section - Segment 2**
  The second segment is a 90 second (1½ minutes) practice exercise. This segment is not scored.
- **Memory Section - Segment 3**
  The third segment is a 5 minute study period during which you try to memorize the Coding Guide.
- **Memory Section - Segment 4**
  This fourth segment is the actual Memory Section test. You have 7 minutes to answer 36 questions. This segment is scored.

There are no answers to mark during the first and third segments. You will be instructed to mark answers for the second segment on a sample answer sheet, not the actual answer sheet. You will be instructed to mark answers for the fourth segment, which is scored, on the actual answer sheet.

Turn to the next page when you are ready to begin Memory Section - Segment 1.

Part C – Coding & Memory

Memory Section – Segment 1

Instructions

Memory Section - Segment 1 is a 3 minute study period during which you try to memorize the information in the Coding Guide. There are no answers to mark during this study period.

Turn the page and begin studying when you are prepared to time yourself for exactly 3 minutes.

Part C – Coding & Memory

Memory Section – Segment 1

CODING GUIDE	
Address Range	**Delivery Route**
1701 – 2700 Lapalco Blvd. 950 – 1349 Beach Blvd. 8600 – 9399 Elkhorn Dr.	A
2701 – 3700 Lapalco Blvd. 9400 – 9899 Elkhorn Dr.	B
11000 – 17000 RR 148 19 – 60 Raceway Rd. 1350 – 1949 Beach Blvd.	C
All mail that doesn't fall in one of the address ranges listed above	D

Part C – Coding & Memory

Memory Section – Segment 2

Instructions

Segment 2 of the Memory Section is a practice exercise where you have 90 seconds to answer 8 questions from memory. The Coding Guide is not shown. You must answer from memory. This segment is not scored. Mark your answers on the sample answer sheet at the bottom of the page, not on the actual answer sheet.

Begin when you are prepared to time yourself for exactly 90 seconds.

Part C – Coding & Memory

Memory Section – Segment 2

QUESTIONS

	Address	Delivery Route			
1.	8794 Elkhorn Dr.	A	B	C	D
2.	1500 Beach Blvd.	A	B	C	D
3.	9443 Elkhorn Dr.	A	B	C	D
4.	975 Beach Blvd.	A	B	C	D
5.	14982 RR 148	A	B	C	D
6.	65 Raceway Rd.	A	B	C	D
7.	930 Beach Blvd.	A	B	C	D
8.	2900 Lapalco Blvd.	A	B	C	D

SAMPLE ANSWER SHEET

1	Ⓐ	Ⓑ	Ⓒ	Ⓓ	5	Ⓐ	Ⓑ	Ⓒ	Ⓓ
2	Ⓐ	Ⓑ	Ⓒ	Ⓓ	6	Ⓐ	Ⓑ	Ⓒ	Ⓓ
3	Ⓐ	Ⓑ	Ⓒ	Ⓓ	7	Ⓐ	Ⓑ	Ⓒ	Ⓓ
4	Ⓐ	Ⓑ	Ⓒ	Ⓓ	8	Ⓐ	Ⓑ	Ⓒ	Ⓓ

The correct answers are 1-A, 2-C, 3-B, 4-A, 5-C, 6-D, 7-D, and 8-B.

Part C – Coding & Memory

Memory Section – Segment 3

Instructions

Memory Section - Segment 3 is a 5 minute study period during which you try to memorize the information in the Coding Guide. There are no answers to mark during this study period.

Turn the page and begin studying when you are prepared to time yourself for exactly 5 minutes.

Part C – Coding & Memory

Memory Section – Segment 3

CODING GUIDE	
Address Range	**Delivery Route**
1701 – 2700 Lapalco Blvd. 950 – 1349 Beach Blvd. 8600 – 9399 Elkhorn Dr.	A
2701 – 3700 Lapalco Blvd. 9400 – 9899 Elkhorn Dr.	B
11000 – 17000 RR 148 19 – 60 Raceway Rd. 1350 – 1949 Beach Blvd.	C
All mail that doesn't fall in one of the address ranges listed above	D

Part C – Coding & Memory

Memory Section – Segment 4

Instructions

Memory Section - Segment 4 is the actual Memory test. You have 7 minutes to answer 36 questions. You must answer from memory. The Coding Guide is not shown. This segment is scored, and the score from this section does affect your overall Exam 473 score. Mark your answers on the actual answer sheet in the section titled Part C - Coding & Memory - Memory Section.

Turn the page and begin when you are prepared to time yourself for exactly 7 minutes.

Part C – Coding & Memory

Memory Section – Segment 4

Questions

	Address	Delivery Route			
37.	9792 Elkhorn Dr.	A	B	C	D
38.	16500 RR 148	A	B	C	D
39.	35 Raceway Rd.	A	B	C	D
40.	1622 Beach Blvd.	A	B	C	D
41.	1994 Lapalco Blvd.	A	B	C	D
42.	9598 Lapalco Blvd.	A	B	C	D
43.	46 Raceway Rd.	A	B	C	D
44.	1741 Beach Blvd.	A	B	C	D
45.	949 Beach Blvd.	A	B	C	D
46.	8761 Elkhorn Dr.	A	B	C	D
47.	2300 Lapalco Blvd.	A	B	C	D
48.	48 Rice Cay Rd.	A	B	C	D
49.	2856 Lapalco Blvd.	A	B	C	D
50.	14000 RR 148	A	B	C	D
51.	9699 Elkhorn Dr.	A	B	C	D
52.	52 Raceway Rd.	A	B	C	D
53.	1454 Beach Blvd.	A	B	C	D
54.	8500 Elkhorn Dr.	A	B	C	D

continued on next page

Part C – Coding & Memory

Memory Section – Segment 4

continued

Questions

	Address	Delivery Route			
55.	9200 Elkhorn Dr.	A	B	C	D
56.	16800 RR 148	A	B	C	D
57.	2461 Lapalco Blvd.	A	B	C	D
58.	1000 RR 148	A	B	C	D
59.	3600 Lapalco Blvd.	A	B	C	D
60.	9527 Elkhorn Dr.	A	B	C	D
61.	21 Raceway Rd.	A	B	C	D
62.	16356 RR 149	A	B	C	D
63.	9800 Elkhorn Dr.	A	B	C	D
64.	13940 RR 148	A	B	C	D
65.	8499 Elkhorn Dr.	A	B	C	D
66.	1268 Beach Blvd	A	B	C	D
67.	1659 Lapalco Blvd.	A	B	C	D
68.	2596 Lapalco Blvd.	A	B	C	D
69.	9782 Elkhorn Dr.	A	B	C	D
70.	1300 Beach Blvd.	A	B	C	D
71.	50 Raceway Rd.	A	B	C	D
72.	3100 Lapalco Blvd.	A	B	C	D

End of Part C – Memory Section – Segment 4

Part D – Personal Characteristics & Experience Inventory

As explained in the guide, it is not possible to practice or prepare for Part D. There are no right or wrong answers, and speed is not an issue. For each question, you simply select the answer that best reflects your own individual personality, temperament, experience, etc.

Since it is not possible to practice or prepare for Part D, no Personal Characteristics & Experience Inventory sample questions are included in this practice exam.

PRACTICE EXAM #5

As detailed below, included in this practice exam are all four parts of the actual exam and an answer sheet.

- **Part A – Address Checking**

Included is a 100% realistic replica of the scored Address Checking test on the actual exam.

- **Part B – Forms Completion**

Included is a 100% realistic replica of the scored Forms Completion test on the actual exam.

- **Part C – Coding & Memory**

Included are 100% realistic replicas of the complete Coding and Memory sections with all seven segments.

- **Part D – Personal Characteristics & Experience Inventory**

As explained in the guide, it is not possible to prepare for this part of the exam. Therefore no Personal Characteristics & Experience Inventory questions are included in the practice test for this part of the exam. However, for realistic formatting, we have included a page in the practice test for this exam part.

- **Answer Sheet**

Included near the back of the book are 100% realistic replicas of the answer sheet from the actual exam. When taking a practice exam, tear out one of these Practice Answer Sheets. Mark your answers to the scored segments of the exam on this answer sheet. As noted above, it is not possible to prepare for Part D. Therefore, bubbles are not included on the answer sheet for Part D. However, for realistic formatting, we have noted where Part D would appear on the answer sheet.

The format of this practice exam is identical to the actual exam, and the instructions are similar to those on the actual exam.

It is imperative that you take this practice exam in as realistic a fashion as possible - meaning that you must time yourself precisely. **Your practice will have no value unless it is done realistically.** Our Timed Practice Test Audio CD and our Test Prep CD-ROM are ideal tools for conveniently having the instructions presented section-by-section and for absolutely precise timing. See the order form in the back of the book or our website *www.PostalExam.com* for details.

Answer keys are provided in the back of your book. It is imperative that you use the formulas given in the book to **score each practice test as you complete it**. Scoring is necessary in order to measure your progress and to identify your individual areas of weakness that may need extra attention.

After completing and scoring each practice exam, move on to the next. **After finishing all six exams, you should be prepared to excel on the actual exam.**

Do not look over the practice exam questions until you are ready to start and to time yourself - usually meaning until you have started either the Timed Practice Test Audio CD or the Postal Test Prep CD-ROM. Similarly, after completing one section of the practice test, do not look over the next one until your are ready to start it. Likewise, stop working and put down your pencil immediately when the allotted period of time has expired. As has been emphasized before but cannot be emphasized enough, your practice is of absolutely no value unless it is done realistically. Also, you must train yourself (1) to not open your test booklet or pick up your pencil until instructed to do so and (2) to close your booklet and put down your pencil immediately upon being so instructed. The Postal Service has zero tolerance on these matters. Any variance may be viewed as cheating and may result in your disqualification.

Turn to the next page when you are ready to begin this Practice Exam.

Important Note about this Practice Exam

The questions, addresses, forms, etc. in this practice exam are very realistic samples, but they are not the actual ones that you will see on the real test. There are hundreds of different versions of this exam, and each version has different questions, addresses, forms, etc. Even if you could get some real questions from one version of the exam, the questions on the version of the exam you take would surely be different.

PRACTICE EXAM #5

Part A – Address Checking

Directions

In Part A consists of 60 questions to be completed in 11 minutes. You are given a **Correct List** of addresses and ZIP codes. A **List to be Checked,** also with addresses and ZIP codes, appears next to the **Correct List**. The **List to be Checked** should be exactly like the **Correct List**, but it may contain errors.

Your task is to compare each row of information in the **Correct List** and the **List to be Checked** to find if there are **No Errors**, an error in the **Address Only**, an error in the **ZIP Code Only**, or an error in **Both** the address and the ZIP code.

After comparing each row of information, select an answer from the below answer choices, and mark your answer on the answer sheet in the section titled Part A - Address Checking.

A. No Errors	B. Address Only	C. ZIP Code Only	D. Both

Turn the page and begin when you are prepared to time yourself for exactly 11 minutes.

Part A – Address Checking

A. No Errors	B. Address Only	C. ZIP Code Only	D. Both

Correct List / **List to be Checked**

	Address	*ZIP Code*	*Address*	*ZIP Code*
1.	4300 Vista Rd. Princeton, N.J.	84457-3214	4300 Vista Rd. Princeton, N.Y.	84457-3214
2.	5390 S Gessner St. Grand Rapids, MI	38310-8496	5390 S Gessner St. Grand Rapids, MI	38310-8496
3.	3115 W Loop South Lexington, Kentucky	54006	3115 W Loop South Lexington, Kentucky	54086
4.	7079 ALLISON DR SHREVEPORT, LA	67938-3541	7070 ALLISON DR SHREVEPORT, LA	67938-3541
5.	19871 Jensen Ave. Biloxi, MS	39440-4812	19871 Jensen Ave. Biloxi, MS	39440-4812
6.	9418 Tally Ho Street Queens, N.Y.	48621-0489	9481 Tally Ho Street Queens, N.Y.	46621-0489
7.	133120 Misty Oak Nashville, TN	74509	131120 Misty Oak Nashville, TN	74500
8.	16938 FANNIN YORK, S.C.	28903-5678	PO BOX 126581 YORK, S.C.	28903-6587
9.	4300 Vista Rd Kimball, TN	60458-2973	4300 Vista Rd Kimball, TN	69458-2973
10.	106211 CRYSTAL DR. ENNIS, T.X.	70084-1056	106211 KRYSTAL DR. ENNIS, T.X.	70088-1056
11.	2631 Fountain Blue Grafton, W.V.	59067-8221	2631 Fountain Blue Grafton, W.V.	59067-8221
12.	92 Beechnut Ct. Rock Springs, WY	81006-7312	98 Beechnut Ct. Rock Springs, WY	81006-7312
13.	124 W 17th Street Fond du Lac, WI	20913-5542	124 W 17th Street Fond du Lac, WI	20913-5542
14.	4825 Fry Rd. Apt. 39 Santa Ana, C.A.	30995	4825 Fry Rd. Apt. 30 Santa Ana, C.A.	30955
15.	7250 HARWIN ABERDEEN, S. D.	94183-5349	7250 HARWIN ABERDEEN, S. C.	94183-5349

continued on next page

Part A – Address Checking

continued

A. No Errors	B. Address Only	C. ZIP Code Only	D. Both

	Correct List		List to be Checked	
	Address	*ZIP Code*	*Address*	*ZIP Code*
16.	P.O. Box 2674 Muskogee, OK	70345-2674	P.O. Box 2674 Muskogee, OK	70345-2674
17.	18 MOORE STREET SHENANDOAH, IA	59164-8453	18 MOORE STREET SHENANDOAH, IA	59164-8453
18.	2005 Long Beach Blvd. Oceanside, CA	42913-8825	2005 Long Beach Blvd. Oceanside, CA	42912-8825
19.	#19 Bakersfield, Apt. 29 Fargo, ND	37619	#19 Bakersfield, Apt. 2A Fargo, ND	37619
20.	9045 Glen Court Salt Lake City, UT	83194-9712	9045 Glen Court Ste E Salt Lake City, UT	83194-9172
21.	110 Village Place St. Springfield, V. T.	62210-5491	110 Village Place St. Springfield, V. T.	62210-5491
22.	89 Coe Rd. Apt. 9 Pleasantville, TX	78210-6513	89 Coe Rd. Apt. 9 Pleasantville, TX	79210-6513
23.	5403 Kirby LN Gallatin, TN	23984-9546	5403 Kirby LN Gallatin, TX	23984-9546
24.	1225 Campbell Ave. York, SC	49907-3819	1220 Campbell Ave. York, SC	49907-3810
25.	6043 Selinsky Eugene, OR	99378	6043 Selinsky Eugene, OK	99378
26.	10056 SHELDON DR DIME BOX, AL	65792-5917	10056 SHELDON DR DIME BOX, AL	65792-5917
27.	550 Sherwood Forest Tampa, F.L.	33094-7391	550 Sherwood Forest Tampa, F.L.	34094-7391
28.	15600 John F. Kennedy San Bernardino, CA	90137-4672	15600 John F. Kennedy San Bernardino, CA	90137-4670
29.	4511 Cherry St. Hartford, C. T.	20065-2613	4511 Cherry St. Hartford, C. T.	20065-2613
30.	3703 Irvington PL Providence, R.I.	11079-3917	3702 Irvington PL Providence, R.I.	11079-3919

continued on next page

Part A – Address Checking
continued

A. No Errors	B. Address Only	C. ZIP Code Only	D. Both

Correct List / **List to be Checked**

	Address	*ZIP Code*	*Address*	*ZIP Code*
31.	9075 GAYLORD AV ANCHORAGE, AK	90975-8826	9075 GAYLORD AV ANCHORAGE, AL	90975-8266
32.	2518 Tangley St. Fresno, CA	95469-3578	2518 Dangy St. Fresno, CA	95469-3578
33.	6156 S Loop East Silver City, CO	80469-4002	6156 S Loop East Silver City, CO	80469-4002
34.	4501 Quail Hollow Dr. Christiansburg, VA	49485	4501 Quail Holler Dr. Christiansburg, VA	49485
35.	3300 Red Cedar Bremerton, W.A.	73021-6512	3300 Red Cedar Bremerton, W.A.	73921-6512
36.	P.O. Drawer 3287 American Fork, Utah	60085-3287	P.O. Drawer 3827 American Fork, Utah	60085-3287
37.	4419 Ironwood Ave. Auburn, G.A.	43012	4419 Ironwood Ave. Auburn, G.A.	43021
38.	2402 Camillia Apt. B McCalla, AL	32156-4378	2402 Camillia Apt. B McCalla, AL	32156-4378
39.	800 Birdsong St. Morro Bay, CA	96521-4457	800 Birdsong St. Morro Bay, CT	96521-4457
40.	1828 125th Ave. Hammond, IN	52136-9100	1828 125th Ave. Hammond, IL	52136-9100
41.	2952 Jasper Circle Wellington, KS	39458-2069	2952 Jasper Circle Wellington, KS	39438-2069
42.	3701 PORTAGE DR BOGALUSA, LA	79612-8431	3701 PORTAGE DR BOGALUSA, LA	79612-8431
43.	403 E. Oskaloosa Festus, MO	56321	403 E. Oskaloosa Fester, MO	56221
44.	4800 NOLAND RD. Wiggins, M.S.	43798-1036	4800 NOLAND RD. Wiggins, M.S.	47398-1036
45.	1436 Dogwood Apt. B Hartford, CT	99452-1006	1436 Dogwood Apt. B Hartford, CT	99452-1006

continued on next page

Part A – Address Checking

continued

A. No Errors	B. Address Only	C. ZIP Code Only	D. Both

Correct List / **List to be Checked**

	Address	ZIP Code	Address	ZIP Code
46.	1201 S Division St. Joliet, IL	77463-1026	1201 W Division St. Joliet, IL	77463-1028
47.	1340 Randall Rd. New Castle, Delaware	26792-7631	1340 Randall Rd. New Castle, Delaware	26792-7631
48.	3855 S Hwy 59 Waterford, C.T.	00154-3719	3855 S Hwy 57 Waterford, C.T.	00154-3719
49.	9499 SHERIDAN CT. BARTOW, FL	43005-7512	9499 SHERIDAN CT. BARNCOW, FL	43005-7521
50.	801 Hover Apt. 24B Hattiesburg, MS	32719-1002	801 Hover Apt. 24B Hattiesburg, MS	32179-1002
51.	4701 N Stone Ave. Mesa, AZ	59127-8437	4701 N Stone Ave. Mesa, AK	59127-8437
52.	1095 Industrial Pky Eagle River, AK	30158-7649	1095 Industrial Pky Eagle River, AK	30158-7649
53.	5401 Beacon Rd. Florence, K.Y.	70694-3791	5401 Beacon Rd. Florence, K.Y.	70694-3791
54.	PO Box 23513 Pratt, K.S.	51349-3513	PO Box 25313 Pratt, K.S.	51349-5313
55.	210 E Tower Park Bastrop, LA	38369-1975	219 E Tower Park Bastrop, LA	38369-1975
56.	218 Cumberline Skowhegan, Maine	02498-6543	218 Cumberline Snowhaven, Maine	02498-6543
57.	167 Northshore Blvd White Marsh, MD	49760-4900	167 Northshore Blvd White Marsh, MD	49160-4900
58.	3301 Pontiac Trail Rd Howell, MI	61039-2163	3301 Pontiac Trail Rd Howell, MI	61039-2163
59.	4740 MAIL DR. OWATONNA, MN	28945-1003	4470 MAIL DR. OWATONNA, MN	28045-1003
60.	601 N. Lincoln Waterbury, CT	03012-9120	601 S. Lincoln Waterbury, CT	03012-9120

End of Part A – Address Checking

PRACTICE EXAM #5

Part B – Forms Completion

Directions

Part B tests your ability to identify information needed to complete various U.S. Postal Service forms. This part of the exam consists of 30 questions to be completed in 15 minutes. You will be shown 5 different forms and be asked to answer 6 questions about each form.

Turn the page and begin when you are prepared to time yourself for exactly 15 minutes.

Part B – Forms Completion

INSURED MAIL RECEIPT		
Postage	1.	1a. ☐ Fragile ☐ Liquid ☐ Perishable
Insurance Fees	2a.	2b. Insurance Coverage
Restricted Delivery Fee	3.	7. Postmark Here
Special Handling Fee	4.	
Return Receipt Fee	5.	
Total Postage & Fees	6.	
8. Sent to:		
9. Street, Apt. No.; or P.O. Box		
10. City, State, ZIP + 4, Country		

continued on next page

Part B – Forms Completion

continued

1. Fees applicable to a particular shipment are postage - $24.90, insurance - $6.40, and restricted delivery - $3.00 for a total of $34.30. Which of these would the entry $34.40 go in?
   A. Box 1
   B. Box 2a
   C. Box 3
   D. Box 6

2. Fees applicable to a particular shipment are postage - $24.90, insurance - $6.40, and restricted delivery - $3.00 for a total of $34.30. Which of these would the entry $24.90 go in?
   A. Box 1
   B. Box 2a
   C. Box 3
   D. Box 6

3. Fees applicable to a particular shipment are postage - $24.90, insurance - $6.40, and restricted delivery - $3.00 for a total of $34.30. Which of these would the entry $6.40 go in?
   A. Box 1
   B. Box 2a
   C. Box 3
   D. Box 6

4. For which of these would the entry "Ed Morrow" be acceptable?
   A. Box 2b
   B. Box 7
   C. Box 8
   D. Box 9

5. Insurance coverage in the amount of $500.00 is purchased for a shipment of valuable tools. Where would the amount of insurance coverage be indicated?
   A. Box 1
   B. Box 1a
   C. Box 2
   D. Box 2b

6. Of the six different types of fees listed on this form, an entry is needed for all except the Special Handling Fee. Which of these must be left blank?
   A. Box 1
   B. Box 2a
   C. Box 3
   D. None of the above

continued on next page

Part B – Forms Completion
continued

Domestic Claim or Registered Mail Inquiry

Mailer Information	Addressee Information
1a. Name	**2a.** Name
1b. Business Name	**2b.** Business Name
1c. Address	**2c.** Address
1d. City, State, ZIP+4	**2d.** City, State, ZIP+4
1e. Telephone (include area code)	**2e.** Telephone (include area code)

Payment Assignment Alternate Payment Address	**Description of Lost or Damaged Article(s)** Add extra sheets as needed				
3a. Who is to receive payment? (Check one) ☐ Mailer ☐ Addressee	Item	Description	Code	Value	Purchase Date
3b. Address	A	**4a.**			
	B	**4b.**			
3c. City, State, ZIP+4	C	**4c.**			
5a. COD amount to be remitted to sender (For business mailer COD claims only) $	**5b.** Total amount claimed for all articles $				

Certification and signature		
6a. Customer submitting claim ☐ Mailer ☐ Addressee	**6b.** Customer signature	**6c.** Date signed

continued on next page

7. Which of these could be an acceptable entry for Box 6c?
   A. Edward Cantrell
   B. Natrona, WY
   C. 8/28/06
   D. $24.50

8. Three items are being claimed on this form. Item A has a value of $60.00, Item B has a value of $23.00, and Item C has a value of $12.50 for a total amount claimed of $95.50. Where should $95.50 be entered?
   A. Box 4a
   B. Box 4b
   C. Box 5a
   D. Box 5b

9. Three items are being claimed on this form. Item A has a value of $60.00, Item B has a value of $23.00, and Item C has a value of $12.50 for a total amount claimed of $95.50. What should be entered in Box 5a?
   A. $60.00
   B. $23.00
   C. $95.50
   D. None of the above

10. For which of these could "(606) 419-1430" be an acceptable entry?
    A. Boxes 1e and 2e
    B. Boxes 1e, 2e, and 3c
    C. Box 2b
    D. None of the above

11. For which of these could a dollar amount be an acceptable entry?
    A. Box 5a
    B. Box 5b
    C. Boxes 5a and 5b
    D. None of the above

12. Which of these could be an appropriate entry for Box 6a?
    A. Evans, Larry
    B. 11/22/05
    C. A check mark
    D. Grand Rapids, MI

continued on next page

Forwarding Order Change Order					Check One **1.** ☐ Entire Family ☐ Individual
2a. Carrier Route No.	**2b.** Carrier/Clerk	**2c.** Receiving Employee	**2d.** Original Order Date	**2e.** This Order Date	**2f.** Expiraton Date
3. *Print* Last Name or Name of Business/Firm *(If more than one last name fill out additional form.)*					
4. *Print* First Name of Each Individual Covered By This Order *(Separate each name by a comma.)*					
Original Address	**5a.** *Print* Number and Street	**5b.** Apt./Suite No.	**5c.** P.O. Box No.	**5d.** Rural Route No.	**5e.** Rural Box No.
	6a. *Print* City		**6b.** State	**6c.** ZIP + 4	
Cancel Forwarding Order	**7a.** *Print* Number and Street	**7b.** Apt./Suite No.	**7c.** P.O. Box No.	**7d.** Rural Route No.	**7e.** Rural Box No.
	8a. *Print* City		**8b.** State	**8c.** ZIP + 4	
New Forwarding Order	**9a.** *Print* Number and Street	**9b.** Apt./Suite No.	**9c.** P.O. Box No.	**9d.** Rural Route No.	**9e.** Rural Box No.
	10a. *Print* City		**10b.** State	**10c.** ZIP + 4	
11a. ☐ Moved no order			**11b.** ☐ Refuses to pay postage due on ALL 4th class		
12a. ☐ No such number			**12b.** ☐ No such street, check forwarding order		
13a. Post Office		**13b.** Station/ Branch		**13c.** By *(Route No., Name)*	

continued on next page

Part B – Forms Completion

continued

13. How would Frank and Mary Jensen indicate that mail for both their names should be forwarded?
    A. Write both full names in Box 3
    B. Write both full names in Box 4
    C. Write their last name in Box 3 and both first names in Box 4
    D. Complete two separate forms.

14. How should you indicate that you do not want to pay postage charges to have 4th class mail forwarded.
    A. Check Box 11a
    B. Check Box 11b
    C. Check Box 12a
    D. Check Box 12b

15. The original address was 1113 Maple St Apt 8A, Ontario, IA 67743-2678. Where should this address be entered?
    A. Boxes 5a, 5d, and 6a
    B. Boxes 5a, 5b, and 6a
    C. Boxes 5a, 5b, 6a, 6b, and 6c
    D. None of the above

16. Andrew Halcomb moved from Missoula to Billings, and shortly afterwards moved to Butte. Into which box should the city name "Missoula" be entered?
    A. Box 5a
    B. Box 6a
    C. Box 8a
    D. Box 10a

17. Which of these could be an acceptable entry for Box 9c?
    A. 11/3/06
    B. Andrew Sullivan
    C. St. Louis, MO
    D. 495

18. What should the Postal representative do if the street name in the forwarding order is incorrect?
    A. Check Box 11a
    B. Check Box 11b
    C. Check Box 12a
    D. Check Box 12b

continued on next page

Application for Post Office Box or Caller Service

Customer: Complete white boxes		Post Office: Complete shaded boxes	
1a. Name(s) to which box number(s) is (are) are assigned			**1b.** Box or Caller Numbers _______ through _______
2a. Name of person applying, Title *(if representing an organization)*, and name of organization *(if different from name in Box 1a above)*			**2b.** Will this box be used for: ☐ Personal use ☐ Business use
3a. Address *(number, street, apt. no., city, state, ZIP code)*. When address changes, cross out address here and put new address on back.			**3b.** Telephone number (include area code)
4a. Date application received	**4b.** Box size needed	**4c.** ID and physical address verified by *(initials)*	**4d.** Dates of service _______ through _______
5a. Two types of identification are required. One must contain a photograph of the addressee(s). Social security cards, credit cards, and birth certificates are unacceptable as identification. Write in identifying information. Subject to verification.		**5b.** Eligibility for Carrier Delivery ☐ City ☐ Rural ☐ HCR ☐ None	**5c.** Service Assigned ☐ Box ☐ Caller ☐ Reserve No.
		6. Name(s) of minors or others receiving mail in individual box.	
WARNING: *The furnishing of false or misleading information on this form or omission of information may result in criminal sanctions (including fines and imprisonment) and/or civil sanctions (including multiple damages and civil penalties).*		**7.** Signature of applicant *(Same as Item 3)*. I agree to comply with all Postal rules regarding Post Office box or caller services.	

continued on next page

19. Where should the types of ID presented be noted?
    A. Box 4a
    B. Box 4c
    C. Box 5a
    D. Box 5b

20. When renting a Post Office Box, where should the beginning and ending dates of service be entered?
    A. Box 1b
    B. Box 4d
    C. Box 4a
    D. None of the above

21. If the street address changes, how should this form be updated?
    A. Complete a new application.
    B. Cross out the old street address and write the new street address on the back of the form.
    C. Cross out the old street address and write the new street address in Box 3a.
    D. Non of the above

22. When renting a Post Office Box to be used for both personal and business purposes, how should this be indicated?
    A. Complete two applications
    B. Attach a letter of explanation
    C. Check both choices in Box 2b.
    D. None of the above

23. Lester Allgood is renting a Post Office Box where he and his three small children will receive mail. Where should the four names be entered?
    A. All four in Box 1a
    B. Lester's name in Box 1a and the three children's names in Box 2a.
    C. Lester's name in Box 1a and the three children's names on the back of the form.
    D. Lester's name in Box 1a and the three children's names in Box 6.

24. Under what circumstances could a social security card be accepted as identification when applying for a Post Office Box?
    A. If a birth certificate is presented also.
    B. If a drivers license is presented also.
    C. If both a birth certificate and a drivers license are presented also.
    D. A social security card is not acceptable as identification under any circumstances.

continued on next page

Part B – Forms Completion

continued

Customs Declaration			
1a. ☐ Gift ☐ Commercial Sample ☐ Documents ☐ Other			I, the undersigned, whose name and address are given on the item, certify that the particulars given in this declaration are correct and that this item does not contain any dangerous article or articles prohibited by legislation or by Postal or customs regulations. This copy will remain at the Post Office for 30 days.
2a. Quantity and detailed description of contents	**2b.** Weight lb. oz.	**2c.** Value US Dollars	**2d.** Sender's Name & Address
3a. For commercial items only (If known, HS tariff number and country of origin)	**3b.** Total Weight	**3c.** Total Value	**3d.** Addressee's Name & Address
4a. Date and sender's signature			**4b.** Date and sender's signature

continued on next page

Part B – Forms Completion

continued

25. Which of these would be an acceptable entry for Box 3b?
    A. 50 lb. 13 oz.
    B. 18 Baseballs
    C. $157.93
    D. Tommy Dambrino

26. Where would you enter the following: 18 rings, 15 necklaces, 8 earrings?
    A. Box 1a
    B. Box 2a
    C. Box 3a
    D. Box 4a

27. Where would you indicate that the total weight of the 18 rings, 15 necklaces and 8 earrings is 5 lb. 3 oz.?
    A. Box 2b
    B. Box 2c
    C. Box 3b
    D. Box 3c

28. Which of these would be an acceptable entry for Box 2b?
    A. $7.00
    B. Pinehurst, SD 77362-1221
    C. Savannah Madden
    D. 10 lb. 4 oz.

29. Which of these would be an acceptable entry for Box 3d?
    A. Reginald A. Smith , 7890 New Brick Rd., Antioch, TX 88903-2345
    B. A check mark
    C. 6:30 a.m.
    D. $29.58

30. Where would you list the monetary value of each item?
    A. Box 2a
    B. Box 2b
    C. Box 2c
    D. Box 3c

End of Part B – Forms Completion

PRACTICE EXAM #5

Part C – Coding & Memory

Part C tests your ability to use codes quickly and accurately both from a Coding Guide and from memory. This part of the exam consists of two sections as detailed below.

- The Coding Section has 36 questions to be answered in 6 minutes. During the Coding section, you will look at a Coding Guide to find answers. The Coding Section is broken down into several segments.
- The Memory Section has 36 questions to be answered in 7 minutes. During the Memory Section, you must answer from memory. The Memory Section is broken down into several segments.

The same Coding Guide will be used throughout both sections of Part C. Four delivery routes (identified by the codes A, B, C, and D) are listed on the Coding Guide. Also listed on the Coding Guide are various address ranges on several streets that are served by these delivery routes.

Each question is an address. To answer each question, you must identify the delivery route that serves the address, and mark as your answer the code (A, B, C, or D) for that delivery route.

Turn the page when you are ready to begin the first section, the Coding Section.

Part C – Coding & Memory

Coding Section

The Coding Section of Part C - Coding & Memory consists of 3 segments as detailed below.

- **Coding Section - Segment 1**
  The first segment is a 2 minute introductory exercise. This segment is not scored.
- **Coding Section - Segment 2**
  The second segment is a 90 second (1½ minutes) practice exercise. This segment is not scored.
- **Coding Section - Segment 3**
  The third segment is the actual Coding Section test. You have 6 minutes to answer 36 questions. This segment is scored.

The Coding Guide is displayed during all 3 segments. You will be instructed to mark answers for the first two unscored segments on sample answer sheets, not the actual answer sheet. You will be instructed to mark answers for the third segment, which is scored, on the actual answer sheet.

Turn to the next page when you are ready to begin Coding Section - Segment 1.

Part C – Coding & Memory

Coding Section – Segment 1

Instructions

Segment 1 of the Coding Section is an introductory exercise to acquaint you with how the questions are to be answered. In this segment, you have 2 minutes to answer 4 questions. The Coding Guide is displayed for your use in answering the questions. This segment is not scored. Mark your answers on the sample answer sheet at the bottom of the question page, not on the actual answer sheet.

Turn the page and begin when you are prepared to time yourself for exactly 2 minutes.

Part C – Coding & Memory

Coding Section – Segment 1

CODING GUIDE	
Address Range	**Delivery Route**
1101 – 1400 Louetta Cir. 770 – 929 Ella Rd. 8300 – 8399 State Rt 16	A
1401 – 1900 Louetta Cir. 8400 – 8499 State Rt 16	B
20 – 50 ALT 90 W 19000 – 22000 Dogwood Trace 930 – 1420 Ella Rd.	C
All mail that doesn't fall in one of the address ranges listed above	D

Part C – Coding & Memory

Coding Section – Segment 1

continued

QUESTIONS

	Address	Delivery Route			
1.	30 ALT 90 W	A	B	C	D
2.	760 Ella Rd	A	B	C	D
3.	1107 Louetta Cir.	A	B	C	D
4.	8432 State Rt 16	A	B	C	D

SAMPLE ANSWER SHEET

1 Ⓐ Ⓑ Ⓒ Ⓓ
2 Ⓐ Ⓑ Ⓒ Ⓓ
3 Ⓐ Ⓑ Ⓒ Ⓓ
4 Ⓐ Ⓑ Ⓒ Ⓓ

The correct answers are 1-C, 2-D, 3-A, and 4-B.

Part C – Coding & Memory

Coding Section – Segment 2

Instructions

Segment 2 of the Coding Section is a practice exercise designed to expose you to the realistic timing demanded. In this segment, you have 90 seconds to answer 8 questions. The Coding Guide is displayed for your use in answering the questions. This segment is not scored. Mark your answers on the sample answer sheet at the bottom of the question page, not on the actual answer sheet.

Turn the page and begin when you are prepared to time yourself for exactly 90 seconds.

Part C – Coding & Memory

Coding Section – Segment 2

CODING GUIDE	
Address Range	**Delivery Route**
1101 – 1400 Louetta Cir. 770 – 929 Ella Rd. 8300 – 8399 State Rt 16	A
1401 – 1900 Louetta Cir. 8400 – 8499 State Rt 16	B
20 – 50 ALT 90 W 19000 – 22000 Dogwood Trace 930 – 1420 Ella Rd.	C
All mail that doesn't fall in one of the address ranges listed above	D

Part C – Coding & Memory

Coding Section – Segment 2

continued

QUESTIONS

	Address	Delivery Route			
1.	1492 Louetta Cir.	A	B	C	D
2.	785 Ella Rd.	A	B	C	D
3.	8368 State Rt 16	A	B	C	D
4.	19562 Dogwood Trace	A	B	C	D
5.	1000 Louetta Cir.	A	B	C	D
6.	941 Ella Rd.	A	B	C	D
7.	8466 State Rt. 16	A	B	C	D
8.	23000 Dogwood Trace	A	B	C	D

SAMPLE ANSWER SHEET

1	Ⓐ	Ⓑ	Ⓒ	Ⓓ	5	Ⓐ	Ⓑ	Ⓒ	Ⓓ
2	Ⓐ	Ⓑ	Ⓒ	Ⓓ	6	Ⓐ	Ⓑ	Ⓒ	Ⓓ
3	Ⓐ	Ⓑ	Ⓒ	Ⓓ	7	Ⓐ	Ⓑ	Ⓒ	Ⓓ
4	Ⓐ	Ⓑ	Ⓒ	Ⓓ	8	Ⓐ	Ⓑ	Ⓒ	Ⓓ

The correct answers are 1-B, 2-A, 3-A, 4-C, 5-D, 6-C, 7-B, and 8-D.

Part C – Coding & Memory

Coding Section – Segment 3

Instructions

Segment 3 of the Coding Section is the actual Coding test. You have 6 minutes to answer 36 questions. The Coding Guide is displayed for your use in answering the questions. This segment is scored, and the score from this section does affect your overall Exam 473 score. Mark your answers on the actual answer sheet in the section titled Part C - Coding & Memory - Coding Section.

Turn the page and begin when you are prepared to time yourself for exactly 6 minutes.

Coding Section – Segment 3

CODING GUIDE	
Address Range	**Delivery Route**
1101 – 1400 Louetta Cir. 770 – 929 Ella Rd. 8300 – 8399 State Rt 16	A
1401 – 1900 Louetta Cir. 8400 – 8499 State Rt 16	B
20 – 50 ALT 90 W 19000 – 22000 Dogwood Trace 930 – 1420 Ella Rd.	C
All mail that doesn't fall in one of the address ranges listed above	D

Coding Section – Segment 3

continued

Questions

	Address	Delivery Route			
1.	42 ALT 90 W	A	B	C	D
2.	1842 Louetta Cir.	A	B	C	D
3.	1367 Ella Rd.	A	B	C	D
4.	1188 Louetta Cir.	A	B	C	D
5.	8429 State Rt 16	A	B	C	D
6.	2100 Louetta Cir.	A	B	C	D
7.	919 Ella Rd.	A	B	C	D
8.	19681 Dagwood Race	A	B	C	D
9.	1690 Louetta Cir.	A	B	C	D
10.	8345 State Rt 16	A	B	C	D
11.	21541 Dogwood Trace	A	B	C	D
12.	1296 Louetta Cir.	A	B	C	D
13.	39 ALT 90 W	A	B	C	D
14.	864 Ella Rd.	A	B	C	D
15.	8413 State Rt 16	A	B	C	D
16.	8370 State Rt 16	A	B	C	D
17.	1800 Louetta Cir.	A	B	C	D
18.	20500 Dogwood Trace	A	B	C	D

continued on next page

Coding Section – Segment 3

continued

CODING GUIDE	
Address Range	**Delivery Route**
1101 – 1400 Louetta Cir. 770 – 929 Ella Rd. 8300 – 8399 State Rt 16	A
1401 – 1900 Louetta Cir. 8400 – 8499 State Rt 16	B
20 – 50 ALT 90 W 19000 – 22000 Dogwood Trace 930 – 1420 Ella Rd.	C
All mail that doesn't fall in one of the address ranges listed above	D

Coding Section – Segment 3

continued

Questions

	Address	Delivery Route			
19.	8472 Louetta Cir	A	B	C	D
20.	1300 Louetta Cir.	A	B	C	D
21.	8488 State Rt 16	A	B	C	D
22.	40 ALT 90 W	A	B	C	D
23.	1803 Louetta Cir.	A	B	C	D
24.	7300 State Rt 16	A	B	C	D
25.	1568 Louetta Cir.	A	B	C	D
26.	21000 Dogwood Trace	A	B	C	D
27.	8377 State Rt 16	A	B	C	D
28.	1255 Ella Rd.	A	B	C	D
29.	26 ALT 90 W	A	B	C	D
30.	22004 Dogwood Trace	A	B	C	D
31.	8396 State Rt 16	A	B	C	D
32.	19400 Dogwood Trace	A	B	C	D
33.	1630 Louetta Cir.	A	B	C	D
34.	797 Ella Rd.	A	B	C	D
35.	1245 Lariat Dr.	A	B	C	D
36.	8405 State Rt 16	A	B	C	D

End of Part C – Coding Section – Segment 3

Part C – Coding & Memory

Memory Section

The Memory Section of Part C - Coding & Memory consists of 4 segments as detailed below.

- **Memory Section - Segment 1**
  The first segment is a 3 minute study period during which you try to memorize the Coding Guide.
- **Memory Section - Segment 2**
  The second segment is a 90 second (1½ minutes) practice exercise. This segment is not scored.
- **Memory Section - Segment 3**
  The third segment is a 5 minute study period during which you try to memorize the Coding Guide.
- **Memory Section - Segment 4**
  This fourth segment is the actual Memory Section test. You have 7 minutes to answer 36 questions. This segment is scored.

There are no answers to mark during the first and third segments. You will be instructed to mark answers for the second segment on a sample answer sheet, not the actual answer sheet. You will be instructed to mark answers for the fourth segment, which is scored, on the actual answer sheet.

Turn to the next page when you are ready to begin Memory Section - Segment 1.

Part C – Coding & Memory

Memory Section – Segment 1

Instructions

Memory Section - Segment 1 is a 3 minute study period during which you try to memorize the information in the Coding Guide. There are no answers to mark during this study period.

Turn the page and begin studying when you are prepared to time yourself for exactly 3 minutes.

Part C – Coding & Memory

Memory Section – Segment 1

CODING GUIDE	
Address Range	**Delivery Route**
1101 – 1400 Louetta Cir. 770 – 929 Ella Rd. 8300 – 8399 State Rt 16	A
1401 – 1900 Louetta Cir. 8400 – 8499 State Rt 16	B
20 – 50 ALT 90 W 19000 – 22000 Dogwood Trace 930 – 1420 Ella Rd.	C
All mail that doesn't fall in one of the address ranges listed above	D

Part C – Coding & Memory

Memory Section – Segment 2

Instructions

Segment 2 of the Memory Section is a practice exercise where you have 90 seconds to answer 8 questions from memory. The Coding Guide is not shown. You must answer from memory. This segment is not scored. Mark your answers on the sample answer sheet at the bottom of the page, not on the actual answer sheet.

Begin when you are prepared to time yourself for exactly 90 seconds.

Part C – Coding & Memory

Memory Section – Segment 2

QUESTIONS

	Address	Delivery Route			
1.	670 Ella Rd.	A	B	C	D
2.	1741 Louetta Cir.	A	B	C	D
3.	46 ALT 90 W	A	B	C	D
4.	8462 State Rt 16	A	B	C	D
5.	1346 Louetta Cir.	A	B	C	D
6.	790 Ella Rd.	A	B	C	D
7.	20999 Dogwood Trace	A	B	C	D
8.	15 ALT 90 W	A	B	C	D

SAMPLE ANSWER SHEET

1 Ⓐ Ⓑ Ⓒ Ⓓ　5 Ⓐ Ⓑ Ⓒ Ⓓ
2 Ⓐ Ⓑ Ⓒ Ⓓ　6 Ⓐ Ⓑ Ⓒ Ⓓ
3 Ⓐ Ⓑ Ⓒ Ⓓ　7 Ⓐ Ⓑ Ⓒ Ⓓ
4 Ⓐ Ⓑ Ⓒ Ⓓ　8 Ⓐ Ⓑ Ⓒ Ⓓ

The correct answers are 1-D, 2-B, 3-C, 4-B, 5-A, 6-A, 7-C, and 8-D.

Part C – Coding & Memory

Memory Section – Segment 3

Instructions

Memory Section - Segment 3 is a 5 minute study period during which you try to memorize the information in the Coding Guide. There are no answers to mark during this study period.

Turn the page and begin studying when you are prepared to time yourself for exactly 5 minutes.

Part C – Coding & Memory

Memory Section – Segment 3

CODING GUIDE	
Address Range	**Delivery Route**
1101 – 1400 Louetta Cir. 770 – 929 Ella Rd. 8300 – 8399 State Rt 16	A
1401 – 1900 Louetta Cir. 8400 – 8499 State Rt 16	B
20 – 50 ALT 90 W 19000 – 22000 Dogwood Trace 930 – 1420 Ella Rd.	C
All mail that doesn't fall in one of the address ranges listed above	D

Part C – Coding & Memory

Memory Section – Segment 4

Instructions

Memory Section - Segment 4 is the actual Memory test. You have 7 minutes to answer 36 questions. You must answer from memory. The Coding Guide is not shown. This segment is scored, and the score from this section does affect your overall Exam 473 score. Mark your answers on the actual answer sheet in the section titled Part C - Coding & Memory - Memory Section.

Turn the page and begin when you are prepared to time yourself for exactly 7 minutes.

Part C – Coding & Memory

Memory Section – Segment 4

Questions

	Address	Delivery Route			
37.	8420 State Rt 16	A	B	C	D
38.	35 ALT 90 W	A	B	C	D
39.	120 Louetta Cir	A	B	C	D
40.	1220 Ellen Rd.	A	B	C	D
41.	8331 State Rt 16	A	B	C	D
42.	37 ALT 90 W	A	B	C	D
43.	1100 Ella Rd.	A	B	C	D
44.	8370 State Rt 16	A	B	C	D
45.	20641 Dogwood Trace	A	B	C	D
46.	1894 Louetta Cir	A	B	C	D
47.	920 Ella Rd.	A	B	C	D
48.	8404 State Rt 16	A	B	C	D
49.	1367 Louetta Cir.	A	B	C	D
50.	29 ALT 90 W	A	B	C	D
51.	915 Ella Rd.	A	B	C	D
52.	1522 Louetta Cir.	A	B	C	D
53.	21682 Dogwood Trace	A	B	C	D
54.	1320 Ella Rd.	A	B	C	D

continued on next page

Part C – Coding & Memory

Memory Section – Segment 4

continued

Questions

	Address	Delivery Route			
55.	8302 State Rt 16	A	B	C	D
56.	39 ALT 90 W	A	B	C	D
57.	21222 Dogwood Trace	A	B	C	D
58.	1121 Ella Rd.	A	B	C	D
59.	1210 Louetta Cir.	A	B	C	D
60.	8490 State Rt 16	A	B	C	D
61.	1010 Louetta Cir.	A	B	C	D
62.	8391 State Rt 16	A	B	C	D
63.	1629 Louetta Cir.	A	B	C	D
64.	19644 Dogwood Raceway	A	B	C	D
65.	859 Baker Rd.	A	B	C	D
66.	43 ALT 90 W	A	B	C	D
67.	1419 Ella Rd.	A	B	C	D
68.	1161 Louetta Cir.	A	B	C	D
69.	19854 Dogwood Trace	A	B	C	D
70.	8401 State Rt 18	A	B	C	D
71.	890 Ella Rd.	A	B	C	D
72.	1700 Louetta Cir.	A	B	C	D

End of Part C – Memory Section – Segment 4

Part D – Personal Characteristics & Experience Inventory

As explained in the guide, it is not possible to practice or prepare for Part D. There are no right or wrong answers, and speed is not an issue. For each question, you simply select the answer that best reflects your own individual personality, temperament, experience, etc.

Since it is not possible to practice or prepare for Part D, no Personal Characteristics & Experience Inventory sample questions are included in this practice exam.

PRACTICE EXAM #6

As detailed below, included in this practice exam are all four parts of the actual exam and an answer sheet.

- **Part A – Address Checking**

Included is a 100% realistic replica of the scored Address Checking test on the actual exam.

- **Part B – Forms Completion**

Included is a 100% realistic replica of the scored Forms Completion test on the actual exam.

- **Part C – Coding & Memory**

Included are 100% realistic replicas of the complete Coding and Memory sections with all seven segments.

- **Part D – Personal Characteristics & Experience Inventory**

As explained in the guide, it is not possible to prepare for this part of the exam. Therefore no Personal Characteristics & Experience Inventory questions are included in the practice test for this part of the exam. However, for realistic formatting, we have included a page in the practice test for this exam part.

- **Answer Sheet**

Included near the back of the book are 100% realistic replicas of the answer sheet from the actual exam. When taking a practice exam, tear out one of these Practice Answer Sheets. Mark your answers to the scored segments of the exam on this answer sheet. As noted above, it is not possible to prepare for Part D. Therefore, bubbles are not included on the answer sheet for Part D. However, for realistic formatting, we have noted where Part D would appear on the answer sheet.

The format of this practice exam is identical to the actual exam, and the instructions are similar to those on the actual exam.

It is imperative that you take this practice exam in as realistic a fashion as possible - meaning that you must time yourself precisely. **Your practice will have no value unless it is done realistically.** Our Timed Practice Test Audio CD and our Test Prep CD-ROM are ideal tools for conveniently having the instructions presented section-by-section and for absolutely precise timing. See the order form in the back of the book or our website *www.PostalExam.com* for details.

Answer keys are provided in the back of your book. It is imperative that you use the formulas given in the book to **score each practice test as you complete it**. Scoring is necessary in order to measure your progress and to identify your individual areas of weakness that may need extra attention.

After completing and scoring each practice exam, move on to the next. **After finishing all six exams, you should be prepared to excel on the actual exam.**

Do not look over the practice exam questions until you are ready to start and to time yourself - usually meaning until you have started either the Timed Practice Test Audio CD or the Postal Test Prep CD-ROM. Similarly, after completing one section of the practice test, do not look over the next one until your are ready to start it. Likewise, stop working and put down your pencil immediately when the allotted period of time has expired. As has been emphasized before but cannot be emphasized enough, your practice is of absolutely no value unless it is done realistically. Also, you must train yourself (1) to not open your test booklet or pick up your pencil until instructed to do so and (2) to close your booklet and put down your pencil immediately upon being so instructed. The Postal Service has zero tolerance on these matters. Any variance may be viewed as cheating and may result in your disqualification.

Turn to the next page when you are ready to begin this Practice Exam.

Important Note about this Practice Exam

The questions, addresses, forms, etc. in this practice exam are very realistic samples, but they are not the actual ones that you will see on the real test. There are hundreds of different versions of this exam, and each version has different questions, addresses, forms, etc. Even if you could get some real questions from one version of the exam, the questions on the version of the exam you take would surely be different.

PRACTICE EXAM III

PRACTICE EXAM #6

Part A – Address Checking

Directions

In Part A consists of 60 questions to be completed in 11 minutes. You are given a **Correct List** of addresses and ZIP codes. A **List to be Checked,** also with addresses and ZIP codes, appears next to the **Correct List**. The **List to be Checked** should be exactly like the **Correct List**, but it may contain errors.

Your task is to compare each row of information in the **Correct List** and the **List to be Checked** to find if there are **No Errors**, an error in the **Address Only**, an error in the **ZIP Code Only**, or an error in **Both** the address and the ZIP code.

After comparing each row of information, select an answer from the below answer choices, and mark your answer on the answer sheet in the section titled Part A - Address Checking.

A. No Errors	B. Address Only	C. ZIP Code Only	D. Both

Turn the page and begin when you are prepared to time yourself for exactly 11 minutes.

Part A – Address Checking

A. No Errors	B. Address Only	C. ZIP Code Only	D. Both

Correct List

	Address	ZIP Code
1.	1404 Wilson Ave Bowie, TX	77362
2.	2309 S. Bridge Greenville, MS	36127-4410
3.	1313 S Main Union City, MI	52149-5548
4.	4801 NW Cooper James Island, S.C.	27103-9412
5.	2254A ASHLEIGH JACKSON, TN	70069-5123
6.	P.O. Box 823 Rapid City, SD	48959
7.	970 E Liberty Ave. San Francisco, C.A.	61259-7812
8.	7600 Greenville Hwy Colorado Springs, CO	84010-6492
9.	853 Broad Blvd Apt. 2C Tulsa, OK	21793-5412
10.	2019 E 81st St Hanover, P.A.	70012-3164
11.	50739 Valley Plaza Warwick, R.I.	23975-5791
12.	1189 Thomas Dr. Bismarck, ND	79781-1462
13.	990 Rebecca Ln. Wilton, NY	84561-3971
14.	26 Hampton House #4 Toms River, N.J.	79462
15.	1000 Roberts Rd. Las Cruces, NM	69731-4987

List to be Checked

Address	ZIP Code
1404 Wilson Ave Bowie, TX	77632
2309 S. Bridge Greenville, MN	36127-4410
1313 S Main Union City, WI	52419-5548
4801 NW Cooper James Island, S.D.	27103-9412
2254A ASHLEIGH JACKSON, TN	70069-5123
P.O. Box 832 Rapid City, SD	48059
970 E Liberty Ave. San Francisco, C.A.	61259-7812
7600 Greenville Hwy Colorado Springs, CO	84100-6492
853 Broad Blvd Apt. 2C Tulsa, OK	21793-4512
2019 E 81st St Handover, P.A.	70112-3164
50739 Valley Plaza Warwick, R.I.	23975-5791
1189 Thomas Dr. Bismarck, NY	79781-1462
990 Rebecca Ln. Wilton, NY	84561-3971
26 Hampton House #4 Toms River, N.J.	79462
100 Roberts Rd. Las Cruces, NM	69731-4987

continued on next page

Part A – Address Checking
continued

A. No Errors	B. Address Only	C. ZIP Code Only	D. Both

Correct List

	Address	ZIP Code
16.	2525 King Ave. Helena, MO	52169-7621
17.	701 Snekter Ave NE Cecil, PA	91203-7522
18.	179 Edgewood Dr. Lake City, SC	37941
19.	2035 Whiskey Rd. S Alcoa, T.N.	79134-6548
20.	1243 Jonathan Ln Vinita, OK	63178-1002
21.	37853 Chardon Rd. Waverly, OH	49872-6547
22.	PO Box 5646379 Gibsonia, P.A.	20897-6379
23.	4141 Jeremy St. Foley, AL	30013-7319
24.	1050 RICHARDSON GLENDALE, AZ	50130
25.	1100 S Beltline Hwy. Kodiak, AK	90640-3197
26.	655 Fieldstone Dr. Red Bluff, C.A.	97800-7391
27.	900 S Bowline St. Florida City, FL	60014-7865
28.	444 W Vine Ave Dover, DE	20614-6521
29.	538 N Church Apt. 34 Petal, MS	36804-6731
30.	705 Dixon Blvd. Utica, N.Y.	09541-5440

List to be Checked

Address	ZIP Code
2525 King Ave. Helen, MO	52769-7621
701 Sneaker Ave NE Cecil, PA	91203-7522
179 Edgewood Dr. Lake City, SC	37941
3025 Whiskey Rd. S Alcoa, T.N.	79134-6548
1243 Jonathan Ln Vinita, OK	63178-1002
37853 Chardon Rd. Waverly, OK	49072-6547
PO Box 5646379 Gibsonia, P.A.	20891-6379
4144 Jeremy St. Foley, AL	30013-7319
1050 RICHARDSON GLENDALE, AZ	50130
1100 S Beltline Hwy. Kodiak, AK	90640-3199
655 Fieldstone Dr. Red Stone, C.A.	97800-7391
900 S Bowline St. Florida City, FL	60014-7865
4444 W Vine Ave Dover, DE	26614-6521
538 N Church Apt. 3B Petal, MS	36804-6731
705 Dixon Blvd. Utica, N.Y.	09541-5400

continued on next page

Part A – Address Checking
continued

A. No Errors	B. Address Only	C. ZIP Code Only	D. Both

	Correct List Address	Correct List ZIP Code	List to be Checked Address	List to be Checked ZIP Code
31.	1538 E Floyd Baker Pierre, SD	72159-9421	1538 E Floyd Baker Pierre, SD	72159-9421
32.	3950 Grandview St. Big Spring, TX	32157	3950 Grandview St. Big Spring, TN	32157
33.	913 Seaboard St. Lenoir City, T.N.	40201-6547	913 Seaboard AV. Lenoir City, T.N.	40200-6547
34.	2377 Dave Lyle Blvd. Rutland, VT	21036-4897	2377 Dave Lilly Blvd. Rutland, VT	21036-4897
35.	3201 E Waco Apt. 3C Sandy, Utah	40691-3321	3201 E Waco Apt. 3B Sandy, Utah	40691-3321
36.	PO BOX 17002 GILLETTE, WY	80128-7002	PO BOX 17002 GILLETTE, WY	80128-7002
37.	234 Springs Way N Logan, WV	70021	234 Springs Hwy N Logan, WV	70012
38.	100 McGinnis Ave. Natchez. MS	39125-7458	100 McGinnis Ave. Natchez. MS	39125-7458
39.	235 Frontage Rd. Lees Summit, MO	41791-5469	235 Frontage Rd. Lees Summit, MO	41791-5469
40.	935 THARP RD VISTA, C.A.	90107-6197	935 THARP RD VISTA, C.A.	90107-6107
41.	21945 9th Ave. Russellville, AL	29130-7391	21495 9th Ave. Russellville, AL	29130-7391
42.	333 Boyd Blvd. Kokomo, IN	49731-9874	333 Boyd Blvd. Kokomo, IN	49731-9784
43.	3240 Southwester Ave. Mt. Pleasant, IA	59871	3240 Southwester Ave. Mt. Pleasanton, IA	59871
44.	4040 Newton St. Wellington, K.S.	65419-3278	4040 Newton St. Wellington, K.S.	65419-2278
45.	735 GOSPEL DR. ABBEVILLE, LA	30069	735 GOSPEL DR. ABBEVILLE, LA	30060

continued on next page

Part A – Address Checking
continued

A. No Errors	B. Address Only	C. ZIP Code Only	D. Both

Correct List / **List to be Checked**

	Correct List: *Address*	Correct List: *ZIP Code*	List to be Checked: *Address*	List to be Checked: *ZIP Code*
46.	1310 N Eisenhower Dr. Appleton, WI	73215-6127	1310 N Eisenhower Dr. Appletown, WI	73215-6127
47.	4 Charles Town Plaza Laurel, MS	34897-5412	4 Charles Town Plaza Laurel, MS	34897-5412
48.	19034 Shows St. Spearfish, SD	90453	19034 Shows St. Spearfish, ND	90543
49.	2401 Augusta Rd. Rock Hill, TN	64500-6471	2401 Augusta Rd. Rock Hill, TN	64509-6471
50.	2795 North Rd Princeton, NJ	13197-3042	2975 North Rd Princeton, NJ	13197-3042
51.	1236 Route 6 Carlsbad, N. M.	59430-2001	1236 Route 6 Carlsbad, N. M.	59430-2001
52.	400 Eubank Blvd. Dexter, MI	49601	400 Eubank Blvd. Nester, MI	49601
53.	89234 THELMA LN ALMA, NEBRASKA	77912-6014	89234 THELMA LN ALMA, NEBRASKA	77912-6014
54.	2401 Foothill Blvd. Sheridan W.Y.	89761-3312	2407 Foothill Blvd. Sheridan W.Y.	89761-3112
55.	2863 Heritage Dr. Dodgeville, W.I.	10365-9812	2868 Heritage Dr. Dodgeville, W.I.	10365-9815
56.	1255 E. Chestnut Arcola, IL	88245	1255 E. Chestnut Arcola, IL	88215
57.	8976 Tompkins Blvd. Crossett, AR	60081-4937	8976 Tompkins Blvd. Crossett, AR	60081-4937
58.	75 Centennial Pky N Humacao, PR	51198-2004	75 Centennial Pky N Sombrero, PR	51198-2004
59.	800 Niagara St. Williston, V.T.	40647-3789	800 Niagara St. Williestown, V.T.	40647-3789
60.	1084 Success Road Pinehurst, TX	77362	1084 Success Road Pinehurst, TX	77362

End of Part A – Address Checking

PRACTICE EXAM #6

Part B – Forms Completion

Directions

Part B tests your ability to identify information needed to complete various U.S. Postal Service forms. This part of the exam consists of 30 questions to be completed in 15 minutes. You will be shown 5 different forms and be asked to answer 6 questions about each form.

Turn the page and begin when you are prepared to time yourself for exactly 15 minutes.

Part B – Forms Completion

Authorization to Hold Mail

Postmaster - Please hold mail for:

1. Name(s)	
2. Address	
3a. Begin Holding Mail (Date)	**3b.** Resume Delivery (Date)
4. ☐ **Option A** I will pick up all accumulated mail when I return and understand that mail delivery will not resume until I do. (This is suggested if your return date may change or if no one will be at home to receive mail.)	
5. ☐ **Option B** Please deliver all accumulated mail and resume normal delivery on the ending date shown above.	
6. Customer Signature	
For Post Office Use Only	
7. Date Received	
8a. Clerk	**8b.** Bin Number
9a. Carrier	**9b.** Route Number
Customer Option A Only	
Carrier: Accumulated mail has been picked up. **10a.** Resume delivery on (date) ______ **10b.** By: ______	

continued on next page

Part B – Forms Completion

continued

1. The customer's name is Helen Crump, the clerk's name is Alicia Peterson, and the carrier's name is Carlos Rodriguez. Where would Alicia Peterson's name be entered on this form?
   A. Box 1
   B. Box 8a
   C. Box 9a
   D. None of the above

2. The customer's name is Helen Crump, the clerk's name is Alicia Peterson, and the carrier's name is Carlos Rodriguez. Where would Helen Crump's name be entered on this form?
   A. Box 1
   B. Box 8a
   C. Box 9a
   D. None of the above

3. The customer's name is Helen Crump, the clerk's name is Alicia Peterson, and the carrier's name is Carlos Rodriguez. Where would Carlos Rodriguez's name be entered on this form?
   A. Box 1
   B. Box 8a
   C. Box 9a
   D. None of the above

4. How would you indicate that you want your accumulated mail delivered on 3/13/05 and that you want your normal delivery to resume on that date?
   A. Enter 3/13/05 in Box 3b.
   B. Check "Option B" in Box 5.
   C. Enter 3/13/05 on Line 10a.
   D. Enter 3/13/05 in Box 3b and check "Option B" in Box 5.

5. If Option A in Box 4 is checked, which of these is correct?
   A. The accumulated mail should be delivered on the date specified.
   B. The accumulated mail should be delivered and delivery should resume on the date specified.
   C. Mail should no longer be held as of the date specified.
   D. None of the above are correct.

6. A date would be an acceptable entry for each of these EXCEPT
   A. Box 3b
   B. Box 6
   C. Box 7
   D. Line 10a

continued on next page

Part B – Forms Completion

continued

EXPRESS MAIL — Mailing Label

ORIGIN (POSTAL USE ONLY)			
PO ZIP Code **1a.**	Day of Delivery **1b.** ☐Next ☐Second	Flat Rate Envelope **1c.** ☐	
Date In **2a.**	**2b.** ☐Noon ☐3 PM	Postage **2c.** $	
Time In **3a.** ☐AM ☐PM	Military **3b.** 2nd Day 3rd Day	Return Receipt Fee **3c.**	
Weight **4a.** lbs. ozs.	Int'l Alpha Country Code **4b.**	COD Fee **4c.**	Insurance Fee **4d.**
No Delivery **5a.** ☐Wknd ☐Holiday	Acceptance Clerk Initials **5b.**	Total Postage & Fees **5c.** $	

DELIVERY (POSTAL USE ONLY)		
Delivery Attempt **1d.** Mo. Day	Time **1e.** ☐AM ☐PM	Employee Signature **1f.**
Delivery Attempt **2d.** Mo. Day	Time **2e.** ☐AM ☐PM	Employee Signature **2f.**
Delivery Attempt **3d.** Mo. Day	Time **3e.** ☐AM ☐PM	Employee Signature **3f.**

6. ☐ WAIVER OF SIGNATURE

NO DELIVERY ☐Weekend ☐Holiday

Customer Signature ______________________

CUSTOMER USE ONLY

Method of Payment **7a.** Express Mail corporate Acct. No.	Federal Agency Acct. No. or **7b.** Postal Service Acct. No.
8a. FROM: (PLEASE PRINT) PHONE: ____________	**8b.** TO: (PLEASE PRINT) PHONE: ____________ ZIP + 4: ______________________

continued on next page

7. An Express Mail is scheduled for delivery by noon the next day. How should this be noted?
   A. Write "Next" in Box 1d.
   B. Write "Next" in Box 2a.
   C. Check "Next" in Box 1b and "Noon" in Box 2b.
   D. Check box 5a

8. An Express Mail package was dropped off at the Post Office on 9/19/05 at 4:00 in the afternoon. How should the drop off time and date be noted?
   A. Write "9/19/05" in Box 2a, write "4:00" in Box 3a, and check "PM" in Box 3a.
   B. Write 9/19/05 in Box 2a and check "AM" in Box 3a.
   C. Write 9/19/05 in Box 1d and check "PM" in Box 1e.
   D. None of the above

9. Which of these could be an acceptable entry for Box 4d?
   A. 10/20/05
   B. 89705
   C. A check mark
   D. $17.65

10. Which of these could be an acceptable entry for Box 1c?
   A. 10/20/05
   B. 89705
   C. A check mark
   D. $17.65

11. Where would you enter the sender's address?
   A. Box 8a
   B. Box 8b
   C. Box 6
   D. The sender's address is not entered on this form.

12. Where does the clerk who accepts the package identify him/herself?
   A. Box 1a
   B. Box 1f
   C. Box 4b
   D. Box 5b

continued on next page

Part B – Forms Completion

<table>
<tr><th colspan="3">RETURN RECEIPT FOR MERCHANDISE</th></tr>
<tr><td>Postage</td><td>1.</td><td rowspan="4">5. Postmark Here</td></tr>
<tr><td>Return Receipt for Merchandise Fee</td><td>2.</td></tr>
<tr><td>Special Handling Fee</td><td>3.</td></tr>
<tr><td>Total Postage & Fees</td><td>4.</td></tr>
<tr><td colspan="3">6. Waiver of Signature ☐ YES ☐ NO</td></tr>
<tr><td colspan="3">7. Recipient's Name (Please print clearly)</td></tr>
<tr><td colspan="3">8. Street, Apt. No.; or P.O. Box</td></tr>
<tr><td colspan="3">9. City, State, ZIP + 4</td></tr>
</table>

continued on next page

13. Janet Cone does not want a waiver of signature. How should she indicate this?
    A. Check "YES" in Box 6
    B. Check "NO" in Box 6
    C. Make a note on the back of the form
    D. None of the above

14. Which of these would be an acceptable entry for Box 8?
    A. $13.57
    B. 07/18/05
    C. Ellen Montgomery
    D. P.O. Box 34778

15. Which of these would be an acceptable entry for Box 7?
    A. $13.57
    B. 07/18/05
    C. Ellen Montgomery
    D. P.O. Box 34778

16. Which of these would be an acceptable entry for Box 1?
    A. 19 47th St. Gulfport, AK
    B. 5:00 p.m.
    C. $29.50
    D. 70042-7899

17. Which of these would be an acceptable entry for Box 6?
    A. Janet Cone
    B. A check mark
    C. 12lbs. 4ozs.
    D. $29.78

18. Which of these would be an acceptable entry for Box 9?
    A. $35.67
    B. A check mark
    C. P.O. Box 1699
    D. Atlanta, GA 89320-6754

continued on next page

Part B – Forms Completion

continued

<table>
<tr><td colspan="7">Certificate of Bulk Mailing</td></tr>
<tr><td colspan="3">Fee for Certificate</td><td rowspan="4">Use Current Rate Chart</td><td colspan="3" rowspan="4">1. Meter stamp or postage (uncancelled) stamps in payment of fee to be affized here and cancelled by postmarking, including date.</td></tr>
<tr><td colspan="3">Up to 1,000 pieces</td></tr>
<tr><td colspan="3">For each additional 1,000 pieces, or fraction</td></tr>
<tr><td colspan="3">Duplicate Copy</td></tr>
<tr><td>2a. Number of identical pieces</td><td>2b. Class of mail</td><td>2c. Postage on each</td><td>2d. Number of pieces per lb.</td><td>2e. Total number of pounds</td><td>2f. Total postage paid</td><td>2g. Fee paid</td></tr>
<tr><td colspan="2">3a. Mailed for</td><td colspan="5">3b. Mailed by</td></tr>
<tr><td colspan="7">Postmaster's Certificate</td></tr>
<tr><td colspan="7">It is hereby certified that the above-described mailing has been received and number of pieces and postage verified.

4. ____
(Postmaster or Designee)</td></tr>
</table>

continued on next page

Part B – Forms Completion

continued

19. Where does the Postmaster sign this form?
    - A. Box 1
    - B. Box 3a
    - C. Box 3b
    - D. Line 4

20. Which of these would be an acceptable entry for Box 2d?
    - A. A check mark
    - B. 90843-6700
    - C. 620 Fawn Run Road
    - D. 35

21. How would you indicate that there are 5,000 identical pieces?
    - A. Enter 5,000 in Line 2a
    - B. Enter 5,000 in Line 2b
    - C. Enter 5,000 in Line 2e
    - D. Enter 5,000 in Line 2g

22. This mailing is to be sent by first class mail. Where would this be indicated?
    - A. Box 1
    - B. Box 2a
    - C. Box 2b
    - D. Box 2c

23. Where should total postage paid be entered?
    - A. Box 2a
    - B. Box 2c
    - C. Box 2f
    - D. Box 2g

24. Which of these would be an acceptable entry for Box 2c?
    - A. 55378-1123
    - B. $0.22
    - C. Sarah Rich
    - D. 11/24/04

continued on next page

Application to Mail at Nonprofit Standard Mail Rates

Part 1 *(For completion by applicant)*

No application fee is required. All information must be complete and typewritten or printed legibly.

1. Complete name of organization *(If voting registration official, include title.)*

2. Street address of organization *(Include apartment or suite number.)*

3. City, state, ZIP+4 code

4a. Telephone *(Include area code.)*

4b. Name of applicant *(Must represent applying organization.)*

5. Type of organization *(Check only one.)*

☐ Religious ☐ Scientific ☐ Agricultural ☐ Veterans' ☐ Qualified political committee
☐ Educational ☐ Philanthropic ☐ Labor ☐ Fraternal ☐ Voting registration official

6. Is this a for-profit organization or does any of the net income inure to the benefit of any private stockholder or individual? ☐ Yes ☐ No

7a. Is this organization exempt from federal income tax? *(If 'Yes', attach a copy of the exemption issued by the Internal Revenue Service that shows the section of the IRS code under which the organization is exempt.)* ☐ Yes ☐ No

7b. Is an application for exempt status pending with the IRS? *(If 'Yes', attach a copy of the application to this form.)* ☐ Yes ☐ No

8. Has this organization previously mailed at the Nonprofit Standard Mail rates? *(If yes, list the Post Offices where mailings were most recently deposited at these rates?* ☐ Yes ☐ No

7c. Has the IRS denied or revoked the organization's federal tax exempt status? *(If 'Yes', attach a copy of the IRS ruling to this form.)* ☐ Yes ☐ No

9. Has your organization had Nonprofit Standard Mail rate mailing privileges denied or revoked? *(If 'Yes', list the Post Office [city and state] where the application was denied or authorization revoked.)* ☐ Yes ☐ No

10. Post Office (not a station or branch) where authorization requested and bulk mailings will be made *(City, state, ZIP code)*

11. Signature of applicant

12. Title

13. Date

Part 2 *(For completion by Postmaster at originating office where application filed)*

14. Signature of Postmaster *(Or designated representative)*

15. Date application filed with Post Office *(Round stamp)*

continued on next page

Part B – Forms Completion

continued

25. How should the type of organization applying be identified if it is devoted to the purpose of religious education?
    A. Check both the "Religious" and the "Educational" choices in Box 5.
    B. Check the "Educational" choice in Box 5 and also write a note about the religious aspect in Box 5.
    C. Check the "Religious" choice in Box 5 and write a note about the educational aspect also in Box 5.
    D. Check either the "Religious" or the "Educational" choice in Box 5, whichever seems more appropriate, but do not check both.

26. Which of these could be an appropriate entry for Box 1?
    A. William Haywood
    B. Calvary Methodist Church
    C. Carl Lee, Voting Registrar, Harris County, TX
    D. Both items B and C above

27. Where on this form is the amount of the application fee noted?
    A. Box 13
    B. Box 8
    C. There is no application fee.
    D. The amount of the fee is dependent upon the location of the Post Office and should therefore be written in Box 10 by the Postmaster.

28. Into which boxes should a city, state, and ZIP code be written?
    A. Boxes 3 and 10
    B. Boxes 2, 3, and 10
    C. Boxes 2, 3, 10 and 13
    D. None of the above

29. A telephone number could be entered into which box or boxes?
    A. Box 1
    B. Box 10
    C. Box 12
    D. None of the above

30. Where does the applicant sign this form?
    A. Box 1
    B. Box 11
    C. Box 13
    D. The applicant does not sign this form.

End of Part B – Forms Completion

PRACTICE EXAM #6

Part C – Coding & Memory

Part C tests your ability to use codes quickly and accurately both from a Coding Guide and from memory. This part of the exam consists of two sections as detailed below.

- The Coding Section has 36 questions to be answered in 6 minutes. During the Coding section, you will look at a Coding Guide to find answers. The Coding Section is broken down into several segments.
- The Memory Section has 36 questions to be answered in 7 minutes. During the Memory Section, you must answer from memory. The Memory Section is broken down into several segments.

The same Coding Guide will be used throughout both sections of Part C. Four delivery routes (identified by the codes A, B, C, and D) are listed on the Coding Guide. Also listed on the Coding Guide are various address ranges on several streets that are served by these delivery routes.

Each question is an address. To answer each question, you must identify the delivery route that serves the address, and mark as your answer the code (A, B, C, or D) for that delivery route.

Turn the page when you are ready to begin the first section, the Coding Section.

Part C – Coding & Memory

Coding Section

The Coding Section of Part C - Coding & Memory consists of 3 segments as detailed below.

- **Coding Section - Segment 1**
  The first segment is a 2 minute introductory exercise. This segment is not scored.
- **Coding Section - Segment 2**
  The second segment is a 90 second (1½ minutes) practice exercise. This segment is not scored.
- **Coding Section - Segment 3**
  The third segment is the actual Coding Section test. You have 6 minutes to answer 36 questions. This segment is scored.

The Coding Guide is displayed during all 3 segments. You will be instructed to mark answers for the first two unscored segments on sample answer sheets, not the actual answer sheet. You will be instructed to mark answers for the third segment, which is scored, on the actual answer sheet.

Turn to the next page when you are ready to begin Coding Section - Segment 1.

Part C – Coding & Memory

Coding Section – Segment 1

Instructions

Segment 1 of the Coding Section is an introductory exercise to acquaint you with how the questions are to be answered. In this segment, you have 2 minutes to answer 4 questions. The Coding Guide is displayed for your use in answering the questions. This segment is not scored. Mark your answers on the sample answer sheet at the bottom of the question page, not on the actual answer sheet.

Turn the page and begin when you are prepared to time yourself for exactly 2 minutes.

Part C – Coding & Memory

Coding Section – Segment 1

CODING GUIDE	
Address Range	**Delivery Route**
801 – 1240 Monmouth Dr. 3300 – 3699 Ince Blvd. 1 – 149 Ellington LN	A
1241 – 1300 Monmouth Dr. 150 – 299 Ellington LN	B
22 – 82 Tolling Wood Terrace 14500 – 16500 Sam Houston Toll RD 3700 – 3999 Ince Blvd.	C
All mail that doesn't fall in one of the address ranges listed above	D

Part C – Coding & Memory

Coding Section – Segment 1

continued

QUESTIONS

	Address	Delivery Route			
1.	14545 Sam Houston Toll RD	A	B	C	D
2.	302 Ellington LN	A	B	C	D
3.	3421 Ince Blvd.	A	B	C	D
4.	160 Ellington LN	A	B	C	D

SAMPLE ANSWER SHEET

1 Ⓐ Ⓑ Ⓒ Ⓓ
2 Ⓐ Ⓑ Ⓒ Ⓓ
3 Ⓐ Ⓑ Ⓒ Ⓓ
4 Ⓐ Ⓑ Ⓒ Ⓓ

The correct answers are 1-C, 2-D, 3-A, and 4-B.

Part C – Coding & Memory

Coding Section – Segment 2

Instructions

Segment 2 of the Coding Section is a practice exercise designed to expose you to the realistic timing demanded. In this segment, you have 90 seconds to answer 8 questions. The Coding Guide is displayed for your use in answering the questions. This segment is not scored. Mark your answers on the sample answer sheet at the bottom of the question page, not on the actual answer sheet.

Turn the page and begin when you are prepared to time yourself for exactly 90 seconds.

Part C – Coding & Memory

Coding Section – Segment 2

CODING GUIDE	
Address Range	**Delivery Route**
801 – 1240 Monmouth Dr. 3300 – 3699 Ince Blvd. 1 – 149 Ellington LN	A
1241 – 1300 Monmouth Dr. 150 – 299 Ellington LN	B
22 – 82 Tolling Wood Terrace 14500 – 16500 Sam Houston Toll RD 3700 – 3999 Ince Blvd.	C
All mail that doesn't fall in one of the address ranges listed above	D

Part C – Coding & Memory

Coding Section – Segment 2

continued

QUESTIONS

	Address	Delivery Route			
1.	3762 Ince Blvd.	A	B	C	D
2.	1258 Monmouth Dr.	A	B	C	D
3.	29 Tolling Wood Terrace	A	B	C	D
4.	967 Monmouth Dr.	A	B	C	D
5.	153 Wellington LN	A	B	C	D
6.	3456 Ince Blvd.	A	B	C	D
7.	20 Tolling Wood Terrace	A	B	C	D
8.	178 Ellington LN	A	B	C	D

SAMPLE ANSWER SHEET

1	A	B	C	D	5	A	B	C	D
2	A	B	C	D	6	A	B	C	D
3	A	B	C	D	7	A	B	C	D
4	A	B	C	D	8	A	B	C	D

The correct answers are 1-C, 2-B, 3-C, 4-A, 5-D, 6-A, 7-D, and 8-B.

Part C – Coding & Memory

Coding Section – Segment 3

Instructions

Segment 3 of the Coding Section is the actual Coding test. You have 6 minutes to answer 36 questions. The Coding Guide is displayed for your use in answering the questions. This segment is scored, and the score from this section does affect your overall Exam 473 score. Mark your answers on the actual answer sheet in the section titled Part C - Coding & Memory - Coding Section.

Turn the page and begin when you are prepared to time yourself for exactly 6 minutes.

Coding Section – Segment 3

CODING GUIDE	
Address Range	**Delivery Route**
801 – 1240 Monmouth Dr. 3300 – 3699 Ince Blvd. 1 – 149 Ellington LN	A
1241 – 1300 Monmouth Dr. 150 – 299 Ellington LN	B
22 – 82 Tolling Wood Terrace 14500 – 16500 Sam Houston Toll RD 3700 – 3999 Ince Blvd.	C
All mail that doesn't fall in one of the address ranges listed above	D

Coding Section – Segment 3

continued

Questions

	Address	Delivery Route			
1.	701 Monmouth Dr.	A	B	C	D
2.	3607 Ince Blvd.	A	B	C	D
3.	199 Ellington LN	A	B	C	D
4.	80 Tolling Wood Terrace	A	B	C	D
5.	822 Monmouth Dr.	A	B	C	D
6.	17500 Sam Houston Toll RD	A	B	C	D
7.	3906 Ince Blvd.	A	B	C	D
8.	92 Ellington LN	A	B	C	D
9.	16218 Sam Houston Toll RD	A	B	C	D
10.	1262 Monmouth Dr.	A	B	C	D
11.	25 Tolling Wild Terrace	A	B	C	D
12.	111 Ellington LN	A	B	C	D
13.	76 Tolling Wood Terrace	A	B	C	D
14.	3489 Ince Blvd.	A	B	C	D
15.	1294 Monmouth Dr.	A	B	C	D
16.	3820 Ince Blvd.	A	B	C	D
17.	1100 Monmouth Dr.	A	B	C	D
18.	253 Ellington LN	A	B	C	D

continued on next page

Coding Section – Segment 3

continued

CODING GUIDE	
Address Range	**Delivery Route**
801 – 1240 Monmouth Dr. 3300 – 3699 Ince Blvd. 1 – 149 Ellington LN	A
1241 – 1300 Monmouth Dr. 150 – 299 Ellington LN	B
22 – 82 Tolling Wood Terrace 14500 – 16500 Sam Houston Toll RD 3700 – 3999 Ince Blvd.	C
All mail that doesn't fall in one of the address ranges listed above	D

Coding Section – Segment 3

continued

Questions

	Address	Delivery Route			
19.	934 Monmouth Dr.	A	B	C	D
20.	41 Tolling Wood Terrace	A	B	C	D
21.	290 Ellington LN	A	B	C	D
22.	1650 Sam Houston Toll RD	A	B	C	D
23.	3890 Ince Blvd.	A	B	C	D
24.	1225 Monmouth Dr.	A	B	C	D
25.	227 Ellington LN	A	B	C	D
26.	3584 Ince Blvd.	A	B	C	D
27.	3741 Ince Blvd.	A	B	C	D
28.	1253 Mammoth Dr.	A	B	C	D
29.	16400 Sam Houston Toll RD	A	B	C	D
30.	27 Ellington LN	A	B	C	D
31.	54 Tolling Wood Terrace	A	B	C	D
32.	119 Ellington LN	A	B	C	D
33.	4220 Ince Blvd.	A	B	C	D
34.	3315 Ince Blvd.	A	B	C	D
35.	1279 Monmouth Dr.	A	B	C	D
36.	15289 Sam Houston Toll RD	A	B	C	D

End of Part C – Coding Section – Segment 3

Part C – Coding & Memory

Memory Section

The Memory Section of Part C - Coding & Memory consists of 4 segments as detailed below.

- **Memory Section - Segment 1**
  The first segment is a 3 minute study period during which you try to memorize the Coding Guide.
- **Memory Section - Segment 2**
  The second segment is a 90 second (1½ minutes) practice exercise. This segment is not scored.
- **Memory Section - Segment 3**
  The third segment is a 5 minute study period during which you try to memorize the Coding Guide.
- **Memory Section - Segment 4**
  This fourth segment is the actual Memory Section test. You have 7 minutes to answer 36 questions. This segment is scored.

There are no answers to mark during the first and third segments. You will be instructed to mark answers for the second segment on a sample answer sheet, not the actual answer sheet. You will be instructed to mark answers for the fourth segment, which is scored, on the actual answer sheet.

Turn to the next page when you are ready to begin Memory Section - Segment 1.

Part C – Coding & Memory

Memory Section – Segment 1

Instructions

Memory Section - Segment 1 is a 3 minute study period during which you try to memorize the information in the Coding Guide. There are no answers to mark during this study period.

Turn the page and begin studying when you are prepared to time yourself for exactly 3 minutes.

Part C – Coding & Memory

Memory Section – Segment 1

CODING GUIDE	
Address Range	**Delivery Route**
801 – 1240 Monmouth Dr. 3300 – 3699 Ince Blvd. 1 – 149 Ellington LN	A
1241 – 1300 Monmouth Dr. 150 – 299 Ellington LN	B
22 – 82 Tolling Wood Terrace 14500 – 16500 Sam Houston Toll RD 3700 – 3999 Ince Blvd.	C
All mail that doesn't fall in one of the address ranges listed above	D

Part C – Coding & Memory

Memory Section – Segment 2

Instructions

Segment 2 of the Memory Section is a practice exercise where you have 90 seconds to answer 8 questions from memory. The Coding Guide is not shown. You must answer from memory. This segment is not scored. Mark your answers on the sample answer sheet at the bottom of the page, not on the actual answer sheet.

Begin when you are prepared to time yourself for exactly 90 seconds.

Part C – Coding & Memory

Memory Section – Segment 2

QUESTIONS

	Address	Delivery Route			
1.	3940 Ince Blvd.	A	B	C	D
2.	136 Ellington LN	A	B	C	D
3.	31 Tolling Wood Terrace	A	B	C	D
4.	1220 Mammoth Dr.	A	B	C	D
5.	184 Ellington LN	A	B	C	D
6.	3352 Ince Blvd.	A	B	C	D
7.	1350 Sam Houston Toll RD	A	B	C	D
8.	1266 Monmouth Dr.	A	B	C	D

SAMPLE ANSWER SHEET

1 Ⓐ Ⓑ Ⓒ Ⓓ   5 Ⓐ Ⓑ Ⓒ Ⓓ
2 Ⓐ Ⓑ Ⓒ Ⓓ   6 Ⓐ Ⓑ Ⓒ Ⓓ
3 Ⓐ Ⓑ Ⓒ Ⓓ   7 Ⓐ Ⓑ Ⓒ Ⓓ
4 Ⓐ Ⓑ Ⓒ Ⓓ   8 Ⓐ Ⓑ Ⓒ Ⓓ

The correct answers are 1-C, 2-A, 3-C, 4-D, 5-B, 6-A, 7-D, and 8-B.

Part C – Coding & Memory

Memory Section – Segment 3

Instructions

Memory Section - Segment 3 is a 5 minute study period during which you try to memorize the information in the Coding Guide. There are no answers to mark during this study period.

Turn the page and begin studying when you are prepared to time yourself for exactly 5 minutes.

Part C – Coding & Memory

Memory Section – Segment 3

CODING GUIDE	
Address Range	**Delivery Route**
801 – 1240 Monmouth Dr. 3300 – 3699 Ince Blvd. 1 – 149 Ellington LN	A
1241 – 1300 Monmouth Dr. 150 – 299 Ellington LN	B
22 – 82 Tolling Wood Terrace 14500 – 16500 Sam Houston Toll RD 3700 – 3999 Ince Blvd.	C
All mail that doesn't fall in one of the address ranges listed above	D

Part C – Coding & Memory

Memory Section – Segment 4

Instructions

Memory Section - Segment 4 is the actual Memory test. You have 7 minutes to answer 36 questions. You must answer from memory. The Coding Guide is not shown. This segment is scored, and the score from this section does affect your overall Exam 473 score. Mark your answers on the actual answer sheet in the section titled Part C - Coding & Memory - Memory Section.

Turn the page and begin when you are prepared to time yourself for exactly 7 minutes.

Part C – Coding & Memory

Memory Section – Segment 4

Questions

	Address	Delivery Route			
37.	52 Tolling Wood Terrace	A	B	C	D
38.	129 Ellington LN	A	B	C	D
39.	16234 Sam Houston Toll RD	A	B	C	D
40.	196 Ellington LN	A	B	C	D
41.	3367 Inch St.	A	B	C	D
42.	812 Monmouth Dr.	A	B	C	D
43.	16550 Sam Houston Toll RD	A	B	C	D
44.	51 Ellington LN	A	B	C	D
45.	1271 Monmouth Dr.	A	B	C	D
46.	3390 Ince Blvd.	A	B	C	D
47.	72 Tolling Wood Terrace	A	B	C	D
48.	1204 Monmouth Dr.	A	B	C	D
49.	279 Ellington LN	A	B	C	D
50.	16000 Sam Houston Toll RD	A	B	C	D
51.	3480 Ince Blvd.	A	B	C	D
52.	35 Tolling Wood Place	A	B	C	D
53.	1290 Monmouth Dr.	A	B	C	D
54.	3900 Ince Blvd.	A	B	C	D

continued on next page

Part C – Coding & Memory

Memory Section – Segment 4

continued

Questions

	Address	Delivery Route			
55.	282 Ellington LN	A	B	C	D
56.	987 Monmouth Dr.	A	B	C	D
57.	15500 Sam Houston Toll RD	A	B	C	D
58.	66 Tolling Wood Terrace	A	B	C	D
59.	3849 Ince Blvd.	A	B	C	D
60.	130 Ellington LN	A	B	C	D
61.	3512 Ince Blvd.	A	B	C	D
62.	35 Tolling Wood Terrace	A	B	C	D
63.	3841 Inch Blvd.	A	B	C	D
64.	144 Ellington LN	A	B	C	D
65.	3670 Ince Blvd.	A	B	C	D
66.	244 Ellington LN	A	B	C	D
67.	14800 Sam Houston Toll RD	A	B	C	D
68.	81 Rolling Wood Terrace	A	B	C	D
69.	1140 Monmouth Dr.	A	B	C	D
70.	3730 Ince Blvd.	A	B	C	D
71.	2849 Main St.	A	B	C	D
72.	1280 Monmouth Dr.	A	B	C	D

End of Part C – Memory Section – Segment 4

Part D – Personal Characteristics & Experience Inventory

As explained in the guide, it is not possible to practice or prepare for Part D. There are no right or wrong answers, and speed is not an issue. For each question, you simply select the answer that best reflects your own individual personality, temperament, experience, etc.

Since it is not possible to practice or prepare for Part D, no Personal Characteristics & Experience Inventory sample questions are included in this practice exam.

Exam 473 Practice Answer Sheet

Answer Sheet Format

When taking the real exam, you fill in information and mark answers on both the front and back of the answer sheet. For realistic practice value, this practice answer sheet is laid out exactly like the real thing. Below are details on what you mark on the answer sheet and where you mark it:

- Front of answer sheet
  - → You fill in information (similar to what you provided when applying for the exam) at the top.
  - → You mark answers for the Address Checking and Forms Completion questions at the bottom.
- Back of answer sheet
  - → You mark answers for the Coding & Memory questions at the top.
  - → You mark answers for the Personality Characteristics & Experience Inventory questions at the bottom.

This page is the front page of the answer sheet. Here at the top of the front page is where (if you were taking the real exam) you would fill in information similar to what you provided when applying. Below, at the bottom of this page, is where you mark answers for the Address Checking and Forms Completion questions.

On the back side of this page is where you mark answers for the Coding & Memory questions at the top and mark answers for the Personality Characteristics & Experience Inventory questions at the bottom.

Ink Color

On real Postal exams, the answer sheets are printed on white paper, but the ink color varies from one test to another. On different exams, the ink may be blue, green, pink, and so on. This is not terribly important, and it should not affect your performance on the exam, but we wanted to make you aware so you will not be surprised by the appearance of the actual answer sheet.

Mark answers for the Address Checking and Forms Completion questions below.

Part A – Address Checking

1 Ⓐ Ⓑ Ⓒ Ⓓ	11 Ⓐ Ⓑ Ⓒ Ⓓ	21 Ⓐ Ⓑ Ⓒ Ⓓ	31 Ⓐ Ⓑ Ⓒ Ⓓ	41 Ⓐ Ⓑ Ⓒ Ⓓ	51 Ⓐ Ⓑ Ⓒ Ⓓ
2 Ⓐ Ⓑ Ⓒ Ⓓ	12 Ⓐ Ⓑ Ⓒ Ⓓ	22 Ⓐ Ⓑ Ⓒ Ⓓ	32 Ⓐ Ⓑ Ⓒ Ⓓ	42 Ⓐ Ⓑ Ⓒ Ⓓ	52 Ⓐ Ⓑ Ⓒ Ⓓ
3 Ⓐ Ⓑ Ⓒ Ⓓ	13 Ⓐ Ⓑ Ⓒ Ⓓ	23 Ⓐ Ⓑ Ⓒ Ⓓ	33 Ⓐ Ⓑ Ⓒ Ⓓ	43 Ⓐ Ⓑ Ⓒ Ⓓ	53 Ⓐ Ⓑ Ⓒ Ⓓ
4 Ⓐ Ⓑ Ⓒ Ⓓ	14 Ⓐ Ⓑ Ⓒ Ⓓ	24 Ⓐ Ⓑ Ⓒ Ⓓ	34 Ⓐ Ⓑ Ⓒ Ⓓ	44 Ⓐ Ⓑ Ⓒ Ⓓ	54 Ⓐ Ⓑ Ⓒ Ⓓ
5 Ⓐ Ⓑ Ⓒ Ⓓ	15 Ⓐ Ⓑ Ⓒ Ⓓ	25 Ⓐ Ⓑ Ⓒ Ⓓ	35 Ⓐ Ⓑ Ⓒ Ⓓ	45 Ⓐ Ⓑ Ⓒ Ⓓ	55 Ⓐ Ⓑ Ⓒ Ⓓ
6 Ⓐ Ⓑ Ⓒ Ⓓ	16 Ⓐ Ⓑ Ⓒ Ⓓ	26 Ⓐ Ⓑ Ⓒ Ⓓ	36 Ⓐ Ⓑ Ⓒ Ⓓ	46 Ⓐ Ⓑ Ⓒ Ⓓ	56 Ⓐ Ⓑ Ⓒ Ⓓ
7 Ⓐ Ⓑ Ⓒ Ⓓ	17 Ⓐ Ⓑ Ⓒ Ⓓ	27 Ⓐ Ⓑ Ⓒ Ⓓ	37 Ⓐ Ⓑ Ⓒ Ⓓ	47 Ⓐ Ⓑ Ⓒ Ⓓ	57 Ⓐ Ⓑ Ⓒ Ⓓ
8 Ⓐ Ⓑ Ⓒ Ⓓ	18 Ⓐ Ⓑ Ⓒ Ⓓ	28 Ⓐ Ⓑ Ⓒ Ⓓ	38 Ⓐ Ⓑ Ⓒ Ⓓ	48 Ⓐ Ⓑ Ⓒ Ⓓ	58 Ⓐ Ⓑ Ⓒ Ⓓ
9 Ⓐ Ⓑ Ⓒ Ⓓ	19 Ⓐ Ⓑ Ⓒ Ⓓ	29 Ⓐ Ⓑ Ⓒ Ⓓ	39 Ⓐ Ⓑ Ⓒ Ⓓ	49 Ⓐ Ⓑ Ⓒ Ⓓ	59 Ⓐ Ⓑ Ⓒ Ⓓ
10 Ⓐ Ⓑ Ⓒ Ⓓ	20 Ⓐ Ⓑ Ⓒ Ⓓ	30 Ⓐ Ⓑ Ⓒ Ⓓ	40 Ⓐ Ⓑ Ⓒ Ⓓ	50 Ⓐ Ⓑ Ⓒ Ⓓ	60 Ⓐ Ⓑ Ⓒ Ⓓ

Part B – Forms Completion

1 Ⓐ Ⓑ Ⓒ Ⓓ	6 Ⓐ Ⓑ Ⓒ Ⓓ	11 Ⓐ Ⓑ Ⓒ Ⓓ	16 Ⓐ Ⓑ Ⓒ Ⓓ	21 Ⓐ Ⓑ Ⓒ Ⓓ	26 Ⓐ Ⓑ Ⓒ Ⓓ
2 Ⓐ Ⓑ Ⓒ Ⓓ	7 Ⓐ Ⓑ Ⓒ Ⓓ	12 Ⓐ Ⓑ Ⓒ Ⓓ	17 Ⓐ Ⓑ Ⓒ Ⓓ	22 Ⓐ Ⓑ Ⓒ Ⓓ	27 Ⓐ Ⓑ Ⓒ Ⓓ
3 Ⓐ Ⓑ Ⓒ Ⓓ	8 Ⓐ Ⓑ Ⓒ Ⓓ	13 Ⓐ Ⓑ Ⓒ Ⓓ	18 Ⓐ Ⓑ Ⓒ Ⓓ	23 Ⓐ Ⓑ Ⓒ Ⓓ	28 Ⓐ Ⓑ Ⓒ Ⓓ
4 Ⓐ Ⓑ Ⓒ Ⓓ	9 Ⓐ Ⓑ Ⓒ Ⓓ	14 Ⓐ Ⓑ Ⓒ Ⓓ	19 Ⓐ Ⓑ Ⓒ Ⓓ	24 Ⓐ Ⓑ Ⓒ Ⓓ	29 Ⓐ Ⓑ Ⓒ Ⓓ
5 Ⓐ Ⓑ Ⓒ Ⓓ	10 Ⓐ Ⓑ Ⓒ Ⓓ	15 Ⓐ Ⓑ Ⓒ Ⓓ	20 Ⓐ Ⓑ Ⓒ Ⓓ	25 Ⓐ Ⓑ Ⓒ Ⓓ	30 Ⓐ Ⓑ Ⓒ Ⓓ

Continued on next page →

Exam 473 Practice Answer Sheet

Continued from previous page

Part C – Coding & Memory

Coding Section

1 Ⓐ Ⓑ Ⓒ Ⓓ	13 Ⓐ Ⓑ Ⓒ Ⓓ	25 Ⓐ Ⓑ Ⓒ Ⓓ
2 Ⓐ Ⓑ Ⓒ Ⓓ	14 Ⓐ Ⓑ Ⓒ Ⓓ	26 Ⓐ Ⓑ Ⓒ Ⓓ
3 Ⓐ Ⓑ Ⓒ Ⓓ	15 Ⓐ Ⓑ Ⓒ Ⓓ	27 Ⓐ Ⓑ Ⓒ Ⓓ
4 Ⓐ Ⓑ Ⓒ Ⓓ	16 Ⓐ Ⓑ Ⓒ Ⓓ	28 Ⓐ Ⓑ Ⓒ Ⓓ
5 Ⓐ Ⓑ Ⓒ Ⓓ	17 Ⓐ Ⓑ Ⓒ Ⓓ	29 Ⓐ Ⓑ Ⓒ Ⓓ
6 Ⓐ Ⓑ Ⓒ Ⓓ	18 Ⓐ Ⓑ Ⓒ Ⓓ	30 Ⓐ Ⓑ Ⓒ Ⓓ
7 Ⓐ Ⓑ Ⓒ Ⓓ	19 Ⓐ Ⓑ Ⓒ Ⓓ	31 Ⓐ Ⓑ Ⓒ Ⓓ
8 Ⓐ Ⓑ Ⓒ Ⓓ	20 Ⓐ Ⓑ Ⓒ Ⓓ	32 Ⓐ Ⓑ Ⓒ Ⓓ
9 Ⓐ Ⓑ Ⓒ Ⓓ	21 Ⓐ Ⓑ Ⓒ Ⓓ	33 Ⓐ Ⓑ Ⓒ Ⓓ
10 Ⓐ Ⓑ Ⓒ Ⓓ	22 Ⓐ Ⓑ Ⓒ Ⓓ	34 Ⓐ Ⓑ Ⓒ Ⓓ
11 Ⓐ Ⓑ Ⓒ Ⓓ	23 Ⓐ Ⓑ Ⓒ Ⓓ	35 Ⓐ Ⓑ Ⓒ Ⓓ
12 Ⓐ Ⓑ Ⓒ Ⓓ	24 Ⓐ Ⓑ Ⓒ Ⓓ	36 Ⓐ Ⓑ Ⓒ Ⓓ

Memory Section

37 Ⓐ Ⓑ Ⓒ Ⓓ	49 Ⓐ Ⓑ Ⓒ Ⓓ	61 Ⓐ Ⓑ Ⓒ Ⓓ
38 Ⓐ Ⓑ Ⓒ Ⓓ	50 Ⓐ Ⓑ Ⓒ Ⓓ	62 Ⓐ Ⓑ Ⓒ Ⓓ
39 Ⓐ Ⓑ Ⓒ Ⓓ	51 Ⓐ Ⓑ Ⓒ Ⓓ	63 Ⓐ Ⓑ Ⓒ Ⓓ
40 Ⓐ Ⓑ Ⓒ Ⓓ	52 Ⓐ Ⓑ Ⓒ Ⓓ	64 Ⓐ Ⓑ Ⓒ Ⓓ
41 Ⓐ Ⓑ Ⓒ Ⓓ	53 Ⓐ Ⓑ Ⓒ Ⓓ	65 Ⓐ Ⓑ Ⓒ Ⓓ
42 Ⓐ Ⓑ Ⓒ Ⓓ	54 Ⓐ Ⓑ Ⓒ Ⓓ	66 Ⓐ Ⓑ Ⓒ Ⓓ
43 Ⓐ Ⓑ Ⓒ Ⓓ	55 Ⓐ Ⓑ Ⓒ Ⓓ	67 Ⓐ Ⓑ Ⓒ Ⓓ
44 Ⓐ Ⓑ Ⓒ Ⓓ	56 Ⓐ Ⓑ Ⓒ Ⓓ	68 Ⓐ Ⓑ Ⓒ Ⓓ
45 Ⓐ Ⓑ Ⓒ Ⓓ	57 Ⓐ Ⓑ Ⓒ Ⓓ	69 Ⓐ Ⓑ Ⓒ Ⓓ
46 Ⓐ Ⓑ Ⓒ Ⓓ	58 Ⓐ Ⓑ Ⓒ Ⓓ	70 Ⓐ Ⓑ Ⓒ Ⓓ
47 Ⓐ Ⓑ Ⓒ Ⓓ	59 Ⓐ Ⓑ Ⓒ Ⓓ	71 Ⓐ Ⓑ Ⓒ Ⓓ
48 Ⓐ Ⓑ Ⓒ Ⓓ	60 Ⓐ Ⓑ Ⓒ Ⓓ	72 Ⓐ Ⓑ Ⓒ Ⓓ

Part D – Personal Characteristics & Experience Inventory

When taking the actual exam, you would mark answers for the Personal Characteristics & Experience Inventory questions here. However, as explained in the guide, it is not really possible to practice or prepare for this part of the exam. With these questions, it is important that you simply answer honestly and sincerely. Therefore, Part D - Personal Characteristics & Experience Inventory was not included in our practice exams or on this practice answer sheet.

Exam 473 Practice Answer Sheet

Answer Sheet Format

When taking the real exam, you fill in information and mark answers on both the front and back of the answer sheet. For realistic practice value, this practice answer sheet is laid out exactly like the real thing. Below are details on what you mark on the answer sheet and where you mark it:

- Front of answer sheet
  - → You fill in information (similar to what you provided when applying for the exam) at the top.
  - → You mark answers for the Address Checking and Forms Completion questions at the bottom.
- Back of answer sheet
  - → You mark answers for the Coding & Memory questions at the top.
  - → You mark answers for the Personality Characteristics & Experience Inventory questions at the bottom.

This page is the front page of the answer sheet. Here at the top of the front page is where (if you were taking the real exam) you would fill in information similar to what you provided when applying. Below, at the bottom of this page, is where you mark answers for the Address Checking and Forms Completion questions.

On the back side of this page is where you mark answers for the Coding & Memory questions at the top and mark answers for the Personality Characteristics & Experience Inventory questions at the bottom.

Ink Color

On real Postal exams, the answer sheets are printed on white paper, but the ink color varies from one test to another. On different exams, the ink may be blue, green, pink, and so on. This is not terribly important, and it should not affect your performance on the exam, but we wanted to make you aware so you will not be surprised by the appearance of the actual answer sheet.

Mark answers for the Address Checking and Forms Completion questions below.

Part A – Address Checking

1 Ⓐ Ⓑ Ⓒ Ⓓ	11 Ⓐ Ⓑ Ⓒ Ⓓ	21 Ⓐ Ⓑ Ⓒ Ⓓ	31 Ⓐ Ⓑ Ⓒ Ⓓ	41 Ⓐ Ⓑ Ⓒ Ⓓ	51 Ⓐ Ⓑ Ⓒ Ⓓ
2 Ⓐ Ⓑ Ⓒ Ⓓ	12 Ⓐ Ⓑ Ⓒ Ⓓ	22 Ⓐ Ⓑ Ⓒ Ⓓ	32 Ⓐ Ⓑ Ⓒ Ⓓ	42 Ⓐ Ⓑ Ⓒ Ⓓ	52 Ⓐ Ⓑ Ⓒ Ⓓ
3 Ⓐ Ⓑ Ⓒ Ⓓ	13 Ⓐ Ⓑ Ⓒ Ⓓ	23 Ⓐ Ⓑ Ⓒ Ⓓ	33 Ⓐ Ⓑ Ⓒ Ⓓ	43 Ⓐ Ⓑ Ⓒ Ⓓ	53 Ⓐ Ⓑ Ⓒ Ⓓ
4 Ⓐ Ⓑ Ⓒ Ⓓ	14 Ⓐ Ⓑ Ⓒ Ⓓ	24 Ⓐ Ⓑ Ⓒ Ⓓ	34 Ⓐ Ⓑ Ⓒ Ⓓ	44 Ⓐ Ⓑ Ⓒ Ⓓ	54 Ⓐ Ⓑ Ⓒ Ⓓ
5 Ⓐ Ⓑ Ⓒ Ⓓ	15 Ⓐ Ⓑ Ⓒ Ⓓ	25 Ⓐ Ⓑ Ⓒ Ⓓ	35 Ⓐ Ⓑ Ⓒ Ⓓ	45 Ⓐ Ⓑ Ⓒ Ⓓ	55 Ⓐ Ⓑ Ⓒ Ⓓ
6 Ⓐ Ⓑ Ⓒ Ⓓ	16 Ⓐ Ⓑ Ⓒ Ⓓ	26 Ⓐ Ⓑ Ⓒ Ⓓ	36 Ⓐ Ⓑ Ⓒ Ⓓ	46 Ⓐ Ⓑ Ⓒ Ⓓ	56 Ⓐ Ⓑ Ⓒ Ⓓ
7 Ⓐ Ⓑ Ⓒ Ⓓ	17 Ⓐ Ⓑ Ⓒ Ⓓ	27 Ⓐ Ⓑ Ⓒ Ⓓ	37 Ⓐ Ⓑ Ⓒ Ⓓ	47 Ⓐ Ⓑ Ⓒ Ⓓ	57 Ⓐ Ⓑ Ⓒ Ⓓ
8 Ⓐ Ⓑ Ⓒ Ⓓ	18 Ⓐ Ⓑ Ⓒ Ⓓ	28 Ⓐ Ⓑ Ⓒ Ⓓ	38 Ⓐ Ⓑ Ⓒ Ⓓ	48 Ⓐ Ⓑ Ⓒ Ⓓ	58 Ⓐ Ⓑ Ⓒ Ⓓ
9 Ⓐ Ⓑ Ⓒ Ⓓ	19 Ⓐ Ⓑ Ⓒ Ⓓ	29 Ⓐ Ⓑ Ⓒ Ⓓ	39 Ⓐ Ⓑ Ⓒ Ⓓ	49 Ⓐ Ⓑ Ⓒ Ⓓ	59 Ⓐ Ⓑ Ⓒ Ⓓ
10 Ⓐ Ⓑ Ⓒ Ⓓ	20 Ⓐ Ⓑ Ⓒ Ⓓ	30 Ⓐ Ⓑ Ⓒ Ⓓ	40 Ⓐ Ⓑ Ⓒ Ⓓ	50 Ⓐ Ⓑ Ⓒ Ⓓ	60 Ⓐ Ⓑ Ⓒ Ⓓ

Part B – Forms Completion

1 Ⓐ Ⓑ Ⓒ Ⓓ	6 Ⓐ Ⓑ Ⓒ Ⓓ	11 Ⓐ Ⓑ Ⓒ Ⓓ	16 Ⓐ Ⓑ Ⓒ Ⓓ	21 Ⓐ Ⓑ Ⓒ Ⓓ	26 Ⓐ Ⓑ Ⓒ Ⓓ
2 Ⓐ Ⓑ Ⓒ Ⓓ	7 Ⓐ Ⓑ Ⓒ Ⓓ	12 Ⓐ Ⓑ Ⓒ Ⓓ	17 Ⓐ Ⓑ Ⓒ Ⓓ	22 Ⓐ Ⓑ Ⓒ Ⓓ	27 Ⓐ Ⓑ Ⓒ Ⓓ
3 Ⓐ Ⓑ Ⓒ Ⓓ	8 Ⓐ Ⓑ Ⓒ Ⓓ	13 Ⓐ Ⓑ Ⓒ Ⓓ	18 Ⓐ Ⓑ Ⓒ Ⓓ	23 Ⓐ Ⓑ Ⓒ Ⓓ	28 Ⓐ Ⓑ Ⓒ Ⓓ
4 Ⓐ Ⓑ Ⓒ Ⓓ	9 Ⓐ Ⓑ Ⓒ Ⓓ	14 Ⓐ Ⓑ Ⓒ Ⓓ	19 Ⓐ Ⓑ Ⓒ Ⓓ	24 Ⓐ Ⓑ Ⓒ Ⓓ	29 Ⓐ Ⓑ Ⓒ Ⓓ
5 Ⓐ Ⓑ Ⓒ Ⓓ	10 Ⓐ Ⓑ Ⓒ Ⓓ	15 Ⓐ Ⓑ Ⓒ Ⓓ	20 Ⓐ Ⓑ Ⓒ Ⓓ	25 Ⓐ Ⓑ Ⓒ Ⓓ	30 Ⓐ Ⓑ Ⓒ Ⓓ

Continued on next page →

Exam 473 Practice Answer Sheet

Continued from previous page

Part C – Coding & Memory

Coding Section

1 Ⓐ Ⓑ Ⓒ Ⓓ	13 Ⓐ Ⓑ Ⓒ Ⓓ	25 Ⓐ Ⓑ Ⓒ Ⓓ
2 Ⓐ Ⓑ Ⓒ Ⓓ	14 Ⓐ Ⓑ Ⓒ Ⓓ	26 Ⓐ Ⓑ Ⓒ Ⓓ
3 Ⓐ Ⓑ Ⓒ Ⓓ	15 Ⓐ Ⓑ Ⓒ Ⓓ	27 Ⓐ Ⓑ Ⓒ Ⓓ
4 Ⓐ Ⓑ Ⓒ Ⓓ	16 Ⓐ Ⓑ Ⓒ Ⓓ	28 Ⓐ Ⓑ Ⓒ Ⓓ
5 Ⓐ Ⓑ Ⓒ Ⓓ	17 Ⓐ Ⓑ Ⓒ Ⓓ	29 Ⓐ Ⓑ Ⓒ Ⓓ
6 Ⓐ Ⓑ Ⓒ Ⓓ	18 Ⓐ Ⓑ Ⓒ Ⓓ	30 Ⓐ Ⓑ Ⓒ Ⓓ
7 Ⓐ Ⓑ Ⓒ Ⓓ	19 Ⓐ Ⓑ Ⓒ Ⓓ	31 Ⓐ Ⓑ Ⓒ Ⓓ
8 Ⓐ Ⓑ Ⓒ Ⓓ	20 Ⓐ Ⓑ Ⓒ Ⓓ	32 Ⓐ Ⓑ Ⓒ Ⓓ
9 Ⓐ Ⓑ Ⓒ Ⓓ	21 Ⓐ Ⓑ Ⓒ Ⓓ	33 Ⓐ Ⓑ Ⓒ Ⓓ
10 Ⓐ Ⓑ Ⓒ Ⓓ	22 Ⓐ Ⓑ Ⓒ Ⓓ	34 Ⓐ Ⓑ Ⓒ Ⓓ
11 Ⓐ Ⓑ Ⓒ Ⓓ	23 Ⓐ Ⓑ Ⓒ Ⓓ	35 Ⓐ Ⓑ Ⓒ Ⓓ
12 Ⓐ Ⓑ Ⓒ Ⓓ	24 Ⓐ Ⓑ Ⓒ Ⓓ	36 Ⓐ Ⓑ Ⓒ Ⓓ

Memory Section

37 Ⓐ Ⓑ Ⓒ Ⓓ	49 Ⓐ Ⓑ Ⓒ Ⓓ	61 Ⓐ Ⓑ Ⓒ Ⓓ
38 Ⓐ Ⓑ Ⓒ Ⓓ	50 Ⓐ Ⓑ Ⓒ Ⓓ	62 Ⓐ Ⓑ Ⓒ Ⓓ
39 Ⓐ Ⓑ Ⓒ Ⓓ	51 Ⓐ Ⓑ Ⓒ Ⓓ	63 Ⓐ Ⓑ Ⓒ Ⓓ
40 Ⓐ Ⓑ Ⓒ Ⓓ	52 Ⓐ Ⓑ Ⓒ Ⓓ	64 Ⓐ Ⓑ Ⓒ Ⓓ
41 Ⓐ Ⓑ Ⓒ Ⓓ	53 Ⓐ Ⓑ Ⓒ Ⓓ	65 Ⓐ Ⓑ Ⓒ Ⓓ
42 Ⓐ Ⓑ Ⓒ Ⓓ	54 Ⓐ Ⓑ Ⓒ Ⓓ	66 Ⓐ Ⓑ Ⓒ Ⓓ
43 Ⓐ Ⓑ Ⓒ Ⓓ	55 Ⓐ Ⓑ Ⓒ Ⓓ	67 Ⓐ Ⓑ Ⓒ Ⓓ
44 Ⓐ Ⓑ Ⓒ Ⓓ	56 Ⓐ Ⓑ Ⓒ Ⓓ	68 Ⓐ Ⓑ Ⓒ Ⓓ
45 Ⓐ Ⓑ Ⓒ Ⓓ	57 Ⓐ Ⓑ Ⓒ Ⓓ	69 Ⓐ Ⓑ Ⓒ Ⓓ
46 Ⓐ Ⓑ Ⓒ Ⓓ	58 Ⓐ Ⓑ Ⓒ Ⓓ	70 Ⓐ Ⓑ Ⓒ Ⓓ
47 Ⓐ Ⓑ Ⓒ Ⓓ	59 Ⓐ Ⓑ Ⓒ Ⓓ	71 Ⓐ Ⓑ Ⓒ Ⓓ
48 Ⓐ Ⓑ Ⓒ Ⓓ	60 Ⓐ Ⓑ Ⓒ Ⓓ	72 Ⓐ Ⓑ Ⓒ Ⓓ

Part D – Personal Characteristics & Experience Inventory

When taking the actual exam, you would mark answers for the Personal Characteristics & Experience Inventory questions here. However, as explained in the guide, it is not really possible to practice or prepare for this part of the exam. With these questions, it is important that you simply answer honestly and sincerely. Therefore, Part D - Personal Characteristics & Experience Inventory was not included in our practice exams or on this practice answer sheet.

Exam 473 Practice Answer Sheet

Answer Sheet Format

When taking the real exam, you fill in information and mark answers on both the front and back of the answer sheet. For realistic practice value, this practice answer sheet is laid out exactly like the real thing. Below are details on what you mark on the answer sheet and where you mark it:

- Front of answer sheet
  → You fill in information (similar to what you provided when applying for the exam) at the top.
  → You mark answers for the Address Checking and Forms Completion questions at the bottom.

- Back of answer sheet
  → You mark answers for the Coding & Memory questions at the top.
  → You mark answers for the Personality Characteristics & Experience Inventory questions at the bottom.

This page is the front page of the answer sheet. Here at the top of the front page is where (if you were taking the real exam) you would fill in information similar to what you provided when applying. Below, at the bottom of this page, is where you mark answers for the Address Checking and Forms Completion questions.

On the back side of this page is where you mark answers for the Coding & Memory questions at the top and mark answers for the Personality Characteristics & Experience Inventory questions at the bottom.

Ink Color

On real Postal exams, the answer sheets are printed on white paper, but the ink color varies from one test to another. On different exams, the ink may be blue, green, pink, and so on. This is not terribly important, and it should not affect your performance on the exam, but we wanted to make you aware so you will not be surprised by the appearance of the actual answer sheet.

Mark answers for the Address Checking and Forms Completion questions below.

Part A – Address Checking

1 Ⓐ Ⓑ Ⓒ Ⓓ	11 Ⓐ Ⓑ Ⓒ Ⓓ	21 Ⓐ Ⓑ Ⓒ Ⓓ	31 Ⓐ Ⓑ Ⓒ Ⓓ	41 Ⓐ Ⓑ Ⓒ Ⓓ	51 Ⓐ Ⓑ Ⓒ Ⓓ
2 Ⓐ Ⓑ Ⓒ Ⓓ	12 Ⓐ Ⓑ Ⓒ Ⓓ	22 Ⓐ Ⓑ Ⓒ Ⓓ	32 Ⓐ Ⓑ Ⓒ Ⓓ	42 Ⓐ Ⓑ Ⓒ Ⓓ	52 Ⓐ Ⓑ Ⓒ Ⓓ
3 Ⓐ Ⓑ Ⓒ Ⓓ	13 Ⓐ Ⓑ Ⓒ Ⓓ	23 Ⓐ Ⓑ Ⓒ Ⓓ	33 Ⓐ Ⓑ Ⓒ Ⓓ	43 Ⓐ Ⓑ Ⓒ Ⓓ	53 Ⓐ Ⓑ Ⓒ Ⓓ
4 Ⓐ Ⓑ Ⓒ Ⓓ	14 Ⓐ Ⓑ Ⓒ Ⓓ	24 Ⓐ Ⓑ Ⓒ Ⓓ	34 Ⓐ Ⓑ Ⓒ Ⓓ	44 Ⓐ Ⓑ Ⓒ Ⓓ	54 Ⓐ Ⓑ Ⓒ Ⓓ
5 Ⓐ Ⓑ Ⓒ Ⓓ	15 Ⓐ Ⓑ Ⓒ Ⓓ	25 Ⓐ Ⓑ Ⓒ Ⓓ	35 Ⓐ Ⓑ Ⓒ Ⓓ	45 Ⓐ Ⓑ Ⓒ Ⓓ	55 Ⓐ Ⓑ Ⓒ Ⓓ
6 Ⓐ Ⓑ Ⓒ Ⓓ	16 Ⓐ Ⓑ Ⓒ Ⓓ	26 Ⓐ Ⓑ Ⓒ Ⓓ	36 Ⓐ Ⓑ Ⓒ Ⓓ	46 Ⓐ Ⓑ Ⓒ Ⓓ	56 Ⓐ Ⓑ Ⓒ Ⓓ
7 Ⓐ Ⓑ Ⓒ Ⓓ	17 Ⓐ Ⓑ Ⓒ Ⓓ	27 Ⓐ Ⓑ Ⓒ Ⓓ	37 Ⓐ Ⓑ Ⓒ Ⓓ	47 Ⓐ Ⓑ Ⓒ Ⓓ	57 Ⓐ Ⓑ Ⓒ Ⓓ
8 Ⓐ Ⓑ Ⓒ Ⓓ	18 Ⓐ Ⓑ Ⓒ Ⓓ	28 Ⓐ Ⓑ Ⓒ Ⓓ	38 Ⓐ Ⓑ Ⓒ Ⓓ	48 Ⓐ Ⓑ Ⓒ Ⓓ	58 Ⓐ Ⓑ Ⓒ Ⓓ
9 Ⓐ Ⓑ Ⓒ Ⓓ	19 Ⓐ Ⓑ Ⓒ Ⓓ	29 Ⓐ Ⓑ Ⓒ Ⓓ	39 Ⓐ Ⓑ Ⓒ Ⓓ	49 Ⓐ Ⓑ Ⓒ Ⓓ	59 Ⓐ Ⓑ Ⓒ Ⓓ
10 Ⓐ Ⓑ Ⓒ Ⓓ	20 Ⓐ Ⓑ Ⓒ Ⓓ	30 Ⓐ Ⓑ Ⓒ Ⓓ	40 Ⓐ Ⓑ Ⓒ Ⓓ	50 Ⓐ Ⓑ Ⓒ Ⓓ	60 Ⓐ Ⓑ Ⓒ Ⓓ

Part B – Forms Completion

1 Ⓐ Ⓑ Ⓒ Ⓓ	6 Ⓐ Ⓑ Ⓒ Ⓓ	11 Ⓐ Ⓑ Ⓒ Ⓓ	16 Ⓐ Ⓑ Ⓒ Ⓓ	21 Ⓐ Ⓑ Ⓒ Ⓓ	26 Ⓐ Ⓑ Ⓒ Ⓓ
2 Ⓐ Ⓑ Ⓒ Ⓓ	7 Ⓐ Ⓑ Ⓒ Ⓓ	12 Ⓐ Ⓑ Ⓒ Ⓓ	17 Ⓐ Ⓑ Ⓒ Ⓓ	22 Ⓐ Ⓑ Ⓒ Ⓓ	27 Ⓐ Ⓑ Ⓒ Ⓓ
3 Ⓐ Ⓑ Ⓒ Ⓓ	8 Ⓐ Ⓑ Ⓒ Ⓓ	13 Ⓐ Ⓑ Ⓒ Ⓓ	18 Ⓐ Ⓑ Ⓒ Ⓓ	23 Ⓐ Ⓑ Ⓒ Ⓓ	28 Ⓐ Ⓑ Ⓒ Ⓓ
4 Ⓐ Ⓑ Ⓒ Ⓓ	9 Ⓐ Ⓑ Ⓒ Ⓓ	14 Ⓐ Ⓑ Ⓒ Ⓓ	19 Ⓐ Ⓑ Ⓒ Ⓓ	24 Ⓐ Ⓑ Ⓒ Ⓓ	29 Ⓐ Ⓑ Ⓒ Ⓓ
5 Ⓐ Ⓑ Ⓒ Ⓓ	10 Ⓐ Ⓑ Ⓒ Ⓓ	15 Ⓐ Ⓑ Ⓒ Ⓓ	20 Ⓐ Ⓑ Ⓒ Ⓓ	25 Ⓐ Ⓑ Ⓒ Ⓓ	30 Ⓐ Ⓑ Ⓒ Ⓓ

Continued on next page →

Exam 473 Practice Answer Sheet

Continued from previous page

Part C – Coding & Memory

Coding Section

1 Ⓐ Ⓑ Ⓒ Ⓓ	13 Ⓐ Ⓑ Ⓒ Ⓓ	25 Ⓐ Ⓑ Ⓒ Ⓓ
2 Ⓐ Ⓑ Ⓒ Ⓓ	14 Ⓐ Ⓑ Ⓒ Ⓓ	26 Ⓐ Ⓑ Ⓒ Ⓓ
3 Ⓐ Ⓑ Ⓒ Ⓓ	15 Ⓐ Ⓑ Ⓒ Ⓓ	27 Ⓐ Ⓑ Ⓒ Ⓓ
4 Ⓐ Ⓑ Ⓒ Ⓓ	16 Ⓐ Ⓑ Ⓒ Ⓓ	28 Ⓐ Ⓑ Ⓒ Ⓓ
5 Ⓐ Ⓑ Ⓒ Ⓓ	17 Ⓐ Ⓑ Ⓒ Ⓓ	29 Ⓐ Ⓑ Ⓒ Ⓓ
6 Ⓐ Ⓑ Ⓒ Ⓓ	18 Ⓐ Ⓑ Ⓒ Ⓓ	30 Ⓐ Ⓑ Ⓒ Ⓓ
7 Ⓐ Ⓑ Ⓒ Ⓓ	19 Ⓐ Ⓑ Ⓒ Ⓓ	31 Ⓐ Ⓑ Ⓒ Ⓓ
8 Ⓐ Ⓑ Ⓒ Ⓓ	20 Ⓐ Ⓑ Ⓒ Ⓓ	32 Ⓐ Ⓑ Ⓒ Ⓓ
9 Ⓐ Ⓑ Ⓒ Ⓓ	21 Ⓐ Ⓑ Ⓒ Ⓓ	33 Ⓐ Ⓑ Ⓒ Ⓓ
10 Ⓐ Ⓑ Ⓒ Ⓓ	22 Ⓐ Ⓑ Ⓒ Ⓓ	34 Ⓐ Ⓑ Ⓒ Ⓓ
11 Ⓐ Ⓑ Ⓒ Ⓓ	23 Ⓐ Ⓑ Ⓒ Ⓓ	35 Ⓐ Ⓑ Ⓒ Ⓓ
12 Ⓐ Ⓑ Ⓒ Ⓓ	24 Ⓐ Ⓑ Ⓒ Ⓓ	36 Ⓐ Ⓑ Ⓒ Ⓓ

Memory Section

37 Ⓐ Ⓑ Ⓒ Ⓓ	49 Ⓐ Ⓑ Ⓒ Ⓓ	61 Ⓐ Ⓑ Ⓒ Ⓓ
38 Ⓐ Ⓑ Ⓒ Ⓓ	50 Ⓐ Ⓑ Ⓒ Ⓓ	62 Ⓐ Ⓑ Ⓒ Ⓓ
39 Ⓐ Ⓑ Ⓒ Ⓓ	51 Ⓐ Ⓑ Ⓒ Ⓓ	63 Ⓐ Ⓑ Ⓒ Ⓓ
40 Ⓐ Ⓑ Ⓒ Ⓓ	52 Ⓐ Ⓑ Ⓒ Ⓓ	64 Ⓐ Ⓑ Ⓒ Ⓓ
41 Ⓐ Ⓑ Ⓒ Ⓓ	53 Ⓐ Ⓑ Ⓒ Ⓓ	65 Ⓐ Ⓑ Ⓒ Ⓓ
42 Ⓐ Ⓑ Ⓒ Ⓓ	54 Ⓐ Ⓑ Ⓒ Ⓓ	66 Ⓐ Ⓑ Ⓒ Ⓓ
43 Ⓐ Ⓑ Ⓒ Ⓓ	55 Ⓐ Ⓑ Ⓒ Ⓓ	67 Ⓐ Ⓑ Ⓒ Ⓓ
44 Ⓐ Ⓑ Ⓒ Ⓓ	56 Ⓐ Ⓑ Ⓒ Ⓓ	68 Ⓐ Ⓑ Ⓒ Ⓓ
45 Ⓐ Ⓑ Ⓒ Ⓓ	57 Ⓐ Ⓑ Ⓒ Ⓓ	69 Ⓐ Ⓑ Ⓒ Ⓓ
46 Ⓐ Ⓑ Ⓒ Ⓓ	58 Ⓐ Ⓑ Ⓒ Ⓓ	70 Ⓐ Ⓑ Ⓒ Ⓓ
47 Ⓐ Ⓑ Ⓒ Ⓓ	59 Ⓐ Ⓑ Ⓒ Ⓓ	71 Ⓐ Ⓑ Ⓒ Ⓓ
48 Ⓐ Ⓑ Ⓒ Ⓓ	60 Ⓐ Ⓑ Ⓒ Ⓓ	72 Ⓐ Ⓑ Ⓒ Ⓓ

Part D – Personal Characteristics & Experience Inventory

When taking the actual exam, you would mark answers for the Personal Characteristics & Experience Inventory questions here. However, as explained in the guide, it is not really possible to practice or prepare for this part of the exam. With these questions, it is important that you simply answer honestly and sincerely. Therefore, Part D - Personal Characteristics & Experience Inventory was not included in our practice exams or on this practice answer sheet.

Exam 473 Practice Answer Sheet

Answer Sheet Format

When taking the real exam, you fill in information and mark answers on both the front and back of the answer sheet. For realistic practice value, this practice answer sheet is laid out exactly like the real thing. Below are details on what you mark on the answer sheet and where you mark it:

- Front of answer sheet
  → You fill in information (similar to what you provided when applying for the exam) at the top.
  → You mark answers for the Address Checking and Forms Completion questions at the bottom.

- Back of answer sheet
  → You mark answers for the Coding & Memory questions at the top.
  → You mark answers for the Personality Characteristics & Experience Inventory questions at the bottom.

This page is the front page of the answer sheet. Here at the top of the front page is where (if you were taking the real exam) you would fill in information similar to what you provided when applying. Below, at the bottom of this page, is where you mark answers for the Address Checking and Forms Completion questions.

On the back side of this page is where you mark answers for the Coding & Memory questions at the top and mark answers for the Personality Characteristics & Experience Inventory questions at the bottom.

Ink Color

On real Postal exams, the answer sheets are printed on white paper, but the ink color varies from one test to another. On different exams, the ink may be blue, green, pink, and so on. This is not terribly important, and it should not affect your performance on the exam, but we wanted to make you aware so you will not be surprised by the appearance of the actual answer sheet.

Mark answers for the Address Checking and Forms Completion questions below.

Part A – Address Checking

1 Ⓐ Ⓑ Ⓒ Ⓓ	11 Ⓐ Ⓑ Ⓒ Ⓓ	21 Ⓐ Ⓑ Ⓒ Ⓓ	31 Ⓐ Ⓑ Ⓒ Ⓓ	41 Ⓐ Ⓑ Ⓒ Ⓓ	51 Ⓐ Ⓑ Ⓒ Ⓓ
2 Ⓐ Ⓑ Ⓒ Ⓓ	12 Ⓐ Ⓑ Ⓒ Ⓓ	22 Ⓐ Ⓑ Ⓒ Ⓓ	32 Ⓐ Ⓑ Ⓒ Ⓓ	42 Ⓐ Ⓑ Ⓒ Ⓓ	52 Ⓐ Ⓑ Ⓒ Ⓓ
3 Ⓐ Ⓑ Ⓒ Ⓓ	13 Ⓐ Ⓑ Ⓒ Ⓓ	23 Ⓐ Ⓑ Ⓒ Ⓓ	33 Ⓐ Ⓑ Ⓒ Ⓓ	43 Ⓐ Ⓑ Ⓒ Ⓓ	53 Ⓐ Ⓑ Ⓒ Ⓓ
4 Ⓐ Ⓑ Ⓒ Ⓓ	14 Ⓐ Ⓑ Ⓒ Ⓓ	24 Ⓐ Ⓑ Ⓒ Ⓓ	34 Ⓐ Ⓑ Ⓒ Ⓓ	44 Ⓐ Ⓑ Ⓒ Ⓓ	54 Ⓐ Ⓑ Ⓒ Ⓓ
5 Ⓐ Ⓑ Ⓒ Ⓓ	15 Ⓐ Ⓑ Ⓒ Ⓓ	25 Ⓐ Ⓑ Ⓒ Ⓓ	35 Ⓐ Ⓑ Ⓒ Ⓓ	45 Ⓐ Ⓑ Ⓒ Ⓓ	55 Ⓐ Ⓑ Ⓒ Ⓓ
6 Ⓐ Ⓑ Ⓒ Ⓓ	16 Ⓐ Ⓑ Ⓒ Ⓓ	26 Ⓐ Ⓑ Ⓒ Ⓓ	36 Ⓐ Ⓑ Ⓒ Ⓓ	46 Ⓐ Ⓑ Ⓒ Ⓓ	56 Ⓐ Ⓑ Ⓒ Ⓓ
7 Ⓐ Ⓑ Ⓒ Ⓓ	17 Ⓐ Ⓑ Ⓒ Ⓓ	27 Ⓐ Ⓑ Ⓒ Ⓓ	37 Ⓐ Ⓑ Ⓒ Ⓓ	47 Ⓐ Ⓑ Ⓒ Ⓓ	57 Ⓐ Ⓑ Ⓒ Ⓓ
8 Ⓐ Ⓑ Ⓒ Ⓓ	18 Ⓐ Ⓑ Ⓒ Ⓓ	28 Ⓐ Ⓑ Ⓒ Ⓓ	38 Ⓐ Ⓑ Ⓒ Ⓓ	48 Ⓐ Ⓑ Ⓒ Ⓓ	58 Ⓐ Ⓑ Ⓒ Ⓓ
9 Ⓐ Ⓑ Ⓒ Ⓓ	19 Ⓐ Ⓑ Ⓒ Ⓓ	29 Ⓐ Ⓑ Ⓒ Ⓓ	39 Ⓐ Ⓑ Ⓒ Ⓓ	49 Ⓐ Ⓑ Ⓒ Ⓓ	59 Ⓐ Ⓑ Ⓒ Ⓓ
10 Ⓐ Ⓑ Ⓒ Ⓓ	20 Ⓐ Ⓑ Ⓒ Ⓓ	30 Ⓐ Ⓑ Ⓒ Ⓓ	40 Ⓐ Ⓑ Ⓒ Ⓓ	50 Ⓐ Ⓑ Ⓒ Ⓓ	60 Ⓐ Ⓑ Ⓒ Ⓓ

Part B – Forms Completion

1 Ⓐ Ⓑ Ⓒ Ⓓ	6 Ⓐ Ⓑ Ⓒ Ⓓ	11 Ⓐ Ⓑ Ⓒ Ⓓ	16 Ⓐ Ⓑ Ⓒ Ⓓ	21 Ⓐ Ⓑ Ⓒ Ⓓ	26 Ⓐ Ⓑ Ⓒ Ⓓ
2 Ⓐ Ⓑ Ⓒ Ⓓ	7 Ⓐ Ⓑ Ⓒ Ⓓ	12 Ⓐ Ⓑ Ⓒ Ⓓ	17 Ⓐ Ⓑ Ⓒ Ⓓ	22 Ⓐ Ⓑ Ⓒ Ⓓ	27 Ⓐ Ⓑ Ⓒ Ⓓ
3 Ⓐ Ⓑ Ⓒ Ⓓ	8 Ⓐ Ⓑ Ⓒ Ⓓ	13 Ⓐ Ⓑ Ⓒ Ⓓ	18 Ⓐ Ⓑ Ⓒ Ⓓ	23 Ⓐ Ⓑ Ⓒ Ⓓ	28 Ⓐ Ⓑ Ⓒ Ⓓ
4 Ⓐ Ⓑ Ⓒ Ⓓ	9 Ⓐ Ⓑ Ⓒ Ⓓ	14 Ⓐ Ⓑ Ⓒ Ⓓ	19 Ⓐ Ⓑ Ⓒ Ⓓ	24 Ⓐ Ⓑ Ⓒ Ⓓ	29 Ⓐ Ⓑ Ⓒ Ⓓ
5 Ⓐ Ⓑ Ⓒ Ⓓ	10 Ⓐ Ⓑ Ⓒ Ⓓ	15 Ⓐ Ⓑ Ⓒ Ⓓ	20 Ⓐ Ⓑ Ⓒ Ⓓ	25 Ⓐ Ⓑ Ⓒ Ⓓ	30 Ⓐ Ⓑ Ⓒ Ⓓ

Continued on next page →

Exam 473 Practice Answer Sheet

Continued from previous page

Part C – Coding & Memory

Coding Section

1 Ⓐ Ⓑ Ⓒ Ⓓ
2 Ⓐ Ⓑ Ⓒ Ⓓ
3 Ⓐ Ⓑ Ⓒ Ⓓ
4 Ⓐ Ⓑ Ⓒ Ⓓ
5 Ⓐ Ⓑ Ⓒ Ⓓ
6 Ⓐ Ⓑ Ⓒ Ⓓ
7 Ⓐ Ⓑ Ⓒ Ⓓ
8 Ⓐ Ⓑ Ⓒ Ⓓ
9 Ⓐ Ⓑ Ⓒ Ⓓ
10 Ⓐ Ⓑ Ⓒ Ⓓ
11 Ⓐ Ⓑ Ⓒ Ⓓ
12 Ⓐ Ⓑ Ⓒ Ⓓ
13 Ⓐ Ⓑ Ⓒ Ⓓ
14 Ⓐ Ⓑ Ⓒ Ⓓ
15 Ⓐ Ⓑ Ⓒ Ⓓ
16 Ⓐ Ⓑ Ⓒ Ⓓ
17 Ⓐ Ⓑ Ⓒ Ⓓ
18 Ⓐ Ⓑ Ⓒ Ⓓ
19 Ⓐ Ⓑ Ⓒ Ⓓ
20 Ⓐ Ⓑ Ⓒ Ⓓ
21 Ⓐ Ⓑ Ⓒ Ⓓ
22 Ⓐ Ⓑ Ⓒ Ⓓ
23 Ⓐ Ⓑ Ⓒ Ⓓ
24 Ⓐ Ⓑ Ⓒ Ⓓ
25 Ⓐ Ⓑ Ⓒ Ⓓ
26 Ⓐ Ⓑ Ⓒ Ⓓ
27 Ⓐ Ⓑ Ⓒ Ⓓ
28 Ⓐ Ⓑ Ⓒ Ⓓ
29 Ⓐ Ⓑ Ⓒ Ⓓ
30 Ⓐ Ⓑ Ⓒ Ⓓ
31 Ⓐ Ⓑ Ⓒ Ⓓ
32 Ⓐ Ⓑ Ⓒ Ⓓ
33 Ⓐ Ⓑ Ⓒ Ⓓ
34 Ⓐ Ⓑ Ⓒ Ⓓ
35 Ⓐ Ⓑ Ⓒ Ⓓ
36 Ⓐ Ⓑ Ⓒ Ⓓ

Memory Section

37 Ⓐ Ⓑ Ⓒ Ⓓ
38 Ⓐ Ⓑ Ⓒ Ⓓ
39 Ⓐ Ⓑ Ⓒ Ⓓ
40 Ⓐ Ⓑ Ⓒ Ⓓ
41 Ⓐ Ⓑ Ⓒ Ⓓ
42 Ⓐ Ⓑ Ⓒ Ⓓ
43 Ⓐ Ⓑ Ⓒ Ⓓ
44 Ⓐ Ⓑ Ⓒ Ⓓ
45 Ⓐ Ⓑ Ⓒ Ⓓ
46 Ⓐ Ⓑ Ⓒ Ⓓ
47 Ⓐ Ⓑ Ⓒ Ⓓ
48 Ⓐ Ⓑ Ⓒ Ⓓ
49 Ⓐ Ⓑ Ⓒ Ⓓ
50 Ⓐ Ⓑ Ⓒ Ⓓ
51 Ⓐ Ⓑ Ⓒ Ⓓ
52 Ⓐ Ⓑ Ⓒ Ⓓ
53 Ⓐ Ⓑ Ⓒ Ⓓ
54 Ⓐ Ⓑ Ⓒ Ⓓ
55 Ⓐ Ⓑ Ⓒ Ⓓ
56 Ⓐ Ⓑ Ⓒ Ⓓ
57 Ⓐ Ⓑ Ⓒ Ⓓ
58 Ⓐ Ⓑ Ⓒ Ⓓ
59 Ⓐ Ⓑ Ⓒ Ⓓ
60 Ⓐ Ⓑ Ⓒ Ⓓ
61 Ⓐ Ⓑ Ⓒ Ⓓ
62 Ⓐ Ⓑ Ⓒ Ⓓ
63 Ⓐ Ⓑ Ⓒ Ⓓ
64 Ⓐ Ⓑ Ⓒ Ⓓ
65 Ⓐ Ⓑ Ⓒ Ⓓ
66 Ⓐ Ⓑ Ⓒ Ⓓ
67 Ⓐ Ⓑ Ⓒ Ⓓ
68 Ⓐ Ⓑ Ⓒ Ⓓ
69 Ⓐ Ⓑ Ⓒ Ⓓ
70 Ⓐ Ⓑ Ⓒ Ⓓ
71 Ⓐ Ⓑ Ⓒ Ⓓ
72 Ⓐ Ⓑ Ⓒ Ⓓ

Part D – Personal Characteristics & Experience Inventory

When taking the actual exam, you would mark answers for the Personal Characteristics & Experience Inventory questions here. However, as explained in the guide, it is not really possible to practice or prepare for this part of the exam. With these questions, it is important that you simply answer honestly and sincerely. Therefore, Part D - Personal Characteristics & Experience Inventory was not included in our practice exams or on this practice answer sheet.

Exam 473 Practice Answer Sheet

Answer Sheet Format

When taking the real exam, you fill in information and mark answers on both the front and back of the answer sheet. For realistic practice value, this practice answer sheet is laid out exactly like the real thing. Below are details on what you mark on the answer sheet and where you mark it:

- Front of answer sheet
  → You fill in information (similar to what you provided when applying for the exam) at the top.
  → You mark answers for the Address Checking and Forms Completion questions at the bottom.
- Back of answer sheet
  → You mark answers for the Coding & Memory questions at the top.
  → You mark answers for the Personality Characteristics & Experience Inventory questions at the bottom.

This page is the front page of the answer sheet. Here at the top of the front page is where (if you were taking the real exam) you would fill in information similar to what you provided when applying. Below, at the bottom of this page, is where you mark answers for the Address Checking and Forms Completion questions.

On the back side of this page is where you mark answers for the Coding & Memory questions at the top and mark answers for the Personality Characteristics & Experience Inventory questions at the bottom.

Ink Color

On real Postal exams, the answer sheets are printed on white paper, but the ink color varies from one test to another. On different exams, the ink may be blue, green, pink, and so on. This is not terribly important, and it should not affect your performance on the exam, but we wanted to make you aware so you will not be surprised by the appearance of the actual answer sheet.

Mark answers for the Address Checking and Forms Completion questions below.

Part A – Address Checking

1 Ⓐ Ⓑ Ⓒ Ⓓ	11 Ⓐ Ⓑ Ⓒ Ⓓ	21 Ⓐ Ⓑ Ⓒ Ⓓ	31 Ⓐ Ⓑ Ⓒ Ⓓ	41 Ⓐ Ⓑ Ⓒ Ⓓ	51 Ⓐ Ⓑ Ⓒ Ⓓ
2 Ⓐ Ⓑ Ⓒ Ⓓ	12 Ⓐ Ⓑ Ⓒ Ⓓ	22 Ⓐ Ⓑ Ⓒ Ⓓ	32 Ⓐ Ⓑ Ⓒ Ⓓ	42 Ⓐ Ⓑ Ⓒ Ⓓ	52 Ⓐ Ⓑ Ⓒ Ⓓ
3 Ⓐ Ⓑ Ⓒ Ⓓ	13 Ⓐ Ⓑ Ⓒ Ⓓ	23 Ⓐ Ⓑ Ⓒ Ⓓ	33 Ⓐ Ⓑ Ⓒ Ⓓ	43 Ⓐ Ⓑ Ⓒ Ⓓ	53 Ⓐ Ⓑ Ⓒ Ⓓ
4 Ⓐ Ⓑ Ⓒ Ⓓ	14 Ⓐ Ⓑ Ⓒ Ⓓ	24 Ⓐ Ⓑ Ⓒ Ⓓ	34 Ⓐ Ⓑ Ⓒ Ⓓ	44 Ⓐ Ⓑ Ⓒ Ⓓ	54 Ⓐ Ⓑ Ⓒ Ⓓ
5 Ⓐ Ⓑ Ⓒ Ⓓ	15 Ⓐ Ⓑ Ⓒ Ⓓ	25 Ⓐ Ⓑ Ⓒ Ⓓ	35 Ⓐ Ⓑ Ⓒ Ⓓ	45 Ⓐ Ⓑ Ⓒ Ⓓ	55 Ⓐ Ⓑ Ⓒ Ⓓ
6 Ⓐ Ⓑ Ⓒ Ⓓ	16 Ⓐ Ⓑ Ⓒ Ⓓ	26 Ⓐ Ⓑ Ⓒ Ⓓ	36 Ⓐ Ⓑ Ⓒ Ⓓ	46 Ⓐ Ⓑ Ⓒ Ⓓ	56 Ⓐ Ⓑ Ⓒ Ⓓ
7 Ⓐ Ⓑ Ⓒ Ⓓ	17 Ⓐ Ⓑ Ⓒ Ⓓ	27 Ⓐ Ⓑ Ⓒ Ⓓ	37 Ⓐ Ⓑ Ⓒ Ⓓ	47 Ⓐ Ⓑ Ⓒ Ⓓ	57 Ⓐ Ⓑ Ⓒ Ⓓ
8 Ⓐ Ⓑ Ⓒ Ⓓ	18 Ⓐ Ⓑ Ⓒ Ⓓ	28 Ⓐ Ⓑ Ⓒ Ⓓ	38 Ⓐ Ⓑ Ⓒ Ⓓ	48 Ⓐ Ⓑ Ⓒ Ⓓ	58 Ⓐ Ⓑ Ⓒ Ⓓ
9 Ⓐ Ⓑ Ⓒ Ⓓ	19 Ⓐ Ⓑ Ⓒ Ⓓ	29 Ⓐ Ⓑ Ⓒ Ⓓ	39 Ⓐ Ⓑ Ⓒ Ⓓ	49 Ⓐ Ⓑ Ⓒ Ⓓ	59 Ⓐ Ⓑ Ⓒ Ⓓ
10 Ⓐ Ⓑ Ⓒ Ⓓ	20 Ⓐ Ⓑ Ⓒ Ⓓ	30 Ⓐ Ⓑ Ⓒ Ⓓ	40 Ⓐ Ⓑ Ⓒ Ⓓ	50 Ⓐ Ⓑ Ⓒ Ⓓ	60 Ⓐ Ⓑ Ⓒ Ⓓ

Part B – Forms Completion

1 Ⓐ Ⓑ Ⓒ Ⓓ	6 Ⓐ Ⓑ Ⓒ Ⓓ	11 Ⓐ Ⓑ Ⓒ Ⓓ	16 Ⓐ Ⓑ Ⓒ Ⓓ	21 Ⓐ Ⓑ Ⓒ Ⓓ	26 Ⓐ Ⓑ Ⓒ Ⓓ
2 Ⓐ Ⓑ Ⓒ Ⓓ	7 Ⓐ Ⓑ Ⓒ Ⓓ	12 Ⓐ Ⓑ Ⓒ Ⓓ	17 Ⓐ Ⓑ Ⓒ Ⓓ	22 Ⓐ Ⓑ Ⓒ Ⓓ	27 Ⓐ Ⓑ Ⓒ Ⓓ
3 Ⓐ Ⓑ Ⓒ Ⓓ	8 Ⓐ Ⓑ Ⓒ Ⓓ	13 Ⓐ Ⓑ Ⓒ Ⓓ	18 Ⓐ Ⓑ Ⓒ Ⓓ	23 Ⓐ Ⓑ Ⓒ Ⓓ	28 Ⓐ Ⓑ Ⓒ Ⓓ
4 Ⓐ Ⓑ Ⓒ Ⓓ	9 Ⓐ Ⓑ Ⓒ Ⓓ	14 Ⓐ Ⓑ Ⓒ Ⓓ	19 Ⓐ Ⓑ Ⓒ Ⓓ	24 Ⓐ Ⓑ Ⓒ Ⓓ	29 Ⓐ Ⓑ Ⓒ Ⓓ
5 Ⓐ Ⓑ Ⓒ Ⓓ	10 Ⓐ Ⓑ Ⓒ Ⓓ	15 Ⓐ Ⓑ Ⓒ Ⓓ	20 Ⓐ Ⓑ Ⓒ Ⓓ	25 Ⓐ Ⓑ Ⓒ Ⓓ	30 Ⓐ Ⓑ Ⓒ Ⓓ

Continued on next page →

Exam 473 Practice Answer Sheet

Continued from previous page

Part C – Coding & Memory

Coding Section

1 Ⓐ Ⓑ Ⓒ Ⓓ	13 Ⓐ Ⓑ Ⓒ Ⓓ	25 Ⓐ Ⓑ Ⓒ Ⓓ
2 Ⓐ Ⓑ Ⓒ Ⓓ	14 Ⓐ Ⓑ Ⓒ Ⓓ	26 Ⓐ Ⓑ Ⓒ Ⓓ
3 Ⓐ Ⓑ Ⓒ Ⓓ	15 Ⓐ Ⓑ Ⓒ Ⓓ	27 Ⓐ Ⓑ Ⓒ Ⓓ
4 Ⓐ Ⓑ Ⓒ Ⓓ	16 Ⓐ Ⓑ Ⓒ Ⓓ	28 Ⓐ Ⓑ Ⓒ Ⓓ
5 Ⓐ Ⓑ Ⓒ Ⓓ	17 Ⓐ Ⓑ Ⓒ Ⓓ	29 Ⓐ Ⓑ Ⓒ Ⓓ
6 Ⓐ Ⓑ Ⓒ Ⓓ	18 Ⓐ Ⓑ Ⓒ Ⓓ	30 Ⓐ Ⓑ Ⓒ Ⓓ
7 Ⓐ Ⓑ Ⓒ Ⓓ	19 Ⓐ Ⓑ Ⓒ Ⓓ	31 Ⓐ Ⓑ Ⓒ Ⓓ
8 Ⓐ Ⓑ Ⓒ Ⓓ	20 Ⓐ Ⓑ Ⓒ Ⓓ	32 Ⓐ Ⓑ Ⓒ Ⓓ
9 Ⓐ Ⓑ Ⓒ Ⓓ	21 Ⓐ Ⓑ Ⓒ Ⓓ	33 Ⓐ Ⓑ Ⓒ Ⓓ
10 Ⓐ Ⓑ Ⓒ Ⓓ	22 Ⓐ Ⓑ Ⓒ Ⓓ	34 Ⓐ Ⓑ Ⓒ Ⓓ
11 Ⓐ Ⓑ Ⓒ Ⓓ	23 Ⓐ Ⓑ Ⓒ Ⓓ	35 Ⓐ Ⓑ Ⓒ Ⓓ
12 Ⓐ Ⓑ Ⓒ Ⓓ	24 Ⓐ Ⓑ Ⓒ Ⓓ	36 Ⓐ Ⓑ Ⓒ Ⓓ

Memory Section

37 Ⓐ Ⓑ Ⓒ Ⓓ	49 Ⓐ Ⓑ Ⓒ Ⓓ	61 Ⓐ Ⓑ Ⓒ Ⓓ
38 Ⓐ Ⓑ Ⓒ Ⓓ	50 Ⓐ Ⓑ Ⓒ Ⓓ	62 Ⓐ Ⓑ Ⓒ Ⓓ
39 Ⓐ Ⓑ Ⓒ Ⓓ	51 Ⓐ Ⓑ Ⓒ Ⓓ	63 Ⓐ Ⓑ Ⓒ Ⓓ
40 Ⓐ Ⓑ Ⓒ Ⓓ	52 Ⓐ Ⓑ Ⓒ Ⓓ	64 Ⓐ Ⓑ Ⓒ Ⓓ
41 Ⓐ Ⓑ Ⓒ Ⓓ	53 Ⓐ Ⓑ Ⓒ Ⓓ	65 Ⓐ Ⓑ Ⓒ Ⓓ
42 Ⓐ Ⓑ Ⓒ Ⓓ	54 Ⓐ Ⓑ Ⓒ Ⓓ	66 Ⓐ Ⓑ Ⓒ Ⓓ
43 Ⓐ Ⓑ Ⓒ Ⓓ	55 Ⓐ Ⓑ Ⓒ Ⓓ	67 Ⓐ Ⓑ Ⓒ Ⓓ
44 Ⓐ Ⓑ Ⓒ Ⓓ	56 Ⓐ Ⓑ Ⓒ Ⓓ	68 Ⓐ Ⓑ Ⓒ Ⓓ
45 Ⓐ Ⓑ Ⓒ Ⓓ	57 Ⓐ Ⓑ Ⓒ Ⓓ	69 Ⓐ Ⓑ Ⓒ Ⓓ
46 Ⓐ Ⓑ Ⓒ Ⓓ	58 Ⓐ Ⓑ Ⓒ Ⓓ	70 Ⓐ Ⓑ Ⓒ Ⓓ
47 Ⓐ Ⓑ Ⓒ Ⓓ	59 Ⓐ Ⓑ Ⓒ Ⓓ	71 Ⓐ Ⓑ Ⓒ Ⓓ
48 Ⓐ Ⓑ Ⓒ Ⓓ	60 Ⓐ Ⓑ Ⓒ Ⓓ	72 Ⓐ Ⓑ Ⓒ Ⓓ

Part D – Personal Characteristics & Experience Inventory

When taking the actual exam, you would mark answers for the Personal Characteristics & Experience Inventory questions here. However, as explained in the guide, it is not really possible to practice or prepare for this part of the exam. With these questions, it is important that you simply answer honestly and sincerely. Therefore, Part D - Personal Characteristics & Experience Inventory was not included in our practice exams or on this practice answer sheet.

Exam 473 Practice Answer Sheet

Answer Sheet Format

When taking the real exam, you fill in information and mark answers on both the front and back of the answer sheet. For realistic practice value, this practice answer sheet is laid out exactly like the real thing. Below are details on what you mark on the answer sheet and where you mark it:

- Front of answer sheet
  → You fill in information (similar to what you provided when applying for the exam) at the top.
  → You mark answers for the Address Checking and Forms Completion questions at the bottom.
- Back of answer sheet
  → You mark answers for the Coding & Memory questions at the top.
  → You mark answers for the Personality Characteristics & Experience Inventory questions at the bottom.

This page is the front page of the answer sheet. Here at the top of the front page is where (if you were taking the real exam) you would fill in information similar to what you provided when applying. Below, at the bottom of this page, is where you mark answers for the Address Checking and Forms Completion questions.

On the back side of this page is where you mark answers for the Coding & Memory questions at the top and mark answers for the Personality Characteristics & Experience Inventory questions at the bottom.

Ink Color

On real Postal exams, the answer sheets are printed on white paper, but the ink color varies from one test to another. On different exams, the ink may be blue, green, pink, and so on. This is not terribly important, and it should not affect your performance on the exam, but we wanted to make you aware so you will not be surprised by the appearance of the actual answer sheet.

Mark answers for the Address Checking and Forms Completion questions below.

Part A – Address Checking

1 (A) (B) (C) (D)	11 (A) (B) (C) (D)	21 (A) (B) (C) (D)	31 (A) (B) (C) (D)	41 (A) (B) (C) (D)	51 (A) (B) (C) (D)
2 (A) (B) (C) (D)	12 (A) (B) (C) (D)	22 (A) (B) (C) (D)	32 (A) (B) (C) (D)	42 (A) (B) (C) (D)	52 (A) (B) (C) (D)
3 (A) (B) (C) (D)	13 (A) (B) (C) (D)	23 (A) (B) (C) (D)	33 (A) (B) (C) (D)	43 (A) (B) (C) (D)	53 (A) (B) (C) (D)
4 (A) (B) (C) (D)	14 (A) (B) (C) (D)	24 (A) (B) (C) (D)	34 (A) (B) (C) (D)	44 (A) (B) (C) (D)	54 (A) (B) (C) (D)
5 (A) (B) (C) (D)	15 (A) (B) (C) (D)	25 (A) (B) (C) (D)	35 (A) (B) (C) (D)	45 (A) (B) (C) (D)	55 (A) (B) (C) (D)
6 (A) (B) (C) (D)	16 (A) (B) (C) (D)	26 (A) (B) (C) (D)	36 (A) (B) (C) (D)	46 (A) (B) (C) (D)	56 (A) (B) (C) (D)
7 (A) (B) (C) (D)	17 (A) (B) (C) (D)	27 (A) (B) (C) (D)	37 (A) (B) (C) (D)	47 (A) (B) (C) (D)	57 (A) (B) (C) (D)
8 (A) (B) (C) (D)	18 (A) (B) (C) (D)	28 (A) (B) (C) (D)	38 (A) (B) (C) (D)	48 (A) (B) (C) (D)	58 (A) (B) (C) (D)
9 (A) (B) (C) (D)	19 (A) (B) (C) (D)	29 (A) (B) (C) (D)	39 (A) (B) (C) (D)	49 (A) (B) (C) (D)	59 (A) (B) (C) (D)
10 (A) (B) (C) (D)	20 (A) (B) (C) (D)	30 (A) (B) (C) (D)	40 (A) (B) (C) (D)	50 (A) (B) (C) (D)	60 (A) (B) (C) (D)

Part B – Forms Completion

1 (A) (B) (C) (D)	6 (A) (B) (C) (D)	11 (A) (B) (C) (D)	16 (A) (B) (C) (D)	21 (A) (B) (C) (D)	26 (A) (B) (C) (D)
2 (A) (B) (C) (D)	7 (A) (B) (C) (D)	12 (A) (B) (C) (D)	17 (A) (B) (C) (D)	22 (A) (B) (C) (D)	27 (A) (B) (C) (D)
3 (A) (B) (C) (D)	8 (A) (B) (C) (D)	13 (A) (B) (C) (D)	18 (A) (B) (C) (D)	23 (A) (B) (C) (D)	28 (A) (B) (C) (D)
4 (A) (B) (C) (D)	9 (A) (B) (C) (D)	14 (A) (B) (C) (D)	19 (A) (B) (C) (D)	24 (A) (B) (C) (D)	29 (A) (B) (C) (D)
5 (A) (B) (C) (D)	10 (A) (B) (C) (D)	15 (A) (B) (C) (D)	20 (A) (B) (C) (D)	25 (A) (B) (C) (D)	30 (A) (B) (C) (D)

Continued on next page →

Exam 473 Practice Answer Sheet

Continued from previous page

Part C – Coding & Memory

Coding Section

1 Ⓐ Ⓑ Ⓒ Ⓓ	13 Ⓐ Ⓑ Ⓒ Ⓓ	25 Ⓐ Ⓑ Ⓒ Ⓓ
2 Ⓐ Ⓑ Ⓒ Ⓓ	14 Ⓐ Ⓑ Ⓒ Ⓓ	26 Ⓐ Ⓑ Ⓒ Ⓓ
3 Ⓐ Ⓑ Ⓒ Ⓓ	15 Ⓐ Ⓑ Ⓒ Ⓓ	27 Ⓐ Ⓑ Ⓒ Ⓓ
4 Ⓐ Ⓑ Ⓒ Ⓓ	16 Ⓐ Ⓑ Ⓒ Ⓓ	28 Ⓐ Ⓑ Ⓒ Ⓓ
5 Ⓐ Ⓑ Ⓒ Ⓓ	17 Ⓐ Ⓑ Ⓒ Ⓓ	29 Ⓐ Ⓑ Ⓒ Ⓓ
6 Ⓐ Ⓑ Ⓒ Ⓓ	18 Ⓐ Ⓑ Ⓒ Ⓓ	30 Ⓐ Ⓑ Ⓒ Ⓓ
7 Ⓐ Ⓑ Ⓒ Ⓓ	19 Ⓐ Ⓑ Ⓒ Ⓓ	31 Ⓐ Ⓑ Ⓒ Ⓓ
8 Ⓐ Ⓑ Ⓒ Ⓓ	20 Ⓐ Ⓑ Ⓒ Ⓓ	32 Ⓐ Ⓑ Ⓒ Ⓓ
9 Ⓐ Ⓑ Ⓒ Ⓓ	21 Ⓐ Ⓑ Ⓒ Ⓓ	33 Ⓐ Ⓑ Ⓒ Ⓓ
10 Ⓐ Ⓑ Ⓒ Ⓓ	22 Ⓐ Ⓑ Ⓒ Ⓓ	34 Ⓐ Ⓑ Ⓒ Ⓓ
11 Ⓐ Ⓑ Ⓒ Ⓓ	23 Ⓐ Ⓑ Ⓒ Ⓓ	35 Ⓐ Ⓑ Ⓒ Ⓓ
12 Ⓐ Ⓑ Ⓒ Ⓓ	24 Ⓐ Ⓑ Ⓒ Ⓓ	36 Ⓐ Ⓑ Ⓒ Ⓓ

Memory Section

37 Ⓐ Ⓑ Ⓒ Ⓓ	49 Ⓐ Ⓑ Ⓒ Ⓓ	61 Ⓐ Ⓑ Ⓒ Ⓓ
38 Ⓐ Ⓑ Ⓒ Ⓓ	50 Ⓐ Ⓑ Ⓒ Ⓓ	62 Ⓐ Ⓑ Ⓒ Ⓓ
39 Ⓐ Ⓑ Ⓒ Ⓓ	51 Ⓐ Ⓑ Ⓒ Ⓓ	63 Ⓐ Ⓑ Ⓒ Ⓓ
40 Ⓐ Ⓑ Ⓒ Ⓓ	52 Ⓐ Ⓑ Ⓒ Ⓓ	64 Ⓐ Ⓑ Ⓒ Ⓓ
41 Ⓐ Ⓑ Ⓒ Ⓓ	53 Ⓐ Ⓑ Ⓒ Ⓓ	65 Ⓐ Ⓑ Ⓒ Ⓓ
42 Ⓐ Ⓑ Ⓒ Ⓓ	54 Ⓐ Ⓑ Ⓒ Ⓓ	66 Ⓐ Ⓑ Ⓒ Ⓓ
43 Ⓐ Ⓑ Ⓒ Ⓓ	55 Ⓐ Ⓑ Ⓒ Ⓓ	67 Ⓐ Ⓑ Ⓒ Ⓓ
44 Ⓐ Ⓑ Ⓒ Ⓓ	56 Ⓐ Ⓑ Ⓒ Ⓓ	68 Ⓐ Ⓑ Ⓒ Ⓓ
45 Ⓐ Ⓑ Ⓒ Ⓓ	57 Ⓐ Ⓑ Ⓒ Ⓓ	69 Ⓐ Ⓑ Ⓒ Ⓓ
46 Ⓐ Ⓑ Ⓒ Ⓓ	58 Ⓐ Ⓑ Ⓒ Ⓓ	70 Ⓐ Ⓑ Ⓒ Ⓓ
47 Ⓐ Ⓑ Ⓒ Ⓓ	59 Ⓐ Ⓑ Ⓒ Ⓓ	71 Ⓐ Ⓑ Ⓒ Ⓓ
48 Ⓐ Ⓑ Ⓒ Ⓓ	60 Ⓐ Ⓑ Ⓒ Ⓓ	72 Ⓐ Ⓑ Ⓒ Ⓓ

Part D – Personal Characteristics & Experience Inventory

When taking the actual exam, you would mark answers for the Personal Characteristics & Experience Inventory questions here. However, as explained in the guide, it is not really possible to practice or prepare for this part of the exam. With these questions, it is important that you simply answer honestly and sincerely. Therefore, Part D - Personal Characteristics & Experience Inventory was not included in our practice exams or on this practice answer sheet.

Answer Key for Practice Exam #1

Address Checking

1. C	31. C
2. A	32. B
3. A	33. B
4. D	34. D
5. D	35. A
6. B	36. A
7. A	37. B
8. C	38. D
9. D	39. B
10. B	40. B
11. C	41. C
12. B	42. A
13. A	43. D
14. A	44. D
15. D	45. A
16. B	46. A
17. B	47. C
18. D	48. B
19. B	49. C
20. A	50. D
21. A	51. A
22. D	52. B
23. B	53. B
24. C	54. C
25. C	55. A
26. C	56. A
27. C	57. D
28. A	58. A
29. B	59. B
30. D	60. B

Forms Completion

1. B
2. D
3. C
4. D
5. B
6. D
7. C
8. A
9. D
10. A
11. B
12. D
13. C
14. C
15. B
16. A
17. B
18. D
19. B
20. D
21. C
22. A
23. B
24. D
25. B
26. A
27. C
28. A
29. C
30. A

Coding & Memory

1. D	37. B
2. B	38. C
3. A	39. B
4. B	40. A
5. C	41. B
6. D	42. D
7. A	43. C
8. C	44. A
9. C	45. B
10. B	46. C
11. A	47. D
12. A	48. A
13. C	49. C
14. B	50. B
15. C	51. D
16. C	52. A
17. D	53. D
18. A	54. A
19. C	55. C
20. B	56. A
21. C	57. A
22. A	58. C
23. D	59. D
24. B	60. A
25. C	61. C
26. B	62. B
27. D	63. D
28. A	64. A
29. C	65. B
30. D	66. C
31. A	67. A
32. D	68. D
33. C	69. C
34. A	70. A
35. C	71. B
36. C	72. C

Answer Key for Practice Exam #2

Address Checking

1. D	31. B
2. A	32. D
3. C	33. C
4. C	34. C
5. C	35. A
6. B	36. B
7. A	37. D
8. B	38. B
9. D	39. D
10. C	40. D
11. A	41. A
12. A	42. A
13. B	43. A
14. A	44. A
15. D	45. C
16. C	46. D
17. A	47. C
18. B	48. B
19. B	49. B
20. D	50. C
21. A	51. D
22. B	52. A
23. C	53. D
24. C	54. C
25. B	55. B
26. A	56. A
27. D	57. B
28. A	58. D
29. B	59. A
30. A	60. B

Forms Completion

1. D
2. D
3. B
4. D
5. C
6. A
7. C
8. C
9. D
10. B
11. A
12. D
13. B
14. A
15. D
16. C
17. B
18. D
19. D
20. D
21. B
22. D
23. B
24. A
25. B
26. D
27. C
28. A
29. A
30. B

Coding & Memory

1. A	37. D
2. B	38. A
3. A	39. A
4. C	40. B
5. A	41. A
6. C	42. C
7. B	43. B
8. C	44. A
9. A	45. C
10. D	46. C
11. C	47. A
12. B	48. C
13. B	49. D
14. C	50. A
15. A	51. B
16. D	52. A
17. C	53. B
18. A	54. A
19. A	55. B
20. B	56. C
21. C	57. C
22. A	58. A
23. C	59. A
24. B	60. B
25. D	61. C
26. A	62. C
27. B	63. D
28. A	64. D
29. C	65. C
30. D	66. D
31. B	67. C
32. C	68. A
33. A	69. B
34. C	70. A
35. A	71. B
36. D	72. C

Answer Key for Practice Exam #3

Address Checking

1. B	31. B
2. A	32. C
3. D	33. A
4. B	34. D
5. C	35. B
6. C	36. D
7. B	37. B
8. A	38. D
9. A	39. A
10. A	40. A
11. B	41. B
12. B	42. B
13. C	43. D
14. D	44. D
15. D	45. A
16. B	46. A
17. C	47. B
18. D	48. B
19. A	49. A
20. A	50. B
21. B	51. D
22. D	52. C
23. A	53. C
24. C	54. B
25. D	55. A
26. B	56. C
27. A	57. B
28. A	58. A
29. C	59. D
30. B	60. D

Forms Completion

1. A
2. A
3. A
4. D
5. C
6. B
7. B
8. A
9. A
10. C
11. D
12. B
13. C
14. A
15. B
16. A
17. D
18. D
19. B
20. D
21. D
22. A
23. C
24. B
25. B
26. B
27. C
28. A
29. D
30. A

Coding & Memory

1. B	37. A
2. C	38. B
3. A	39. C
4. C	40. A
5. B	41. C
6. C	42. A
7. A	43. C
8. C	44. B
9. D	45. D
10. C	46. C
11. A	47. B
12. B	48. C
13. C	49. A
14. A	50. B
15. D	51. C
16. B	52. A
17. D	53. A
18. B	54. D
19. A	55. D
20. A	56. A
21. D	57. C
22. C	58. C
23. A	59. A
24. C	60. B
25. D	61. C
26. A	62. A
27. B	63. B
28. C	64. D
29. B	65. C
30. A	66. C
31. C	67. D
32. C	68. A
33. D	69. B
34. C	70. A
35. D	71. D
36. A	72. A

Answer Key for Practice Exam #4

Address Checking

1. B	31. A
2. D	32. B
3. A	33. D
4. C	34. A
5. A	35. B
6. C	36. B
7. D	37. A
8. A	38. C
9. B	39. B
10. D	40. C
11. C	41. A
12. A	42. D
13. B	43. C
14. C	44. B
15. D	45. A
16. B	46. C
17. D	47. B
18. A	48. A
19. C	49. A
20. B	50. D
21. A	51. C
22. D	52. D
23. B	53. A
24. A	54. A
25. C	55. D
26. D	56. C
27. D	57. D
28. B	58. A
29. A	59. A
30. D	60. B

Forms Completion

1. C
2. D
3. D
4. A
5. D
6. B
7. D
8. B
9. B
10. A
11. D
12. B
13. D
14. A
15. D
16. A
17. C
18. B
19. A
20. A
21. C
22. D
23. B
24. D
25. C
26. C
27. A
28. A
29. B
30. C

Coding & Memory

1. D	37. B
2. A	38. C
3. B	39. C
4. C	40. C
5. D	41. A
6. A	42. D
7. B	43. C
8. C	44. C
9. A	45. D
10. C	46. A
11. C	47. A
12. D	48. D
13. A	49. B
14. C	50. C
15. B	51. B
16. B	52. C
17. A	53. C
18. C	54. D
19. C	55. A
20. B	56. C
21. B	57. A
22. C	58. D
23. D	59. B
24. C	60. B
25. A	61. C
26. C	62. D
27. D	63. B
28. B	64. C
29. C	65. D
30. A	66. A
31. C	67. D
32. D	68. A
33. B	69. B
34. C	70. A
35. A	71. C
36. D	72. B

Answer Key for Practice Exam #5

Address Checking

1. B	31. D
2. A	32. B
3. C	33. A
4. B	34. B
5. A	35. C
6. D	36. B
7. D	37. C
8. B	38. A
9. C	39. B
10. D	40. B
11. A	41. C
12. B	42. A
13. A	43. D
14. D	44. C
15. B	45. A
16. A	46. D
17. A	47. A
18. C	48. B
19. B	49. D
20. D	50. C
21. A	51. B
22. C	52. A
23. B	53. A
24. D	54. D
25. B	55. B
26. A	56. B
27. C	57. C
28. C	58. A
29. A	59. D
30. D	60. B

Forms Completion

1. D
2. A
3. B
4. C
5. D
6. D
7. C
8. D
9. D
10. A
11. C
12. C
13. C
14. B
15. C
16. B
17. D
18. D
19. C
20. B
21. B
22. C
23. D
24. D
25. A
26. B
27. C
28. D
29. A
30. B

Coding & Memory

1. C	37. B
2. B	38. C
3. C	39. D
4. A	40. D
5. B	41. A
6. D	42. C
7. A	43. C
8. D	44. A
9. B	45. C
10. A	46. B
11. C	47. A
12. A	48. B
13. C	49. A
14. A	50. C
15. B	51. A
16. A	52. B
17. B	53. C
18. C	54. C
19. D	55. A
20. A	56. C
21. B	57. C
22. C	58. C
23. B	59. A
24. D	60. B
25. B	61. D
26. C	62. A
27. A	63. B
28. C	64. D
29. C	65. D
30. D	66. C
31. A	67. C
32. C	68. A
33. B	69. C
34. A	70. D
35. D	71. A
36. B	72. B

Answer Key for Practice Exam #6

Address Checking

1. C	31. A
2. B	32. B
3. D	33. D
4. B	34. B
5. A	35. B
6. D	36. A
7. A	37. D
8. C	38. A
9. C	39. A
10. D	40. C
11. A	41. B
12. B	42. C
13. A	43. B
14. A	44. C
15. B	45. C
16. D	46. B
17. B	47. A
18. A	48. D
19. B	49. C
20. A	50. B
21. D	51. A
22. C	52. B
23. B	53. A
24. A	54. D
25. C	55. D
26. B	56. C
27. A	57. A
28. D	58. B
29. B	59. B
30. C	60. A

Forms Completion

1. B
2. A
3. C
4. D
5. D
6. B
7. C
8. A
9. D
10. C
11. A
12. D
13. B
14. D
15. C
16. C
17. B
18. D
19. D
20. D
21. A
22. C
23. C
24. B
25. D
26. D
27. C
28. A
29. D
30. B

Coding & Memory

1. D	37. C
2. A	38. A
3. B	39. C
4. C	40. B
5. A	41. D
6. D	42. A
7. C	43. D
8. A	44. A
9. C	45. B
10. B	46. A
11. D	47. C
12. A	48. A
13. C	49. B
14. A	50. C
15. B	51. A
16. C	52. D
17. A	53. B
18. B	54. C
19. A	55. B
20. C	56. A
21. B	57. C
22. D	58. C
23. C	59. C
24. A	60. A
25. B	61. A
26. A	62. C
27. C	63. D
28. D	64. A
29. C	65. A
30. A	66. B
31. C	67. C
32. A	68. D
33. D	69. A
34. A	70. C
35. B	71. D
36. C	72. B

Postal Phone Directory

The following phone numbers were confirmed to be valid as of the publish date of this guide. However, it is possible that some numbers may change from time to time. If one of these numbers does not work when you try it, call another nearby location and ask for the updated number.

The "RECORDING" column contains "Hiring & Testing Hotline" numbers that can be called 24/7 to hear recorded announcements of employment and testing opportunities. The numbers with 800, 866, 877, and 888 area codes are all toll free calls.

The "EXAM OFFICE" numbers ring into exam and human resources offices where you can speak to a person to ask specific questions.

STATE, ETC.	CITY	RECORDING	EXAM OFFICE
Alabama	Birmingham	205-521-0214	205-521-0272
Alabama	Huntsville		256-461-6636
Alabama	Mobile	251-694-5921	251-694-5920
Alabama	Montgomery	334-244-7551	334-244-7553
Alaska	Anchorage	907-564-2964	907-564-2962
Arizona	Phoenix	602-223-3624	602-223-3633
Arizona	Tucson	520-388-5191	520-388-5103
Arkansas	Little Rock	501-945-6665	501-945-6668
California	Anaheim	714-662-6375	714-662-6235
California	Bakersfield	661-392-6261	661-392-6251
California	Fresno	559-497-7636	559-497-7770
California	Los Angeles	323-586-1351	323-586-1392
California	Modesto	209-983-6490	209-983-6492
California	Oakland	510-251-3040	510-251-3041
California	Sacramento	916-373-8448	916-373-8679
California	San Bernardino	909-335-4339	909-335-4329
California	San Diego	858-674-0577	858-674-2626
California	San Francisco	415-550-5534	415-550-5330
California	San Jose	408-437-6986	
California	San Mateo	650-377-1124	
California	Santa Ana	626-855-6339	626-855-6355
California	Santa Barbara	805-278-7668	805-278-7648
California	Van Nuys	661-775-7014	661-775-7035
Colorado	Colorado Springs	719-570-5316	719-570-5443
Colorado	Denver	877-482-3238	303-853-6041
Connecticut	Hartford	860-524-6120	860-524-6259
Delaware	See Bellmawr, NJ		
District of Columbia	Washington	301-324-5837	301-499-7737
Florida	Fort Myers	800-533-9097	239-768-8025
Florida	Jacksonville	904-359-2737	904-359-2979
Florida	Lake Mary	888-771-9056	407-444-2014
Florida	Miami	888-725-7295	305-470-0782
Florida	Orlando	888-771-9056	407-850-6314
Florida	Pensacola	850-434-9167	850-434-9169
Florida	Tallahassee	850-216-4248	850-216-4250

STATE, ETC.	CITY	RECORDING	EXAM OFFICE
Florida	Tampa	800-533-9097	813-872-3501
Georgia	Atlanta	770-717-3500	770-717-3470
Georgia	Macon	478-752-8465	478-752-8473
Georgia	Savannah	912-235-4629	912-235-4628
Hawaii	Honolulu	808-423-3690	808-423-3613
Idaho	Boise	208-433-4415	
Illinois	Bedford Park	708-563-7496	708-563-7494
Illinois	Carol Stream	630-260-5200	630-260-5633
Illinois	Chicago		312-983-8522
Illinois	Peoria	309-671-8835	309-671-8865
Illinois	Rockford		815-229-4752
Illinois	Springfield	217-788-7437	217-788-7480
Indiana	Indianapolis	317-870-8500	317-870-8564
Iowa	Des Moines	515-251-2061	515-251-2214
Kansas	See Omaha, NE		
Kansas	Topeka	785-295-9164	785-295-9145
Kansas	Wichita	316-946-4596	316-946-4613
Kansas	Wichita		316-946-4621
Kentucky	Lexington	859-231-6755	859-231-6851
Kentucky	Louisville	502-454-1625	502-454-1641
Louisiana	Baton Rouge	888-421-4887	225-763-3788
Louisiana	New Orleans	888-421-4887	504-589-1171
Louisiana	Shreveport	888-421-4887	318-677-2321
Maine	Bangor	207-941-2064	207-941-2084
Maine	Portland	207-828-8520	207-828-8576
Maryland	Baltimore	410-347-4320	410-347-4473
Massachusetts	Boston	617-654-5569	617-654-5608
Massachusetts	North Reading	978-664-7665	978-664-7711
Massachusetts	Springfield	413-731-0425	413-785-6323
Massachusetts	Worcester		508-795-3676
Michigan	Detroit	888-442-5361	313-226-8007
Michigan	Detroit		313-226-8265
Michigan	Grand Rapids		616-336-5323
Michigan	Royal Oak	248-546-7104	248-546-7157
Minnesota	St Paul	877-293-3364	651-293-3009
Mississippi	Gulfport	228-831-5438	228-831-5419
Mississippi	Jackson	601-351-7099	601-351-7269
Missouri	Kansas City	816-374-9346	816-374-9163
Missouri	St Louis	314-436-3855	314-436-4489
Montana	Billings	406-657-5763	406-657-5765
Montana	Missoula		406-329-2227
Nebraska	Lincoln	402-473-1669	402-473-1665
Nebraska	Omaha	402-348-2523	402-255-3989
Nevada	Las Vegas	702-361-9564	702-361-9320
Nevada	Reno	775-788-0656	775-788-0630
New Hampshire	Manchester	603-644-4065	603-644-4061

STATE, ETC.	CITY	RECORDING	EXAM OFFICE
New Jersey	Bellmawr	856-933-4314	856-933-4288
New Jersey	Edison	732-819-4334	732-819-3832
New Jersey	Elizabeth	908-820-8454	
New Jersey	Newark	866-665-3562	973-693-5153
New Mexico	Albuquerque	505-346-8780	505-346-8793
New York	Albany	518-452-2445	518-452-2450
New York	Binghamton		607-773-2152
New York	Buffalo	716-846-2478	716-846-2472
New York	Long Island	631-582-7530	631-582-7543
New York	New York	212-330-3633	212-330-3641
New York	Queens	718-529-7000	718-529-7011
New York	Rochester		716-272-5705
New York	Syracuse	315-452-3616	315-452-3436
New York	White Plains	914-697-5400	914-697-7048
North Carolina	Charlotte	704-393-4490	704-393-4557
North Carolina	Fayetteville	910-486-2321	910-486-2425
North Carolina	Greensboro	866-839-7826	336-668-1258
North Carolina	Raleigh	919-420-5284	919-420-5282
North Dakota	Fargo	888-725-7854	701-241-6161
Ohio	Akron	330-996-9530	330-996-9532
Ohio	Canton	330-438-6425	330-996-9522
Ohio	Cincinnati	513-684-5449	513-684-5481
Ohio	Cleveland	216-443-4210	216-443-4241
Ohio	Columbus	614-469-4356	614-469-4322
Ohio	Dayton	937-227-1146	937-227-1144
Ohio	Toledo		419-245-6825
Ohio	Youngstown		330-740-8932
Oklahoma	Oklahoma City	405-553-6159	405-553-6173
Oregon	Eugene	541-341-3625	541-341-3625
Oregon	Portland	503-294-2270	503-294-2283
Pennsylvania	Devon		610-964-6461
Pennsylvania	Erie	800-868-6835	814-898-7310
Pennsylvania	Harrisburg	717-257-2191	717-257-2173
Pennsylvania	Johnstown	814-533-4926	814-533-4818
Pennsylvania	Lehigh Valley		610-882-3290
Pennsylvania	Philadelphia	215-895-8830	215-895-8850
Pennsylvania	Pittsburgh	412-359-7516	412-359-7974
Pennsylvania	Scranton		570-969-5156
Puerto Rico	San Juan	787-767-3351	787-622-1834
Rhode Island	Providence		401-276-3941
South Carolina	Charleston	843-760-5343	843-760-5341
South Carolina	Columbia	803-926-6400	803-926-6437
South Carolina	Greenville	864-282-8374	864-282-8320
South Dakota	Sioux Falls	888-725-7854	605-333-2690
Tennessee	Chattanooga	423-499-8348	423-499-8355
Tennessee	Knoxville	865-558-4540	865-558-4596

STATE, ETC.	CITY	RECORDING	EXAM OFFICE
Tennessee	Memphis	901-521-2550	901-576-2119
Tennessee	Nashville	615-885-9190	615-872-5722
Texas	Austin	512-342-1139	512-342-1150
Texas	Corpus Christi	361-886-2281	361-886-2288
Texas	Dallas	214-760-4531	972-393-6714
Texas	El Paso		915-780-7534
Texas	Fort Worth	817-317-3366	817-317-3356
Texas	Houston	713-226-3872	713-226-3968
Texas	Lubbock	806-799-6547	806-799-1756
Texas	Midland		432-560-5108
Texas	San Angelo		325-659-7710
Texas	San Antonio	210-368-8400	210-368-8401
Texas	Waco		254-399-2244
Utah	Salt Lake City	801-974-2209	801-974-2219
Vermont	See Springfield, MA		
Virgin Islands	See San Juan, Puerto Rico		
Virginia	Merrifield	703-698-6561	703-698-6398
Virginia	Norfolk	757-629-2225	757-629-2208
Virginia	Richmond	804-775-6290	804-775-6196
Washington	Seattle	206-442-6240	206-442-6237
Washington	Spokane	509-626-6896	509-626-6820
Washington	Tacoma	253-471-6148	
West Virginia	Charleston	304-561-1266	304-561-1256
Wisconsin	Green Bay	920-498-3831	
Wisconsin	Madison	608-246-1268	
Wisconsin	Milwaukee	414-287-1835	414-287-1815
Wyoming	See Denver, CO		

Web Directory

Listed below are various web addresses that may be of benefit as you seek Postal Employment. These addresses were confirmed to be good as of the publish date of of this guide. If one of the addreses does not work when you try it, go the Postal Service website *www.usps.com* and look for job related links that may lead to the information you need.

Postal Exam Information and Test Prep Guides - *www.PostalExam.com*

Postal Job information - *www.Postal-Job.com* (Dash must be included between "Postal" and "Job".)

Postal Service homepage - *www.usps.com*

Exam & job announcement page - *http://uspsapps.hr-services.org/UspsLocate.asp?strExam=*

Postal online exam & casual job application form - *http://uspsapps.hr-services.org/*

Postal professional & corporate jobs page - *http://www.usps.com/employment/corporatejobs.htm*

Postal general employment information -
http://www.usps.com/employment/welcome.htm?from=global&page=employment

POSTAL EXAM NEWSLETTER

Pathfinder publishes an online Postal Exam Newsletter to keep our customers 100% up-to-date with news related to Postal exams, Postal jobs, and Postal test prep tools. Visit the newsletter when you first start your test preparation to check for any news related to your particular exam or study guide. To access the newsletter, simply go to *www.PostalExam.com* and click on the Postal Exam Newsletter link.

TEST PREP SUPPORT

The information, instructions, and strategies discussed in this guide are presented as simply as possible to assure full understanding. If a subject seems confusing, reading over that section again will usually clear it up. You may want to review the subject more than once - perhaps after each practice test. Experiencing the subject on a practice test is frequently the best way to grasp it. For assistance with urgent matters, our Test Prep Support Group is available Monday through Friday (except holidays) from 8:00 AM to 5:00 PM CST. Contact info for the Test Prep Support Group is provided below. When requesting test prep assistance, you must confirm your status as a Pathfinder customer by providing the code number found at the bottom of page 3 in your book.

Test Prep Support e-mail address: support@pathfinderdc.com
Test Prep Support phone number: 281-259-2302

Postal Exam 473 & 473-C

Study Guides & Accessories

The Original Postal Exam Study Guide

Exam 473 & 473-C • Only $19.95 + S/H

Complete instruction on every detail of the exam. Featuring ...

- Free Live Support – Test prep answers & advice by phone or e-mail
- Fully up-to-date with the new exam. Choose carefully. Obsolete guides are a widespread problem.
- Six realistic practice exams – Practice is the key to performance, to a high score, and to a job.
- Test taking tips & strategies – Master the unfamiliar job-related skills tested on this exam.

New Postal Exam Computer-Based Course with CD-ROM

Exam 473 & 473-C • Only $29.95 + S/H

The ultimate test prep technology. Featuring a CD-ROM loaded with ...

- Series of self-paced test prep classes – Comprehensive test prep instruction
- Timed practice tests – Just like the real exam – The most realistic way to practice
- Plus Pathfinder's best-selling Postal Exam 473 & 473-C Study Guide
- Free Live Support – Test prep answers & advice by phone or e-mail

Complete Postal Exam Training Program with 2 Audio CD's

Exam 473 & 473-C • Only $29.95 + S/H

Listen and learn the quick & easy way. Featuring ...

- Postal Exam Training Course Audio CD – Your own personal test prep class
- Postal Exam Timed Practice Test Audio CD – The most realistic way to practice
- Plus Pathfinder's best-selling Postal Exam 473 & 473-C Study Guide
- Free Live Support – Test prep answers & advice by phone or e-mail

Test Scoring & Speed Marking System

Only $9.95 + S/H

Science and common sense combine to take test-taking technology to a new level.

- The system features a set of exclusive Test Scoring & Speed Marking Pencils with ...
- Specially formulated #2 lead to assure 100% perfect scanning success
- Oversized lead enables you to mark answers more than twice as fast as a normal pencil.
- Also included is a booklet of speed and performance boosting strategies.

Postal Test Prep CD-ROM

Exam 473 & 473-C • Only $14.95 + S/H

The ultimate test prep technology assures maximum performance ...

- Series of self-paced test prep classes – Comprehensive test prep instruction
- Timed practice tests – Just like the real exam – The most convenient and realistic way to practice
- Compatible with any internet ready version of Windows®. (You don't have to be hooked up to internet.)
- Just pop it in your CD drive – Automatically opens & runs

Continued on next page ...

Postal Exam 473 & 473-C

Study Guides & Accessories

Postal Exam Training Course Audio CD

Exam 473 & 473-C • Only $9.95 + S/H

Your own personal test prep class. Featuring ...

- Complete up-to-date facts – What's on the exam, how to prepare, and more
- Step-by-step instructions for all four sections of the test with exact exam format
- Simple explanations for the all important test taking strategies
- Master the skills and speed needed to achieve your highest possible score.

Postal Exam Timed Practice Test Audio CD

Exam 473 & 473-C • Only $9.95 + S/H

The most convenient way to practice realistically and time yourself precisely ...

- Accurately timing yourself is the most important part of practicing realistically.
- Finding someone to time you day after day for extended periods can be difficult.
- Timing yourself is distracting, and you simply cannot afford to be distracted on this exam.
- The Timed Practice Test CD does the timing for you conveniently and precisely.

2 Audio CD Test Prep Combo

Exam 473 & 473-C • Only $14.95 + S/H

Combo package includes both Pathfinder test prep audio CD's at a special price ...

- Postal Exam 473 & 473-C Training Course CD – Your own personal test prep class
- Postal Exam Timed Practice Test CD – The most convenient and realistic way to practice
- Listen and learn the quick & easy way.
- Save money when buying both CD's together in this special combo package.

Audio CD Upgrade Kit with Test Scoring & Speed Marking Pencils

Exam 473 & 473-C • Only $19.95 + S/H

Upgrade your Study Guide with audio CD's and pencils at a special combo price ...

- Postal Exam 473 & 473-C Training Course CD – Your own personal test prep class
- Postal Exam Timed Practice Test CD – The most convenient and realistic way to practice
- Set of exclusive Test Scoring & Speed Marking Pencils
- Save money when buying all three items together in this special combo package.

CD-ROM Upgrade Kit with Test Scoring & Speed Marking Pencils

Exam 473 & 473-C • Only $19.95 + S/H

Upgrade your Study Guide with the CD-ROM and pencils at a special combo price ...

- Series of self-paced test prep classes – Comprehensive test prep instruction
- Timed practice tests – Just like the real exam – The most convenient and realistic way to practice
- Set of exclusive Test Scoring & Speed Marking Pencils
- Save money when buying both products together in this special combo package.

Continued on next page ...

Rural Carrier Associate Exam 460

Study Guides

Postal Exam 460 Quick Course Book

Only ~~$15.95 + S/H~~ Special offer for valued customers – only $9.95 + S/H

Complete test preparation in less that 12 hours ...

- Free Live Support – Test prep answers & advice by phone or e-mail
- Fully up-to-date with all four section of the exam
- Test taking tips make the exam manageable – Especially the difficult memory section.
- Six complete practice exams – Practice is the key to a high score and to getting a job.

Postal Exam 460 Quick Course Book with CD-ROM

Only ~~$24.95 + S/H~~ Special offer for valued customers – only $14.95 + S/H

The Postal Exam Quick Course book with a test prep CD-ROM featuring ...

- Series of Six Self-Paced Test Prep Classes – Comprehensive instruction
- Timed practice tests – Just like the real exam – The most realistic way to practice
- Following Oral Instructions Practice Tests – Presentation of all 6 oral practice tests in the book
- Compatible with any internet ready version of Windows®. (You don't have to be hooked up to internet.)

Postal Exam 460 Quick Course Book with 3 Audio CD's

Only ~~$29.95 + S/H~~ Special offer for valued customers – only $19.95 + S/H

Includes the Postal Exam Quick Course book plus 3 audio CD's featuring ...

- Postal Exam Training Course CD – Your own personal test prep class
- Postal Exam Timed Practice Test CD – The most realistic way to practice
- Following Oral Instructions Practice Tests CD – All 6 oral practice tests from the book
- Listen and learn the quick & easy way.

Continued on next page ...

Postal Exams 710, 931, 932 & 933

Downloadable Study Guides

Downloadable Postal Exam 710 Quick Course

Clerical Abilities Exam / Data Conversion Operator Exam • Only $9.95

A complete downloadable study guide for exam 710 featuring ...

- Three complete & realistic practice tests
- All seven sections of the exam – 100% up-to-date
- Quick & easy to use – Just download, study, and print as needed.
- Visit our website *www.PostalExam.com* to order this downloadable guide.

Downloadable Postal Exam 931 Quick Course

General Maintenance Mechanic Exam • Only $9.95

A complete downloadable study guide for exam 931 featuring ...

- Six complete practice tests for the Following Oral Instructions section
- Actual Postal sample questions for the technical section
- Quick & easy to use – Just download, study, and print as needed.
- Visit our website *www.PostalExam.com* to order this downloadable guide.

Downloadable Postal Exam 932 Quick Course

Electronic Technician Exam • Only $9.95

A complete downloadable study guide for exam 932 featuring ...

- Six complete practice tests for the Following Oral Instructions section
- Actual Postal sample questions for the technical section
- Quick & easy to use – Just download, study, and print as needed.
- Visit our website *www.PostalExam.com* to order this downloadable guide.

Downloadable Postal Exam 933 Quick Course

Mail Processing Equipment Mechanic Exam • Only $9.95

A complete downloadable study guide for exam 933 featuring ...

- Six complete practice tests for the Following Oral Instructions section
- Actual Postal sample questions for the technical section
- Quick & easy to use – Just download, study, and print as needed.
- Visit our website *www.PostalExam.com* to order this downloadable guide.

Note: All downloadable guides must be ordered online at *www.PostalExam.com.*

The products on this page are all downloadable study guides. After ordering one of these guides online at *www.PostalExam.com*, you will receive an e-mail message with downloading instructions. The instructions will include a web address where you can find the guide on the internet and details on how to download it.

Continued on next page ...

How to Order

Order Online

Visit our website *www.PostalExam.com* to order Pathfinder products online with a credit card. Order with confidence. Pathfinder's online orders are processed in a totally secure environment. Online orders are usually shipped within 24 hours. **Downloadable guides must be ordered online.**

Order by Phone

Call 1-800-748-1819 to order by phone using a credit card. Phone orders are usually shipped within 24 hours. This toll free number is answered by Customer Service Representatives prepared to assist you with orders, but they are not trained to provide test prep support, and they cannot connect you to the Test Prep Support Group. For test prep support, you must call the Support Line phone number given on page 377.

Order by Mail

To order by mail, send a check or money order for the proper amount to the below address along with the order form found on the next page. It is important that you send the completed order form to assure we understand exactly which item or items you wish to order. Mail orders are usually shipped within 24 hours once your payment is received at our office.

Pathfinder Distributing Co.
P.O. Box 1368
Pinehurst, TX 77362-1368

Shipping & Handling

- **Priority Mail**
  For fast, accurate, traceable, and economical delivery, Pathfinder's standard form of shipping is Priority Mail. Typical delivery time is 2 - 3 Postal working days. This delivery time does not include the shipping date and is not guaranteed. However, in our experience, Priority Mail is almost always delivered within this time frame. For your benefit, Pathfinder charges a flat $5.00 shipping and handling fee per order for Priority Mail. No matter how many items you order, the most you will pay for shipping and handling per order is $5.00. Depending on weight and address, our cost can exceed $5.00, but Pathfinder absorbs any shipping costs over this amount.
- **Express Mail**
  For even faster delivery, Express Mail is available for a flat fee of only $15.00. Express Mail offers guaranteed next day delivery to metropolitan addresses and second day delivery to rural addresses. Call for details.

Prices, shipping charges, and/or products are subject to change without notice. All sales are final.

Continued on next page ...